Foundations of Organisational Economics

Foundations of Organisational Economics: Histories and Theories of the Firm and Production delves into a range of key topics to do with the history of the mainstream approach to the theory of production and the theory of the firm. This includes the frameworks used to analyse production, the division of labour and its application to the firm and the development of the neoclassical model of production.

The first topic explored is the change from a normative approach to a largely positive approach to the analysis of the theory of production, which occurred around the seventeenth century. The next topic is an examination of the relationship (or the lack of a relationship) between the division of labour and the theory of the firm. In the fourth chapter, the focus is on the development of the proto-neoclassical approach to production. Here, the development of the theories of monopoly, oligopoly and perfect competition are discussed, as well as the theory of input utilisation. Chapter 5 looks at Marshall's idea of the representative firm, which was the main early neoclassical approach to the theory of industry-level production. The penultimate chapter considers the criticisms made of the neoclassical model between 1940 and 1970.

This work is an illuminating reference for students and researchers of the history of economic thought, industrial organisation, microeconomic theory and organisational studies.

Paul Walker is an economist based in Christchurch, New Zealand. He received his PhD in economics from the University of Canterbury, Christchurch, New Zealand. His research is mainly to do with the history of economic thought and the theory of the firm. He is author of *The Theory of the Firm: An Overview of the Economic Mainstream* and *A Brief Prehistory of the Theory of the Firm*, both published by Routledge.

I0894805

Routledge Studies in the History of Economics

A History of Feminist and Gender Economics
Giandomenica Becchio

The Theory of Transaction in Institutional Economics
A History
Massimiliano Vatiero

F.A. Hayek and the Epistemology of Politics
The Curious Task of Economics
Scott Scheall

Classical Liberalism and the Industrial Working Class
The Economic Thought of Thomas Hodgskin
Alberto Mingardi

English Economic Thought in the Seventeenth Century
Rejecting the Dutch Model
Seiichiro Ito

Poverty in the History of Economic Thought
From Mercantilism to Neoclassical Economics
Edited by Mats Lundahl, Daniel Rauhut and Neelambar Hatti

Macroeconomic Analysis in the Classical Tradition
The Impediments of Keynes's Influence
James C.W. Ahiakpor

Foundations of Organisational Economics
Histories and Theories of the Firm and Production
Paul Walker

For more information about this series, please visit: www.routledge.com/series/SE0341

Foundations of Organisational Economics

Histories and Theories of the Firm and Production

Paul Walker

Routledge
Taylor & Francis Group
LONDON AND NEW YORK

First published 2021
by Routledge
2 Park Square, Milton Park, Abingdon, Oxon OX14 4RN

and by Routledge
52 Vanderbilt Avenue, New York, NY 10017

Routledge is an imprint of the Taylor & Francis Group, an informa business

British Library Cataloguing-in-Publication Data
A catalogue record for this book is available from the British Library

Library of Congress Cataloging-in-Publication Data
A catalog record for this book has been requested

ISBN: 978-0-367-65143-5 (hbk)
ISBN: 978-0-367-72249-4 (pbk)
ISBN: 978-1-003-12847-2 (ebk)

Typeset in Bembo
by Apex CoVantage, LLC

Contents

Preface and acknowledgements

Micklethwait and Wooldridge (2003: xv) see the business firm as the most important organisation we have for enhancing our well-being.

> The most important organization in the world is the company: the basis of the prosperity of the West and the best hope for the future of the rest of the world.

Not everyone, however, is willing to fully embrace Micklethwait and Wooldridge's proposition, but even for those who do not it should still be obvious that the firm is one of the most important[1] organisations in the modern economy. It would also seem obvious that, given this importance, a proper understanding of how an economy functions would require a sophisticated theoretical understanding of the nature and structure of firms and production. And yet

> [t]he theory of the firm has been a neglected area of study in mainstream economics. Despite Ronald Coase bringing the issue up for discussion in 1937, it was not on the research agenda until the 1970s. Even now, as both Coase and Oliver Williamson, the founder of and prominent scholar in the transaction cost-focusing analysis of firm organization, have received the Nobel Prize in economics,[2] the area remains in the periphery of economic analysis.
>
> (Bylund 2011: 189)

When talking, in a 2013 interview, about the approach taken to production in contemporary economics, Ronald Coase stated that "[m]odern economics shows little interest in production. I am not sure production function tells us anything about production in the economy" (Wang 2014: 118).

How did we get to a situation of such apathy towards the theory of production and the theory of the firm? An analysis of the past of the theories of production and the firm is necessary to help cultivate an understanding of the historical developments that have resulted in the contemporary theories of the firm and production and, somewhat paradoxically, a lack of interest in production and the firm. This inquiry helps add depth to our knowledge of ideas commonly used today but whose origins lie in past debates to do with production and the firm. It also allows us to see how and why changes in thinking took place. The chapters that make up this book set out to examine some of the steps that have been taken to get to our modern approach to production and the firm.

This book has no pretensions to originality. A substantial portion of the subject matter covered here is a component of any introduction to economics. All microeconomics textbooks will discuss the theory of production, and it is taught to all undergraduate students. Sometimes, less often, the modern theory of the firm is also taught. But the theory is presented in an ahistorical manner; the theory just emerges, fully formed, from nowhere.[3] How the theory got to be the way it is is never explained. Students do not learn about the theory's history since most of their teachers cannot explain how the theory developed.

Students see little in the way of material to do with the history of economic thought, in general, as part of a standard undergraduate training in economics. But, as noted, they see even less in the way of material on the history of economic thought to do with the theory of production and the theory of the firm. These chapters will, with luck, help rectify this shortcoming, if only to a small degree. Topics discussed include the change from a normative perspective to a more positive one, the relationship between the division of labour and the theory of the firm, the influence of the proto-neoclassicals on the theory of production, Marshall's (in)famous, if short lived, concept of the 'representative firm' and the challenges to the neoclassical theory that arose in the 1940–1970 period.

The following chapters will be, hopefully, understandable to students – and their teachers – and will give them an introduction to some of the more under-appreciated and understudied topics in the history of economic thought. They will also give some background as to how the theory we see today got to be that theory.

Hopefully these essays will be of interest not only to economics students but also to historians of economic thought, organisational economists, industrial organisation economists and others interested in the history of ideas in economics.

Aside from advantages inherent in a better understanding of the development of ideas to do with "the ordinary business of life", with "that part of individual and social action which is most closely connected with the attainment and with the use of the material requisites of wellbeing",[4] why should anyone, even if not one of those mentioned in the previous paragraph, read this book? The best reason comes from G.L.S. Shackle, "I would like you to read it, in the words of the Dean of Faculties of Columbia University, 'for your own sinister pleasure'" (Shackle 1968: vii).[5]

Acknowledgements

I wish to thank (but not implicate) Glenn Boyle, Philip Meguire, Ulrich Schwalbe, Yoshinori Shiozawa and the publisher's anonymous referees for comments on previous drafts of the manuscript. All remaining errors are the fault of the author. The chapters presented in this volume draw on material from Walker (2020a, b). These works are revised versions of Walker (2016, 2018), respectively.

- Walker, Paul (2016). *The Theory of the Firm: An Overview of the Economic Mainstream*, London: Routledge.
- Walker, Paul (2018). *A Brief Prehistory of the Theory of the Firm*, London: Routledge.
- Walker, Paul (2020a). 'The Theory of the Firm: An Overview of the Economic Mainstream: Revised Edition', Working Paper. Available at: http://ssrn.com/abstract=2000431
- Walker, Paul (2020b). 'A Brief Prehistory of the Theory of the Firm: Revised Edition', Working Paper. Available at: http://ssrn.com/abstract=2911699

I am grateful to the Oxford University Press for permission to reproduce an adapted version of the figure from page 44 of D. H. Macgregor, *Economic Thought and Policy*, Oxford: Oxford University Press, 1949. www.oup.com/

Notes

1 Cowen (2019: 1) emphasises the importance of firms by noting that they have two essential virtues, "[f]irst, business makes most of the stuff we enjoy and consume. Second, business is what gives most of us jobs. The two words that follow most immediately from the world of business are 'prosperity' and 'opportunity'". He goes on to identify some of the various contributions that firms have make to our wellbeing.

"Without business we would not have:

- Ships, trains, and cars
- Electricity, lighting, and heating equipment
- Most of our food supply
- Most of our lifesaving pharmaceuticals
- Clothes for our children
- Our telephones and smartphones
- The books we love to read
- The ability to access, more or less immediately, so much of the world's online" (Cowen 2019: 2).

More than 60 years earlier Bowen (1955: 1) had also highlighted the importance of firms to people's wellbeing when he wrote,

> [t]he business enterprise is one of the most pervasive and influential institutions of our society, and one in which innumerable important decisions and responses are made. These decisions and responses, in small and large enterprises, are links in the chain of factors determining the range of products available to consumers, the level of national income, the degree of economic security, the rate and direction of economic progress, and the distribution of income. These decisions and responses also significantly influence the character of human relations in industry, the quality of the lives of those who work in industry, and even the power structure of our society.

2 Since Bylund wrote this, a third Nobel Prize has been awarded for work in organisational economics. The 2016 prize was awarded to Oliver Hart and Bengt Holmstrom, both of whom have made seminal contributions to the theory of the firm.

3 This is also true of the theory of the consumer. A short historical survey tracing the development of consumer theory is given in Katzner (1970: 5–13).
4 Alfred Marshall wrote

> [p]olitical economy or economics is a study of mankind in the ordinary business of life; it examines that part of individual and social action which is most closely connected with the attainment and with the use of the material requisites of wellbeing.
> (Marshall 2009: 1)

5 Shackle's reference is to a comment by Jacques Barzun, the Dean of the Graduate School, Dean of Faculties, and Provost at Columbia University from 1955 to 1968: "Some men are so selfish that they read a book or go to a concert for their own sinister pleasure, instead of doing it to improve social conditions, as the good citizen does when drinking cocktails or playing bridge" (Jacques Barzun, *The Saturday Evening Post*, 3 May 1958).

References

Bowen, Howard R. (1955). *The Business Enterprise as a Subject for Research: Prepared for the Committee on Business Enterprise Research*, Social Science Research Council, Pamphlet No. 11, New York: Social Science Research Council.

Bylund, Per L. (2011). 'Division of Labor and the Firm: An Austrian Attempt at Explaining the Firm in the Market', *Quarterly Journal of Austrian Economics*, 14(2): 188–215.

Cowen, Tyler (2019). *Big Business: A Lover Letter to an American Anti-Hero*, New York: St. Martin's Press.

Katzner, Donald W. (1970). *Static Demand Theory*, New York: The Macmillan Company.

Marshall, Alfred (2009). *Principles of Economics*, Unabridged 8th edn., New York: Cosimo, Inc. Eighth edition first published 1920. First edition 1890.

Micklethwait, John and Adrian Wooldridge (2003). *The Company: A Short History of a Revolutionary Idea*, New York: The Modern Library.

Shackle, G. L. S. (1968). *Economics for Pleasure*, 2nd edn., Cambridge: Cambridge University Press.

Wang, Ning (2014). 'A Life in Pursuit of "Good Economics": Interview with Ronald Coase by NingWang', *Man and the Economy*, 1(1) June: 99–120.

1 Introduction

Preliminaries

According to Robert Ekelund and Robert Hébert, there are a number of benefits that accrue to the study of the history of economic thought:

> [o]ne of the things that can be gained from a study of the past is a better understanding of the creative process. All the great intellectual pioneers held a skeptical, almost iconoclastic, attitude toward traditional ideas and maintained an open, almost naive, credulity toward new concepts. Out of this combination came the crucial capacity to see a familiar situation or problem in a new light. The creative process is always a wrenching away of a concept from its traditional context or meaning.
>
> Another benefit from a study of the past is an appreciation for the kind of ideas that have staying power. What separates good ideas from bad ideas? Why do certain ideas survive in economic theory long after their emergence on the intellectual scene? Why do other ideas fizzle quickly? Traditional economics courses have little time for such issues, yet they are entirely appropriate within the context of intellectual history, and, it turns out, the answers have an enormous impact on the content of economics at any particular point of time.
>
> Yet another benefit is a keener understanding of contemporary economic theory by exposure to the shortcomings of past theories and the obstacles overcome by the principles that survive. Some students will find the abstract theory of economics more palatable – indeed, more understandable – when it is presented in a historical context. But in the final analysis the only justification needed for studying the history of economic thought may be that the subject is interesting.
>
> (Ekelund and Hébert 2013: 3)

However, not everyone today shares Ekelund and Hébert's view. Many, if not most, economists do not. The history of thought is largely ignored in contemporary mainstream economics. Historian of economic thought Mark Blaug has lamented the state of the history of thought within modern economics:

> [i]t is no secret that the study of the history of economic thought is held in low esteem by mainstream economists and sometimes openly disparaged as a type of antiquarianism. There is nothing new in this. Practically every commentator on the role of history of economic thought in modern economics in the last 30 years has lamented the steady decline of interest in the area since the end of World War II and its virtual disappearance from university curricula, not just at the graduate but sometimes even at the undergraduate level.
>
> (Blaug 2001: 145)

David Laidler has commented on the declining importance of the history of economic thought [HET] within modern economics:

> [b]ut my pleasure tonight is tempered by the apprehension that many of us feel about HET's future. Though matters are not so far gone in Europe as in North America, its serious study as a branch of economics seems to be in decline everywhere.
>
> (Laidler 2012: 2)

Dieter Bögenhold also sees HET in decline:

> [d]uring the last decades, HET has mostly been abolished or has disappeared in many contemporary teaching curricula in economics. When latest methods in econometrics and mathematical procedures are put into the reading schedule in university education, reading of the history of the own discipline appears to be nearly forgotten.
>
> (Bögenhold 2017: 2)

But the history of thought to do with the theory of production and the theory of the firm[1] receives even less attention than the subject in general. If you look at, for example, Backhouse (2002), a well-regarded introduction to the history of economic thought, it devotes, roughly, one page out of a total of 369 to the history of the theory of the firm. Another well-used introduction, Sandmo (2011), does even worse in that none of its almost 500 pages deals with the theory of the firm. Heilbroner (1999), one of the most famous introductions to the history of economic thought, has no discussion of the questions which we today think of as making up the theory of the firm.[2] In 1893, when Edwin Cannan published the first of three editions of his *A History of the Theories of Production and Distributions from 1776 to 1848*, he commented that "I have been able to obtain surprisingly little assistance from previous writers" (Cannan 1893: v). Since then, sadly, little appears to have changed. There is still little assistance from the literature for those who are interested in the history of thought to do with production or the firm. In fact, in the more than one hundred years since Cannan wrote there seems to have been only three additional books (in English at least) published that directly deal with the topic of the history of thought to do with either the theory of production or the theory of the firm: George Stigler published a revised version of his PhD thesis as *Production and Distribution Theories: The Formative Period* in 1941; in 1978, Philip L. Williams published his PhD thesis as *The Emergence of the Theory of the Firm: From Adam Smith to Alfred Marshall*; and Paul Walker published *A Brief Prehistory of the Theory of the Firm* in 2018.

Hopefully, the essays presented here will shed light on a few of the wide array of interesting topics that can be investigated under the rubric of the history of the theory of production and the theory of the firm. The emphasis is on the pre-1970 mainstream literature on production and the firm. 1970 is used as a convenient, if not entirely accurate, dividing line between what constitutes the 'past' and the 'present' of the theory of the firm, since it was around this time that the theory of production began to be supplemented by a genuine theory of the firm. Pre-1970, what went under the heading of the 'theory of the firm' was, in fact, a microeconomic theory of production.[3] It was in the 1970s that the present mainstream – largely Coaseian inspired – approaches to the firm started to develop, with works such as Williamson (1971, 1973, 1975), Alchian and Demsetz (1972), Jensen and Meckling (1976) and Klein, Crawford and Alchian (1978). The major difference between the mainstream theories of the past (the neoclassical theory of production) and the mainstream theories of the present (the theory of the firm), at least as far as they are conceived of here, is that the focus – in terms of the questions the theory attempts to answer – of the post-1970 mainstream literature is markedly different from that of the earlier mainstream (neoclassical) theory. The theory of the firm for Ronald Coase, Oliver Williamson, Bengt Holmström or Oliver Hart is a very different thing from the theory of production associated with the likes of Arthur Pigou, Lionel Robbins, Jacob Viner, Joan Robinson and Edward Chamberlin.

The questions the theory seeks to answer have changed from being about how the firm acts in its various markets, how it prices its outputs or how it combines its inputs to questions about the firm's existence, boundaries[4] and internal organisation. That is, within the mainstream theory there has been a movement away from seeing the theory of the firm as simply developing one component (albeit an important component) of price theory, namely the element concerned with the factor and product market behaviour of producers, to the theory being concerned with the firm as an important economic institution in its own right.

The focus here is on the mainstream[5] microeconomic theory of production and the firm, and both the 'mainstream' and 'microeconomic' terms matter. The concentration on the mainstream means that the heterodox[6] approaches to the firm are not discussed, while the microeconomic focus means that the macroeconomic theory of production[7] and its associated controversies are not examined. The chapters are written in the—perhaps forlorn—hope that they will stimulate interest in the history of the mainstream theory of production and the firm.

The essays have been written as introductions to the topics covered and are intended to be accessible to undergraduate students and general readers. With this in mind, any background needed is provided and any mathematics used is explained either in the text or chapter notes. Given this, each chapter can be read independently of all the others, and thus readers can sample as they see fit. A cost to this approach is that there is some repetition between chapters.

Outline of the rest of the book

The second chapter looks at the change from a largely normative approach to the theory of production to a largely positive approach. Today we take a positive approach to the firm for granted, but before the mercantilists in the period, roughly, from the sixteenth to the eighteenth centuries the standard approach to production, and economics more generally, was predominately normative.

Chapter 3 considers the relationship between the division of labour and the theory of the firm since, as Ronald Coase has put it, "[t]o understand production, we have to go back to Adam Smith's division of labor" (Wang 2014: 118). However, the main conclusion to be drawn here is about just how little impact the division of labour has had on the development of the theory of production and the firm. Before the twentieth century, the division of labour played little part in the development of the theory of the firm. Starting in the twentieth century, the manufacturing division of labour did begin to play a role, but it is a limited role within the contemporary mainstream theory of the firm. This literature has taken a more contractually based approach.

In Chapter 4 we consider some aspects of the development of the neoclassical approach to production, in particular the proto-neoclassical formulation of the theory of production. The case is made that much of what we call the neoclassical theory of production was in fact created before the 'neoclassical revolution' of the 1870s. The theories of monopoly, oligopoly, input utilisation and even the theory of perfect competition were developed before the 1870s.

Chapter 5 looks at Alfred Marshall's 'representative firm'. This was a concept that first appeared in the 1890s[8] as a way for Marshall to construct an industry supply curve without having to assume that all firms in an industry were identical. It allowed him to marry his dynamic view of firms with a static view of industry. But the idea did not last long; it fell victim to the 'cost controversy' of the 1920s and was driven out of the economics literature by 1930.

The criticisms of the neoclassical approach to production that originated in the period 1940 to 1970 are briefly covered in Chapter 6. This chapter includes discussions of the full cost controversy that took place in the UK and the related marginalist controversy which occurred in the US. This is followed by an examination of some of the first attempts to look inside the black box of the neoclassical 'firm', namely the behavioural, managerial and X-inefficiency theories of the firm. These models took issue with a number of aspects of the neoclassical model including the notion that there are no principal agent problems in the firm, the use of profit maximisation as the objective for the firm, or in one case the use of the maximising assumption at all, and the idea that a firm operates in a technically efficient manner.

The final chapter is the conclusion.

Notes

1 Spulber (2008: 5, footnote 8) gives the origin of the word 'firm' as "[t]he word 'firm' derives from the Latin word 'firmare' referring to a signature that confirmed an agreement by designating the name of the business".
2 Some more advanced texts do better. Blaug (1997), for example, covers aspects of the theory of production and the theory of the firm. From an earlier era, Whittaker (1940) has a 40-page chapter on production.
3 Even today, if an undergraduate microeconomic has a chapter on the theory of the firm, what it contains is the neoclassical theory of production.
4 Determining firm boundaries amounts to a theory of firm integration, or non-integration
5 Colander, Holt and Rosser (2004: 490) argue that the "[m]ainstream consists of the ideas that are held by those individuals who are dominant in the leading academic institutions, organizations, and journals at any given time, especially the leading graduate research institutions. Mainstream economics consists of the ideas that the elite in the profession finds acceptable, where by elite we mean the leading economists in the top graduate schools. It is not a term describing a historically determined school, but is instead a term describing the beliefs that are seen by the top schools and institutions in the profession as intellectually sound and worth working on". While Dequech (2007: 281) says "that mainstream economics is that which is taught in the most prestigious universities and colleges, gets published in the most prestigious journals, receives funds from the most important research foundations, and wins the most prestigious awards". In this survey we do not distinguish the 'orthodoxy' from the 'mainstream'. The terms are used interchangeably in what follows. See Colander, Holt and Rosser (2004, 2005) for a more sophisticated discussion of the concepts which draws a distinction between them.
6 Here the term heterodox is used in a general way to cover dissenting schools of economic thought such as the Austrians, the resource-based theory of the firm, the knowledge-based view, the capabilities approach, the evolutionary approach, the (Old) Institutionalists, Marxists and post-Keynesians, among others.
7 Ferguson (1969: part II) discusses the neoclassical macroeconomic theories of production and distribution. Felipe and McCombie (2013) offers a critique of the neoclassical aggregate production function. Blaug (1974) reviews one of the most significant attacks on neoclassical macroeconomics during the 1940–1975 period, the famous 'Cambridge Controversy'.
8 The term "representative firm" first appeared explicitly in the second edition of Marshall's *Principles of Economics*, originally published in 1891. The first edition had appeared in 1890, the third in 1895, the fourth in 1898, the fifth in 1907, the sixth in 1910, the seventh in 1916 and the eighth edition in 1920. A 9th (Variorum) edition appeared in 1961.

References

Alchian, Armen and Harold Demsetz (1972). 'Production, Information Costs and Economic Organization', *American Economic Review*, 62(5) December: 777–95.

Backhouse, Roger E. (2002). *The Ordinary Business of Life: A History of Economics From the Ancient World to the Twenty-First Century*, Princeton, NJ: Princeton University Press.

Blaug, Mark (1974). *The Cambridge Revolution: Success or Failure*, London: The Institute of Economic Affairs.

Blaug, Mark (1997). *Economic Theory in Retrospect*, 5th edn., Cambridge: Cambridge University Press.

Blaug, Mark (2001). 'No History of Ideas, Please, We're Economists', *Journal of Economic Perspectives*, 15(1) Winter: 145–64.

Bögenhold, Dieter (2017). 'History of Economic Thought as Analytic Tool: Why Historiography of Ideas is More than Watching old Movies', paper presented at the 58th Annual Conference of the Italian Economic Association – Società Italiana degli Economisti (SIE) annual conference at the Università della Calabria, Arcavacata di Rende, Italy, October 19–21.

Cannan, Edwin (1893). *A History of the Theories of Production and Distribution in English Political Economy From 1776 to 1848*, London: Percival & Co. Second edition 1903, third edition 1917.

Colander, David, Richard Holt and J. Barkley Rosser Jr. (2004). 'The Changing Face of Mainstream Economics', *Review of Political Economy*, 16(4): 485–99.

Colander, David, Richard Holt and J. Barkley Rosser Jr. (2005). *The Changing Face of Economics: Conversations with Cutting Edge Economists*, Ann Arbor: University of Michigan Press.

Dequech, David (2007). 'Neoclassical, Mainstream, Orthodox, and Heterodox Economics', *Journal of Post Keynesian Economics*, 30(2): 279–302.

Ekelund Jr. Robert B. and Robert F. Hébert (2013). *A History of Economic Theory and Method*, 6th edn., Long Grove, IL: Waveland Press.

Felipe, Jesus and John S. L. McCombie (2013). *The Aggregate Production Function and the Measurement of Technical Change: 'Not Even Wrong'*, Cheltenham, UK: Edward Elgar.

Ferguson, C. E. (1969). *The Neoclassical Theory of Production & Distribution*, Cambridge: Cambridge University Press.

Heilbroner, Robert L. (1999). *The Worldly Philosophers: The Lives, Times, and Ideas of the Great Economic Thinkers*, 7th edn., New York: Simon & Schuster.

Jensen, Michael C. and William H. Meckling (1976). 'Theory of the Firm: Managerial Behaviour, Agency Costs, and Ownership Structure', *Journal of Financial Economics*, 3(4) October: 305–60.

Klein, Benjamin, Robert G. Crawford and Armen A. Alchian (1978). 'Vertical Integration, Appropriable Rents, and the Competitive Contracting Process', *Journal of Law and Economics*, 21(2) October: 297–326.

Laidler, David (2012). 'Today's Standards and Yesterday's Economics – Two Short Occasional Essays: Eliminating History from Economic Thought and Mark Blaug on the Quantity Theory', Economic Policy Research Institute, EPRI Working Papers, 2012–6 November, London, ON: Department of Economics, University of Western Ontario.

Marshall, Alfred (1890). *Principles of Economics*, London: Macmillan and Co.

Sandmo, Agnar (2011). *Economics Evolving: A History of Economic Thought*, Princeton: Princeton University Press.

Spulber, Daniel F. (2008). 'Discovering the Role of the Firm: The Separation Criterion and Corporate Law', Northwestern Law & Economics Research Paper No. 08–23, December 6.

Stigler, George J. (1941). *Production and Distribution Theories: The Formative Period*, New York: The Macmillan Company.

Walker, Paul (2018). *A Brief Prehistory of the Theory of the Firm*, London: Routledge.

Wang, Ning (2014). 'A Life in Pursuit of "Good Economics": Interview with Ronald Coase by Ning Wang', *Man and the Economy*, 1(1) June: 99–120.

Whittaker, Edmund (1940). *A History of Economic Ideas*, New York: Longmans, Green and Co.

Williams, Philip L. (1978). *The Emergence of the Theory of the Firm: From Adam Smith to Alfred Marshall*, London: The Macmillan Press.

Williamson, Oliver E. (1971). 'The Vertical Integration of Production: Market Failure Considerations', *American Economic Review*, 61(2) May: 112–23.

Williamson, Oliver E. (1973). 'Markets and Hierarchies: Some Elementary Considerations', *American Economic Review*, 63(2) May: 316–25.

Williamson, Oliver E. (1975). *Markets and Hierarchies: Analysis and Antitrust Implications*, New York: The Free Press.

2 Normative versus positive analysis in the history of the theory of production

Introduction

William Letwin sees the development of economics as a positive science as signalling the end for the Roman Catholic Church as the supreme authority on economic matters.

> The final outcome of the decline in the authoritativeness of theological pronouncements on economic matters was the emergence of economics as an inquiry independent of religious and ethical considerations.
>
> (Letwin 1964: 87)

Letwin illustrates this idea with the example of the literature on usury. During the medieval period, much had been written with regard to the moral condemnation of usury. But "[a]fter 1640, and especially after 1660, such works cease, and although much is written on 'interest', the word 'usury' almost disappears; the moral aspect of the question has been superseded by the economic one" (Letwin 1964: 88).

When discussing the case of international trade, Dorobăţ (2015: 107) writes

> [u]p until the Middle Ages, philosophers and theoreticians did not undertake any systematic study of international trade, and early theories are rather fragmented, laced with ethical and political considerations.

Looking at the history of the theory of production/the firm, the replacement of a normative framework of analysis with a positive one also stands out. Before the seventieth century, the predominant mode of enquiry was a descriptive/normative one. Looking back at ancient China, India and Greece or to medieval Islam and Christianity, we see that the little that was written on production was written within a descriptive/normative framework. The frameworks applied were ethical and/or religious. The questions asked were about what should be produced or what production or occupations would find favour with God or what production was ethically justified. The important point is that these normative frameworks did not give rise to a theory of production, such a theory had to wait for the mercantilists, and a more positive approach to economics before it stated to develop.

A clear recognition of a formal distinction between normative and positive analysis goes back, at least, as far as John Neville Keynes. Keynes wrote

> [a]s the terms are here used, a *positive science* may be defined as a body of systematized knowledge concerning what is; a *normative* or *regulative science* as a body of systematized knowledge relating to criteria of what ought to be, and concerned therefore with the ideal as distinguished from the actual; an art as a system of rules for the attainment of a given end. The object of a positive science is the establishment of *uniformities*, of a normative science the determination of *ideals*, of an art the formulation of *precepts*.
>
> (Keynes 1917: 34–5; emphasis in the original)

Carl Menger also saw a difference, with regard to ethical considerations, between theoretical economics (positive economics) and economic policy (normative economics). In *Investigations into the Method of the Social Sciences with Special Reference to Economics* Menger criticises what he calls the "ethical orientation" of the German historical school (Menger 1883: 235). He writes with regard to theoretical economics that

> [w]hat we should like to stress here particularly is the fact that we cannot rationally speak of an *ethical* orientation of *theoretical* economics either in respect to the exact orientation of theoretical research or to the empirical-realistic orientation.

But normative considerations do enter into economic policy:

> Economic policy, the science of the basic principles for suitable advancement (appropriate to conditions) of "national economy" on the part of the public authorities.
>
> (Menger 1883: 211)

The important word here is 'suitable'. You cannot determine what is suitable without value judgements.

John Stuart Mill makes a similar distinction when he differentiates between science and art.

> These two ideas [science and art] differ from one another as the understanding differs from the will, or as the indicative mood in grammar differs from the imperative. The one deals in facts, the other in precepts. Science is a collection of *truths*; art, a body of *rules*, or directions for conduct. The language of science is, This is, or, This is not; This does, or does not, happen. The language of art is, Do this; Avoid that. Science takes cognizance

> of a *phenomenon*, and endeavours to discover its *law*; art proposes to itself an *end*, and looks out for *means* to effect it.
>
> (Mill 1844: 124)

One of the major changes that has taken place in the history of economic thought to do with production/the firm has been the shifting of analysis from an emphasis on the descriptive/normative to an emphasis on the positive. It was only with the development of a positive approach to economic analysis that a theory of production began to emerge.

Ancient China, India and Greece

James Bonar makes the point that the little economic thinking that can be found in the works of the ancient Greek philosophers is dependent on their moral and political philosophies.

> Such economical doctrine as is traceable in the writings of the Greek philosophers grows out of their moral and political philosophy.
>
> (Bonar 1893: 5)

Bonar goes on to say

> [t]he conceptions of Wealth, Production, Distribution, and of the economical functions of the State and Society are treated by Plato, some incidentally, others at length, but always in subordination to Ethics, and never as (even in theory) separate from ethical considerations.
>
> (Bonar 1893: 11)

Hannah Sewall argues in a similar vein.

> The Greeks, in common with most ancient peoples, had no conception of "rational laws governing the phenomena of the distribution of wealth." They studied human conduct to discover a man's duty, or to ascertain what kind of actions constituted noble lives, rather than to know the ultimate relations of all actions.
>
> (Sewall 1901: 1)

Aristotle argued that wealth cannot be the chief end for man. Wealth is a collection of means to an end.

> All human action and enterprise involve the pursuit of ends, and some of the ends are subordinate to others, while all are subordinate to one chief end, which ethical and political philosophy must define and explains.
>
> (Bonar 1893: 32)

Ancient Indian texts attached importance to wealth. For example,

> in the ancient Tamil treatise, *Tirukkural*, written sometime between the 1st and 3*rd* century BCE, the author Thiruvalluvar underscores the importance of wealth. There are 700 aphorism devoted to the subject of wealth in Book II titled *Kural*. For example, verse 1040 in Kural (Pope *et al*, 1886) mentions that the mother earth will laugh at the prospect of those who plead poverty but lead an idle life. Moreover, verse 1036 suggests that if farmers were to give up their dexterous life, even the ascetics will have hard time to live.
>
> (Deodhar 2018: 9)

Ancient Buddhist texts took a favourable view of economic activity, including the acquisition of wealth, and thus productive activity. Dasgupta (1993: chapter 2) argues in support of this point. "A recurrent theme in Buddhist texts is that the worldly and the spiritual spheres of activity are not different *in kind*, and that the qualities required for success in them have a large overlap" (Dasgupta 1993: 14). It is argued that "[h]ad Buddha himself turned his talents to worldly rather than spiritual matters, he would, according to the *Dighanikaya* have been a great success" (Dasgupta 1993: 15). Also,

> [t]he favourable attitude of Buddhism to economic activity also comes out in the role that is prescribed to the laity or householder. . . . True mediation, says Vimalakirti, lies not in just 'sitting there' but rather, in holding on to the *Dhamma* while remaining active in the ordinary business of life.
>
> (Dasgupta 1993: 15)

"Gombrich (1988: 78) sums up succinctly, 'Buddha never suggests that layman should eschew property, he commends wealth which is righteously acquired by one's own efforts'" (Dasgupta 1993: 17).

Turning to the Arthasastra,[1] a fourth century BCE text that incorporates Hindu philosophy, we find an outline of how a king should act to increase and keep his wealth and power.

> [T]he Arthasastra, despite its title, which literally means the science of wealth, was not an enquiry into the causes of wealth of nations, but rather a work of polity offering advice to the ruler on how to increase and preserve his wealth and power.
>
> (Dasgupta 1993: 28)

In the case of production, the advice is to give the state the dominant role. Dasgupta (1993) writes "[t]he government was not merely tax gatherer but also agriculturist, cowherd, road-builder, cattle-breeder, miner, forester, manufacturer and merchant. Private economic activity other than crop production was only residual and even then subject to strict government regulation and control" (Dasgupta 1993: 29) and

> [w]hat scope is left for private enterprise in industry? Hardly any, apart from production carried out by artisans and craftsmen. There were master artisans, employing a number of artisans to do the actual work for the customers, and earning a profit. There were also artisans working independently with their own capital and in their own workshops. In the latter case, the guild (*serni*), to which the artisan belonged, guaranteed the customer against, damage, etc. caused by the artisan (4.1.2–3). . . . Even artisans were subject to state-control: delay in delivery and failure to carry out the customer's instructions were offences punishable by the state (4.1.5–7). The required percentage increase or decrease in raw material during the process of manufacture, to which the artisans must conform, are stated (4.1.89, 13, 36ff).
>
> (Dasgupta 1993: 33)

Here we see an overlapping of the economic and religious thinking, with the normative emphasis being dominant.

If we turn to ancient China, we see that during the Western Zhou Dynasty (1066–771 BCE), agriculture was considered to be the most important form of production. From the *Rites of the Zhou Dynasty* we see that the working people were divided into nine professions: "Among these professions the first four fall within the scope of agriculture in the broad sense: farmers, gardeners, foresters and fishermen, and animal breeders and fanciers" (Hu 1988: 5).

While agriculture was given the most prominent position with regard to production, handicrafts were still afforded a high status. "On the previous list of nine profession, handcrafts was put in fifth place, just below agriculture in the broad sense" (Hu 1988: 6).

Of the various schools of thought in ancient China, the two most influential were Confucianism and Daoism.[2] Both schools originated from the Spring and Autumn (770–480 BCE) and Warring States (480–221 BCE) periods, and each had its texts which have influenced the intellectual development of Chinese thought since that time: *Analects of Confucius* and *Laozi*[3] (or Daodejing), respectively.

Confucians had a largely positive attitude towards the production of wealth. The author of *Da Xue*[4] saw the importance of land in the production of wealth, while the author of *Zhong Yong*[5] recognised that industrial production could also produce wealth. The Confucian approach to production was, however, a sort of ethical production outlook. Confucius emphasised that production and the acquisition of wealth should conform to an ethical standard. He set justice against profit. Those in the ruling class were born with a liking for justice, while workers, those involved in the productive activities, know only profit. Gentlemen (*junzi*) do not carry out manual labour; this was the role of the *xiaoren* (lowly person). "But the fact that he classifies people into junzi and xiaoren shows the reactionary nature of his belittling of productive labour from the ethical viewpoint" (Tang 2014: 124).

Daoists also took a mostly positive view of productive labour, except where it provided the rulers with luxurious consumer products. Laozi takes a positive attitude towards agricultural production which conforms to natural law but is more negative with regard to handicraft industry and commercial production. Laozi places emphasis on the natural essence of things and sees handicraft production as being about changing the form and structure of natural things to meet people's needs, and this is to be avoided. Anything that changes the essence of things, including production, is rejected. Zhuangzi[6] believed that all forms of farming, industry and commerce stressed the body and spirit and enslaved the people to material things.

Medieval thought

Douglas Irwin, a historian of thought concerning international trade, has highlighted the ethical-centric basis of and largely antagonistic attitude towards economics and commerce among scholars from within the medieval Church:

> the early Christian Fathers treated economics as a branch of ethics and, somewhat like the Greeks and Romans before them, condemned commerce as abetting fraud, promoting avarice, and encouraging worldly gains.
>
> (Irwin 1996: 17)

The negative attitude of the early Christian church towards wealth was summarised by the economic historian W. J. Ashley as

> [t]he teaching of the Gospel as to worldly goods had been unmistakable. It had repeatedly warned men against the pursuit of wealth, which would alienate them from the service of God and choke the good seed. It had in one striking instance associated spiritual perfection with the selling of all that a man had that he might give it to the poor. It had declared the poor and hungry blessed, and had prophesied woes to the rich. Instead of anxious thought for the food and raiment of the morrow, it had taught trust in God instead of selfish appropriation of whatever a man could obtain, a charity which gave freely to all who asked. And in the members of the earliest Christian Church it presented an example of men who gave up their individual possessions, and had all things in common.
>
> (Ashley 1919: 126)

Historian Diana Wood contends that the church acted as a brake on economic development since its emphasis was on spiritual rather than material matters. The (normative) environment the church created was not conducive to the acquisition of wealth, to entrepreneurial activities and thus to developing a positive attitude towards production.

> The other-worldly aim of the Church meant that in theory at least the concerns of this world were secondary. Temporal ends and temporal affairs, the merely transient and mundane, always had to be subordinated to the higher, spiritual purpose of life. Because material matters were thought to be of so little account, the Church put a firm brake on economic development. It actively discouraged people form wanting to better themselves because to be socially ambitious, to want to be upwardly mobile, was a sin. . . . The only justifications for working to earn more than mere sustenance were to perform pious works, to make reasonable provision for future emergencies, or to support offspring. . . . This was hardly the commercial or entrepreneurial attitude necessary for an economic take-off.
>
> (Wood 2002: 3–4)

Whittaker (1940) also explains that, in the early Christian period, attention was focused on the form of production. The (normative) question of which occupations should be pursued, and thus what goods and services should be produced, was emphasised.

> In production, as in everything else, the Christian man was to be a servant of God, occupying himself only in those activities that received divine favor. But occasionally, especially as time went by, comments appeared on the efficiency of production.
>
> (Whittaker 1940: 362)

Attitudes towards wealth, and thus by implication towards production, changed over time. Saint Augustine's attitude was a neutral one; wealth was useful and was to be used by men throughout their life, but it was not to be desired for its own sake. Such an attitude endured until the twelfth century (Wood 2002: 50). Views changed in the thirteenth century. Changes in the theoretical approach to wealth were driven, in part, by the increased availability of Aristotle's works. "For Aristotle, there is a minimum amount of wealth required to avoid a life of toil and there is a maximum amount above which full happiness or *eudaimonia* cannot be achieved" (DesRoches 2014: 387). Saint Thomas Aquinas also thought a certain amount of wealth was needed in the pursuit of virtue but beyond this amount wealth became an evil (Wood 2002: 51). In addition, Aquinas "followed Aristotle as regards disparagement of retail trade as a profession" (Robbins 1998: 29). But by the mid-fifteenth century wealth was no longer being seen as evil.

> The Florentine Leonardo Bruni provides a good example. In the Preface to his translation of the pseudo-Aristotelian *Economics* (c. 1420) he observed "As health is the goal of medicine, so riches are the goal of the household.

> For riches are useful both for ornamenting their owners as well as for helping nature in the struggle for virtue". Matteo Palmieri, too, thought that riches were instruments in the pursuit of virtue. Poggio Bracciolini turned ecclesiastical values on their head by predicting that without avarice civilized life would be destroyed. Many of the Italian civic funeral orations of the fifteenth century praised the deceased humanists for acquiring wealth by diligence and hard work, for the brilliance of their lifestyle, and for their contributions to the life of the city through charity, patronage of the arts, and financing of magnificent buildings.
>
> (Wood 2002: 52)

Lionel Robbins notes a more positive regard for trade and manufacturing in writings of the fifteenth century, an example being the works of San Bernardino of Siena.

> San Bernardino recognises trade and manufacture as useful. He praises them. He praises the upright tradesman. . . . [H]e reverts to the fact that good entrepreneurship, good managerial ability, was rare, and he has no objection to them being rewarded.
>
> (Robbins 1998: 29)

These changes in the (normative) view of wealth and trade imply the development of a more favourable view of the creation of wealth, that is, production.

Using a normative framework for thinking to do with economic issues did not apply just to work on production, the use of the framework covered most of the areas of economic enquiry. And much of the early moral evaluation was negative.

> Some of the Fathers[7] looked upon commerce as sinful, or as easily conducive to sin and disreputable. . . . Even as late as in the year 1078 a Roman Council, presided over by Gregory VII, promulgated Canons, the fifth of which declared that whereas soldiers and merchants could not carry on their trade without sin, there was no salvation for them unless they turned to other occupations.
>
> (Beer 1938: 18)

Beer also noted that

> [t]he ultimate authority of the laws and regulations that circumscribed the economic activities of the mediaeval merchant, trader, and craftsman were Scripture and Aristotle. High Writ gave the precepts, and their truths were established by the moral philosophy, the logic and dialectic of Aristotle as interpreted by the schoolmen.
>
> (Beer 1938: 228)

One of the most advanced contributors to medieval thinking to do with economic issues was the School of Salamanca, yet even they took an ethical approach. When discussing the Salamanca School's view of economic issues Alves and Moreira (2013: 65) write

> this approach is characterized, among other factors, by a realistic natural-law outlook (that takes into account actual human ends without forfeiting an ethical evaluation of those ends) and also by a "first-person" ethics, in which individual agents – and not society as a whole – are taken to be, at the end of the line, the ones who bear responsibility for formulating moral judgements and deciding in conscience how to act on the market.

Pre-fifteenth century Muslim scholars took a more positive view of production[8] than their Christian equivalents.

> Inspired by the Qur'anic considerations that engaging in lawful economic activities is seeking "'bounty of Allah" (cf. the Qur'an 62:10 and 73:20) and inspired by the Prophet's (peace be upon him) saying that planting a plant is also a good deed (cf. Al-Qurashi, 1987. pp. 115–16), the Muslim scholars gave high value to productive activities.
>
> (Islahi 2014: 29)

The Muslim scholars' approach, while seeing production more positively, was still employing a religious-based framework. One example where this framework was counterproductive for production had to do with the corporation, in particular the lack of the corporate form in Islamic law.

> No collective economic actor appears in the Quran, let alone a collectivity considered a legal person. Islam's most authoritative source of guidance harbors nothing obvious, then, that might have inspired or supported the corporate form of organization, or justified borrowing it from an outside source.
>
> (Kuran 2011: 106)

Experimentation with organisational form, including the corporation, from around 1100[9] was one reason for western Europe's growing economic advantage over the Islamic world.[10]

It could be argued that the beginnings of the development of economics proper had to wait for the writings of the mercantilists and the physiocrats starting in the seventeenth century. Before then,

> [e]conomic questions were considered peripheral to ethical and other related concerns. . . . Greek and Roman writers have passages on the division of labor, but their attention was largely directed elsewhere; the scholastics were mainly interested in ethical aspects of economic activity and

> deriving codes of conduct in the marketplace from divine law; the natural law thinkers tried to create objective moral standards that were in accord with the law of nature.
>
> (Irwin 1996: 25)

The mercantilists and the physiocrats were the two leading pre-classical groups of authors interested in economic issues. Both groups put forward a rudimentary analysis of (macro-level) production. Importantly for this chapter, their approach required a more positive analytical framework.

Mercantilism

Whittaker (1940: 716) argues that, in medieval Europe, economic thought was subordinate to Christian morals, and it was only with the appearance of mercantilism[11] that this changed. He suggests that the state[12] replaced God in the discussion of wealth and production. But while there are discussions concerning the state control and direction of production and firms to be found within the mercantilist[13] literature, when it came to firms, it is a limited discussion—limited in the sense that it deals not with issues to do with firms per se but rather with the effects of firms on more macro issues such as the balance of trade. It was also limited in that it largely deals only with the regulated companies[14] and their monopolies.[15] When discussing the period 1649–1690, Magnusson (1994: 101–3) argues that several mercantilist writers attacked the regulated companies. Some authors argued for the adoption of measures to end the monopoly position that regulated companies such as the Merchant Adventurers, the Russian Company, the Levant Company and the East India Company held. There were also debates about the effects of companies like the East India Company on the balance of trade. Gerrad Malynes, for example, argued that the East India Company was exporting money "beyond the seas" (Magnusson 1994: 102) and thus hurting England's balance of trade. More voices where added to the chorus against the regulated companies as the seventeenth century progressed. In 1645, for example, an anonymous writer, in a pamphlet entitled *A Discourse Consisting of Motives for the Enlargement and Freedome of Trade*, attacked the Merchant Adventurers. The author argued that there is nothing more "pernicious and destructive to any Kingdom or Common-wealth than Monopolies".

But regulated companies also had their defenders. In 1601, John Wheeler defended the Merchant Adventurers, saying that its traffic in cloth led to a situation where "a number of laboring men are set to work and gain much monie, besides that which the Merchant gaineth". That is, what's good for the Adventurers is good for the country! He also argued that the Adventures were not a monopoly:

> He began with a Latin quotation according to which monopoly meant trading concentrated into one hand, and he considered the charge sufficiently refuted when he pointed out that the Company had no "bank or

> common stock" and no common factor for buying and selling. Not only, he asserted, was it not a monopoly, but its "stint" even rendered it diametrically opposed to any monopolistic tendency, for it prevented the rich from taking bread from the poor.
>
> (Heckscher 1994, vol. 1: 386)

In 1641 Lewell Roberts recommended that more regulated companies should be set up. He was of the opinion that if people were to "joyn one with another in a corporation and Company, and not to kase their Traffike by themselves asunder, or apart", it would lead to increased strength and maximum benefits for a trading nation. In addition, Thomas Mun, Edward Misselden and Sir Josiah Child had all defended the East India Company from attack at different times.

It should be noted, however, that many of these debates were partisan rent seeking with each side just dressing up their position in terms of the public good. Importantly, such attacks are more policy relevant than economics revenant. It is worth observing that although such arguments involve firms, they do not require a theory of the firm or of production. Just accepting that the firms exist and transact is enough for policy evaluation; there is no need for an explanation of what a firm is, what its boundaries are or what its internal organization is.

So what we see here is, much like the situation with the later classical economists, a largely macroeconomic-originated outlook which had no need for a meaningful theory of micro-level production. But significantly, their mode of analysis did move away from the normative towards the positive. Their discussion of the balance of trade, the effects of monopoly, employment, etc., requires more than just a normative framework.

Physiocrats

The aim of the physiocrats[16] was to analyse the determinants of the general level of economic activity, and again this aim required a more positive approach to analysis. For the physiocrats, the key variable affecting the level of activity was the capacity of agriculture to yield a 'net product'.[17] The physiocrats saw the wealth of a nation as being determined by the size of any surplus of agricultural production over and above that needed to support agriculture (by feeding farm labourers, etc.). They argued that it was only when labour was applied to land that it created a surplus over and above what was required for its maintenance. It was out of this surplus that all other classes in society were supported. Agriculture alone was productive; it alone produces the 'net product'. Other classes in society were stipendiary, sterile or unproductive.

To see the difference between productive and unproductive note that the physiocrats believed that the artisan sold his output for a payment that covered (1) his production costs plus (2) subsistence wages for himself, while the cultivator received an amount that covered (1) his production costs plus (2) his subsistence wages plus (3) a surplus, which would be paid to the landowner as a rent. Thus productive means productive of a surplus (Whittaker 1940: 369–70).

Johnson (1966: 617) describes the physiocrats' approach to production briefly as

> [t]he physiocratie theory of production and the associated theory of commodity circulation formed the basis of François Quesnay's famous Tableau *économique*. This table summarized reproduction and distribution in an extensive agricultural kingdom with a population of thirty million similar to France. The population was divided into three classes: the "productive" comprising one half the population who were engaged in agriculture, fishing, and mining; the "sterile," the quarter of the population which included manufacturers, artisans, distributors, artists, professionals, and domestic servants; and the "proprietary," the quarter who owned the lands or those, such as crown officials and church personnel, who got their support immediately from proprietor revenue. The Quesnay analysis suggested that the economy was in a state of self-perpetuating equilibrium with the ratios of its components remaining always the same. Economic growth operated with equal force in all directions without altering the proportions. The reproduction process once underway was thus essentially circular.

For our purposes, the relevant point in all of this is that this is a positive, if misguided, description of the aggregate economy.

When commenting on Turgot's *Réflexions Sur La Formation et la Distribution des Richesses* (Reflections on the Formulation and the Distributions of Riches), Edmund Whittaker writes

> the *Réflexions* furnished an integrated treatment of wealth, divorced from ethical or political considerations.
>
> (Whittaker 1940: 720)

Classical economists

The classical economists did develop a theory of production, but it was predominately a theory of macro production aimed at explaining the production of an entire economy rather than being a microeconomic theory of firm production.[18] O'Brien (2003: 112) remarks that

> [c]lassical economics ruled economic thought for about 100 years [approximately 1770–1870]. It focused on macroeconomic issues and economic growth. Because the growth was taking place in an open economy, with a currency that (except during 1797–1819) was convertible into gold, the classical writers were necessarily concerned with the balance of payments, the money supply, and the price level. Monetary theory occupied a central

> place, and their achievements in this area were substantial and – with their trade theory – are still with us today.

Foss and Klein (2006: 7–8) note that from at least the time of the mercantilists and carrying on into the classical economics period, economics was largely carried out at the aggregate level, with microeconomic analysis being harnessed, generally, in the service of the macroeconomic concerns,

> [e]conomics began to a large extent in an aggregative mode, as witness, for example, the "Political Arithmetick" of Sir William Petty, and the dominant interest of most of the classical economists in distribution issues. Analysis of pricing, that is to say, analysis of a phenomenon on a lower level of analysis than distributional analysis, was to a large extent only a means to an end, namely to analyze the functional income distribution.

Lionel Robbins remarked that the classical theories of production and distribution were about determining the total wealth, or total product, of the nation:

> [t]he traditional approach to Economics, at any rate among English-speaking economists, has been by way of an enquiry into the causes determining the production and distribution of wealth. Economics has been divided into two main divisions, the theory of production and the theory of distribution, and the task of these theories has been to explain the causes determining the size of the "total product" and the causes determining the proportions in which it is distributed between different factors of production and different persons.
>
> (Robbins 1935: 64)

This emphasis on macro-level analysis could help explain why the classical economists missed the opportunities they had to develop either a theory of micro-level production or a theory of the firm. As an example of such a missed opportunity, consider Adam Smith, who opens his magnum opus, *An Inquiry into the Nature and Causes of the Wealth of Nations*, with a discussion of the division of labour at the microeconomic level, the famous pin factory example,[19] but quickly moves the analysis to the market level. When discussing Smith's approach to the division of labour McNulty (1984: 237–8) comments,

> [h]aving conceptualized division of labor in terms of the organization of work within the enterprise, however, Smith subsequently failed to develop or even to pursue systematically that line of analysis. His ideas on the division of labor could, for example, have led him toward an analysis of task assignment, management, or organization. Such an intra-firm approach would have foreshadowed the much later—indeed, quite recent—efforts in this direction by Herbert Simon, Oliver Williamson, Harvey Leibenstein, and others, a body of work which Leibenstein calls

> "micro-microeconomics". . . . But, instead, Smith quickly turned his attention away from the internal organization of the enterprise, and outward toward the market and the realm of exchange, perhaps because he found therein both the source of division of labor, in the "propensity in human nature . . . to truck, barter and exchange" and its effective limits.

Another such missed opportunity is when, from the third edition on, Smith discusses 'joint-stock companies'. When considering the internal organisation of such firms Smith raises, but does not develop a theory of what we would call today the principal-agent problems that arise from the separation of ownership from control.[20] Perhaps his most famous remark is:

> [t]he directors of such companies, however, being the managers rather of other people's money than of their own, it cannot well be expected, that they should watch over it with the same anxious vigilance with which the partners in a private copartnery frequently watch over their own. Like the stewards of a rich man, they are apt to consider attention to small matters as not for their master's honour, and very easily give themselves a dispensation from having it. Negligence and profusion, therefore, must always prevail, more or less, in the management of the affairs of such a company.
>
> (Smith 1776: Book V, Chapter 1, Part III, p. 741)

But Smith does not go on to develop the ideas of agency problems or of corporate governance.

When writing about Adam Smith's approach to the firm, Williams (1978: 11) says:

> [t]he firm was disembodied and became a unit in which resources congeal in the productive process. When we come to examine the equilibrium/value theory of *The Wealth of Nations* it will be shown that, in that context, the firm is little more than a passive conduit which assists in the movement of resources between alternative activities.

But, again, we see a more positive approach to the economic analysis of production in Smith's work.

One economist from the classical period who did analyse production at a slightly disaggregated level was Robert Torrens. Torrens (2019) considers the production of wealth at a level less than that of the whole economy. Torrens begins by defining wealth as

> those material articles which are useful or desirable to man, and which it requires some portion of voluntary exertion to produce or to preserve.
>
> (Torrens 2019: 1)

He then defined production as "the original acquisition of wealth" (Torrens 2019: 66).

For Torrens, there were the three standard instruments of production: land, labour and capital. Importantly, in Torrens's approach, these three factors can be utilised in many different ways to create wealth. But all the different combinations of the three instruments can be allocated to one of four different general categories or 'industries': the 'appropriate industry', those activities which involve the mere collecting or appropriating of things spontaneously supplied by nature; the 'manufacturing industry', those activities for which exertion is required for the purpose of adapting factors supplied by nature for use by man; the 'agricultural industry', activities to increase the quantity of outputs from nature's endowments for useful purposes; and the 'commercial industry', which involves the transportation and exchange of articles of wealth acquired by the three previous methods.

Thus, Torrens gives us, at best, a theory of large-scale groupings of firms, a theory of aggregated industries rather than a theory of firm-level production or a theory of the firm in the modern sense.

Historian of economic thought Mark Blaug summed up the classical economics approach to the firm by arguing that the classical economists simply "had no theory of the firm" (Blaug 1958: 226). Bowen (1955: 5–6) argues in a similar fashion:

> economists of the classical tradition had usually assumed that the level and distribution of income and the allocation of resources were determined by forces that could be understood without a detailed theory of the firm. . . . Everything else would be settled by the impersonal forces of the market, and there would be no need to consider in detail the decisions and actions of the individual firm.

Again, what we see with the classical economists is a macro-level theory of production, not a theory of the firm[21] or even a theory of micro-production.[22] But importantly, their theory is a positive theory of aggregate production without the ethical overtones of the pre-seventeenth-century writers. This set the tone for all the theories that followed.

Neoclassical economics

The early neoclassical economists wrote little of significance on the theory of production or the theory of the firm. As Kenneth Boulding has written "[i]t is well to remember that for all practical purposes there was no theory of the firm in economics before Marshall and no theory of the individual consumer before Jevons and the Austrians" (Boulding 1952: 42). Or as D. P. O'Brien has put it,

> [s]erious discussion of the history of the theory of the firm has to start with Alfred Marshall. There is no doubt that he inherited relevant material from Classical economics; but an attempt to construct a pre-Marshallian theory of the firm from the materials available is likely to be unsuccessful.
>
> (O'Brien 1984: 25)

If we look at the work of Alfred Marshall, the quintessential neoclassical economist, we see that he favoured analysing economic phenomena, including production, from a positive perspective.[23] As Dzionek-Kozłowska (2015) writes,

> [h]is adoption of such an attitude [conducting economics as a positive science] is understandable as it was, in a way, a natural consequence of the development of the 19th century methodological reflections formulated by John Stuart Mill (1844; 1974), William Nassau Senior (1836, 1852), John Elliot Cairnes (1875) and John Neville Keynes (1891). It may be treated as signum temporis too, as the last quarter of that century was the time of professionalisation of economics, recognizing it is a science focused on researching facts, free from subjective evaluation, providing instead objective knowledge about certain aspects of social reality. The ideal of economics as a positive science facilitated it in establishing its position as an independent science and academic discipline.
>
> (Dzionek-Kozłowska 2015: 2)

and

> [a]t the start one need once again to look at an idea which Marshall, over the course of his 50-year-long scientific career, invariably supported – the idea that economists should strive to explain the facts and to analyse the economic reality as objectively as possible, shying away from presenting economic laws as tenets of economic policy, and all the more as moral imperatives.
>
> (Dzionek-Kozłowska 2015: 2)

The development of his approach to production utilising the 'representative firm' is an example of the positive approach. Marshall's investigations of real-world industries told him that even for a given industry there would be firms of different sizes, making different amounts of profit, producing different quantities of output. There would be firms who had just entered the market and would be willing, in the short-term at least, to make a loss in the hope of gaining a foothold in the market and making profits latter on. On the other hand, there would also be firms who are well established and would be making profits now. For Marshall, firms were dynamic, heterogeneous, in disequilibrium and they progressed through a life cycle in much the same way as people. Marshall wanted to "summarise" this real-world variability so that he could create an industry supply curve without having to assume that all firms were the same. The representative firm was the way he did this.

Scott Moss highlights the point that "[t]he representative firm is composed of the salient characteristics of all firms in the industry" (Moss 1984a: 308), while Philip L. Williams notes that,

> [i]t [the representative firm] would need to be in some sense "representative" both of the cost and of the sales position of other firms within the

> industry. For this to be true it would need to be "representative" with respect to its business ability, age, luck, size and its access to net external economies.
>
> (Williams 1978: 102)

The important point here is that Marshall is taking a positive approach to his theory of production. He did not ask what firms should do; he looked at what firms actually did and used that information to create his representative firm.

The representative firm was driven out of the economics literature during the cost controversy of the 1920s and replaced[24] by A. C. Pgiou's equilibrium firm. But again the equilibrium firm was a positive construction. Moss argues that Pigou assumed

> that an equilibrium firm could be constructed from the law of returns (increasing, constant or diminishing) obeyed by any industry.
>
> (Moss 1984a: 313)

and

> that the notion of a "representative firm" with characteristics deduced from the known characteristics of an industry is useful in the exposition of a limited range of concepts. Pigou adopted the same strictures with regard to his "equilibrium firm".
>
> (Moss 1984b: 65)

It was the equilibrium firm that gave rise to the now standard textbook theory of the firm.[25]

Conclusion

The outline of the history of the theory of production/the firm given here highlights the idea that up until the seventeenth century the discussion of production was dominated by normative analysis. The questions asked were about what production would find favour with the predominant religious or ethical framework of the time. But over time, ethical considerations were replaced by more positive concerns. By 1913 Herbert J. Davenport could write, with regard to the question of what is production, that ethical tests are irrelevant.

> Nor, again, does it at all matter to the purpose what may be the artistic merit of the service or its moral quality – whether the advice be wholesome, the acting skillful, the music classic, the play clean, the teaching scholarly, the lecture conservative, the preaching godly. Each of these questions is irrelevant except in so far as it may have some bearing upon the price that will be bid. Peruna, Hop Bitters, obscene literature, indecent paintings, picture hats and corsets are wealth, irrespective of any ethical or

> conventional test to which they may or may not conform. Being marketable, price-bearing, they are wealth. So likewise of services; in no case is economic productivity a matter of piety or of merit or of social deserving.
> (Davenport 1913: 126)

That normative analysis had lost its predominant position in the theory of production became indisputable in the seventeenth century. It was with the development of mercantilism that positive questions began to come to the fore. Only then did a more realistic theory of production begin to be developed. For the mercantilists, physiocrats and classical economists, production meant aggregate production, but they laid the foundations for the later theories of micro-level production and, eventually, the theory of the firm. All these theories were driven by asking positive questions; normative questions were relegated to a secondary level of importance.

In the conclusion to his paper 'A Short History of Economics As a Moral Science', James Alvey concisely summaries the decline of economics as a moral science:

> [a]fter the introductory remarks, I set out in the first section a brief history of economics before Adam Smith, showing that it was generally (with the exception of the mercantilists) conceived of as a part of moral philosophy. In the second section I presented elements of the new interpretation of Smith, which show the latter as a developer of economics as a moral science. In the third section of the paper I showed that even after Smith, up to the beginning of the present century, a number of leading economic theorists conceived of economics as a moral science, either in theory or in practice. In the fourth section I sketched the decline of economics as a moral science. The key factor was the emergence and influence of positivism. The current view of the detachment of economics from moral science and morals, in particular, is alien to much of the history of the discipline.
> (Alvey 1999: 68)

This does raise two important questions for future study: first, whether the example of production is just one case of a more general movement in economics away from the normative to the positive (taking into consideration Letwin's example of usury and Dorobăţ's example of international trade suggests that answer could be yes), and second, whether economics is just one example of a more general movement in scientific thinking in the seventeenth century.

Notes

1 The Arthasastra is normally attributed to Kautilya (also known as Canakya and Vishnupta) who was the Chief Minister of Emperor Candragupta Mourya. Mourya was the founder of the Maurya Empire in ancient India. His reign covered the period c. 321–c. 297 BCE. The Arthasastra is thought to have been written sometime around the end of the fourth century BCE.

2 Also called Taoism.
3 One of the two foundational texts of Daoism.
4 One of *The Four Books* in Confucianism. These books are the classic texts illustrating the belief system of Confucianism.
5 Another of *The Four Books* in Confucianism.
6 One of the two foundational texts of Daoism. Attributed to Zhuang Zhou – usually known as "Zhuangzi" (Master Zhuang).
7 Beer notes that "from the Fathers, such as Ambrose, Augustine, Chrysostom, Cassiodor" (Beer 1938: 24).
8 Muslim scholars took a positive view of commerce in general. "Traditionally, commerce was assigned high value by the Muslim scholars, because, perhaps, it was once the occupations of the Prophet (pbuh) himself and it was the main source of earning in the Arabian Peninsula" (Islahi 2014: 29).
9

> Following the split of Christianity in 1054, and during the struggle to emancipate religion from the control of emperors, kings, and feudal lords (1075–1122), the Roman Catholic Church began calling itself a corporation and running its affairs according to a new canon law (*jus novum*).
>
> (Kuran 2011: 102)

10 See Kuran (2011) for a discussion of the reasons for the Islamic world relative economic decline.
11 The meaning we should attach to 'mercantilism' is not clear. As Lars Magnusson has written, "[i]n his *Predecessors to Adam Smith*, E. A. J. Johnson labelled 'mercantilism' an 'unhappy word'. As our future discussion will reveal, this might not be totally inaccurate. Hence, this word has been used in a confusing number of senses and for many different designs. As any common consent with regard to the interpretation of "mercantilism has been difficult to accomplish, discussions dealing with this phenomenon have often been blurred" (Magnusson 1994: 8).
12 Mercantilism requires a dominant state to provide and enforce monopolies as well as to regulate and control both domestic and international trade and to direct the economy in general. Beer (1939: 13, footnote 1) lists the characteristics of mercantilism as:

> (i) Conception of money (coin and bullion or treasure) as the essence of wealth. (This conception prevailed from the end of the Middle Ages up to the end of the seventeenth century.) (ii) Regulating foreign trade with a view to bringing in money by the balance of trade. (iii) Making the balance of trade the criterion of national prosperity or decline. (iv) Promotion of manufacture by supplying it with cheap raw materials and cheap labour. (v) Protective customs duties on, or prohibition of, import of manufactured commodities. (vi) The view that the economic interests of nations are mutually antagonistic.

Higgs (1897: 16) explains "[t]he Mercantilists seem always to have propounded to themselves the problem, How can Government make this nation prosperous? Nationalism, state-regulation, and particularism are the essence of their policy", while Backhouse (2002: 58) notes "[m]ercantilist policies include the use of state power to build up industry, to obtain and increase the surplus of exports over imports, and to accumulate stocks of precious metals". "In France during this period [mid-1700s] the concept [mercantilism] was utilized in order to describe an economic policy regime characterized by direct state intervention, intended to protect domestic merchants and manufacturers" (Magnusson 2003: 46) When discussing the general economic background to the development of the mercantile chartered companies in England, Griffiths (1974) explains that "[t]he right—and the duty—of the Crown to control the economy was taken for granted and according to Coke 'the royal prerogative had an ancient and special force in the government of trade'" (p. ix) and "[t]he underlying concepts were those of monopolies, collective trading or regulation of trade and the right of the Crown to control the economy" (p. 3). In a comment on Eli Heckscher's view of mercantilism, Deepak Lal writes that

> Heckscher had argued that the mercantilist system arose as the Renaissance princes sought to consolidate the weak states they had inherited or acquired from the ruins of the Roman Empire. These were states encompassing numerous feuding and disorderly groups which the new Renaissance princes sought to curb to create a nation. The purpose was to achieve 'unification and power,' making the 'State's purposes decisive in a uniform economic sphere and to make all economic activity subservient to considerations corresponding to the requirements of the State'. The mercantilist policies–with their industrial regulations, state-created monopolies, import and export restrictions, price controls–were partly motivated by the objective of granting royal favors in exchange for revenue to meet the chronic fiscal crisis of the state . . . . Another objective was to extend the span of government control over the economy to facilitate its integration.
>
> (Lal 2006: 307).

13 For a detailed discussion of mercantilism see Heckscher (1994), Viner (1937), Beer (1938: Chapter VI), Magnusson (1994, 2003, 2015) and Ekelund and Tollison (1997).

14 See Cawston and Keane (1896), Griffiths (1974) and Ekelund and Tollison (1997: chapters 6 and 7) for general histories of the regulated companies.

15 Erikson and Hamilton (2018: 112) argue that the development of the regulated companies "was a significant factor driving the sudden increase in innovative economic works" in seventeenth-century England. But as argued here, the reverse was not true. The increased interest in things economic did not stimulate an interest in the firm, or at least in the theory of the firm.

16 For discussions of physiocracy see Beer (1939), Higgs (1897), Meek (1962) and Vaggi (1987).

17 There were a number of pre-fifteenth century Muslim scholars who also saw agriculture as the most important economic activity (Islahi 2014: 29–30).

18 Waldauer, Zahka and Pal (1996) argues that in areas such as international trade, taxation and the labour theory of value the Arthasastra anticipated classical economic thought by more than 2,000 years.

19 For a discussion of the origins of Smith's pin making example, see Peaucelle (2006) and Peaucelle and Guthrie (2011).

20 See Guthrie (2017) for an introduction to the modern approach to these issues.

21 This had to wait till the 1970s to develop; see Walker (2016).

22 This developed as part of neoclassical economics.

23 Dzionek-Kozłowska (2015) notes that despite his calls for avoiding value judgments in theoretical economics, Marshall's texts contain many normative discussions.

24 Newman (1960: 591, footnote 5) argues that the equilibrium firm is the "representative firm with the representativeness with respect to size left out".

25 The move from the equilibrium firm to the textbook model involved two additional changes.

> First, Pigou himself did not assume that the industry was comprised entirely of equilibrium firms, but only that an equilibrium firm could be constructed from the law of returns (increasing, constant or diminishing) obeyed by any industry. Second, Pigou did not assume the firm qua production function to be facing household preference functions. It was the inclusion of these two elements that constituted the third step in the creation of the firm analysed in the neoclassical theory of the firm.
>
> (Moss 1984a: 313)

These two steps were completed, in the main, by Robinson (1933) and Chamberlin (1933).

References

Alves, André A. and José M. Moreira (2013). *The Salamanca School* (Major Conservative and Libertarian Thinkers, Series Editor: John Meadowcroft, vol. 9), New York: Bloomsbury Academic.

Alvey, James E. (1999). 'A Short History of Economics as a Moral Science', *Journal of Markets & Morality*, 2(1) Spring: 53–73.

Anonymous (1645). *A Discourse Consisting of Motives for the Enlargement and Freedome of Trade: Especially That of Cloth, and Other Woollen Manufactures, Engrossed at Present Contrary to the Law of Nature, the Law of Nations, and the Lawes of This Kingdome*, London: printed by Richard Bishop for Stephen Bowtell to be sold at his shop at the signe of the Bible in Popes-Head Alley.

Ashley, W. J. (1919). *An Introduction to English Economic History and Theory: Part One – The Middle Ages*, 4th edn., One Volume Edition, New York: Augustus M. Kelly Publishers, 1966. First edition 1888.

Backhouse, Roger E. (2002). *The Ordinary Business of Life: A History of Economics from the Ancient World to the Twenty-First Century*, Princeton, NJ: Princeton University Press.

Beer, M. (1938). *Early British Economics: From the Thirteenth to the Middle of the Eighteenth Century*, London: George Allen and Unwin Ltd.

Beer, M. (1939). *An Inquiry into Physiocracy*, London: George Allen and Unwin Ltd.

Blaug, Mark (1958). 'The Classical Economists and the Factory Acts – A ReExamination', *Quarterly Journal of Economics*, 72(2) May: 211–26.

Bonar, James (1893). *Philosophy and Political Economy in Some of Their Historical Relations*, London: Swan, Sonnenschein & Co.

Boulding, Kenneth E. (1952). 'Implications for General Economics of More Realistic Theories of the Firm', *American Economic Review*, 42(2) Papers and Proceedings of the Sixty-fourth Annual Meeting of the American Economic Association May: 35–44.

Bowen, Howard R. (1955). *The Business Enterprise as a Subject for Research: Prepared for the Committee on Business Enterprise Research*, Social Science Research Council, Pamphlet No. 11, New York: Social Science Research Council.

Cawston, George and A. H. Keane (1896). *The Early Chartered Companies (A.D. 1296–1858)*, London: Edward Arnold.

Chamberlin, Edward H. (1933). *The Theory of Monopolistic Competition*, Cambridge, MA: Harvard University Press.

Dasgupta, Ajit (1993). *A History of Indian Economic Thought*, London: Routledge.

Davenport, Herbert J. (1913). *The Economics of Enterprise*, New York: Augustus M. Kelley Publishers, 1968.

Deodhar, Satish (2018). 'Indian Antecedents to Modern Economic Thought', WP No. 2018–01–02 January, Indian Institute of Management, Ahmedabad.

DesRoches, Tyler C. (2014). 'On Aristotle's Natural Limit', *History of Political Economy*, 46(3) Fall: 387–407.

Dorobăț, Carmen, E. (2015). 'A Brief History Of International Trade Thought: From Pre-Doctrinal Contributions to the 21st Century Heterodox International Economics', *The Journal of Philosophical Economics: Reflections on Economic and Social Issues*, 8(2): 106–37.

Dzionek-Kozłowska, Joanna (2015). 'Alfred Marshall's Puzzles. Between Economics as a Positive Science and Economic Chivalry', Lodz Economics Working Papers 5/2015.

Ekelund, Robert B. Jr. and Robert D. Tollison (1997). *Politicized Economies: Monarchy, Monopoly, and Mercantilism*, College Station: Texas A&M University Press.

Erikson, Emily and Mark Hamilton (2018). 'Companies and the Rise of Economic Thought: The Institutional Foundations of Early Economics in England, 1550–1720', *American Journal of Sociology*, 124(1) July: 111–49.

Foss, Nicolai J. and Peter G. Klein (2006). 'The Emergence of the Modern Theory of the Firm', Center for Strategic Management and Globalization, Copenhagen Business School, SMG Working Paper 1/2006, January.

Griffiths, Percival (1974). *A Licence to Trade: A History of the English Chartered Companies*, London: Ernest Benn Limited.

Guthrie, Graeme (2017). *The Firm Divided: Manager-Shareholder Conflict and the Fight for Control of the Modern Corporation*, Oxford: Oxford University Press.

Heckscher, Eli F. (1994). *Mercantilism*, 2 vols., London: Routledge. First published, in Swedish, in 1931. First published in English in 1935.

Higgs, Henry (1897). *The Physiocrats: Six Lectures on The French Économistes of the 18th Century*, London: Macmillan and Co., Limited.

Hu, Jichuang (1988). *A Concise History of Chinese Economic Thought*, Beijing: Foreign Languages Press.

Irwin, Douglas A. (1996). *Against the Tide: An Intellectual History of Free Trade*, Princeton: Princeton University Press.

Islahi, Abdul Azim (2014). *History of Islamic Economic Thought: Contributions of Muslim Scholars to Economic Thought and Analysis*, Cheltenham, UK: Edward Elgar Publishing Ltd.

Johnson, Jerah (1966). 'The Role of Spending in Physiocratic Theory', *Quarterly Journal of Economics*, 80(4) November: 616–32.

Keynes, John Neville (1917). *The Scope and Method of Political Economy*, 4th edn., New York: Augustus M. Kelley Publishers, 1986.

Kuran, Timur (2011). *The Long Divergence: How Islamic Law Held Back the Middle East*, Princeton: Princeton University Press.

Lal, Deepak (2006). 'The Contemporary Relevance of Heckscher's Mercantilism'. In Ronald Findlay, Rolf G. H. Henriksson, Håkan Lindgren and Mats Lundahl (eds.), *Eli Heckscher, International Trade, and Economic History* (305–19), Cambridge, MA: MIT Press.

Letwin, William (1964). *The Origins of Scientific Economics*, New York: Doubleday & Company, Inc.

Magnusson, Lars G. (1994). *Mercantilism: The Shaping of Economic Language*, London: Routledge.

Magnusson, Lars G. (2003). 'Mercantilism'. In Warren J. Samuels, Jeff E. Biddle and John B. Davis (eds.), *A Companion to the History of Economic Thought* (46–60), Oxford: Blackwell Publishing Ltd.

Magnusson, Lars G. (2015). *The Political Economy of Mercantilism*, London: Routledge.

McNulty, Paul J. (1984). 'On the Nature and Theory of Economic Organization: The Role of the Firm Reconsidered', *History of Political Economy*, 16(2) Summer: 233–53.

Meek, Ronald L. (1962). *The Economics of Physiocracy*, London: George Allen and Unwin Ltd.

Menger, Carl (1883). *Investigations into the Method of the Social Sciences with Special Reference to Economics*, formerly published under the title: Problems of Economics and Sociology (Untersuchungen uber die Methode der Socialwissenschaften und der Politischen Oekonomie insbesondere), with an introduction by Lawrence H. White, edited by Louis Schneider, translated by Francis J. Nock, New York: New York University Press, 1985.

Mill, John Stuart (1844). *Essays on Some Unsettled Questions of Political Economy*, London: John W. Parker.

Moss, Scott (1984a). 'The History of the Theory of the Firm from Marshall to Robinson and Chamberlin: The Source of Positivism in Economics', *Economica*, n.s. 51(203) August: 307–18.

Moss, Scott (1984b). 'O'Brien's "The Evolution of the Theory of the Firm": A Discussion'. In Frank H. Stephen (ed.), *Firms, Organization and Labour* (63–8), London: The Macmillan Press Ltd.

Newman, Peter (1960). 'The Erosion of Marshall's Theory of Value', *Quarterly Journal of Economics*, 74(4) November: 587–99.

O'Brien, D. P. (1984). 'The Evolution of the Theory of the Firm'. In Frank H. Stephen (ed.), *Firms, Organization and Labour* (25–62), London: The Macmillan Press Ltd.

O'Brien, Denis P. (2003). 'Classical Economics'. In Warren J. Samuels, Jeff E. Biddle and John B. Davis (eds.), *A Companion to the History of Economic Thought* (112–29), Oxford: Blackwell Publishing Ltd.

Peaucelle, Jean-Louis (2006). 'Adam Smith's Use of Multiple References for His Pin Making Example', *European Journal of the History of Economic Thought*, 13(4) December: 489–512.

Peaucelle, Jean-Louis and Cameron Guthrie (2011). 'How Adam Smith Found Inspiration in French Texts on Pin Making in the Eighteenth Century', *History of Economic Ideas*, 19(3): 41–67.

Robbins, Lionel (1935). *An Essay on the Nature & Significance of Economic Science*, 2nd edn., Revised and Extended, London: Macmillan and Co. Limited.

Robbins, Lionel (1998). *A History of Economic Thought: The LSE Lectures*, Steven G. Medema and Warren J. Samuels (eds.), Princeton, NJ: Princeton University Press.

Robinson, Joan (1933). *The Economics of Imperfect Competition*, London: Macmillan and Co., Ltd.

Sewall, Hannah R. (1901). *The Theory of Value Before Adam Smith*, New York: Augustus M. Kelly Publishers, 1971.

Smith, Adam (1776). *An Inquiry into the Nature and Causes of the Wealth of Nations*, Volumes I and II, R. H. Campbell and A. S. Skinner (general eds.), W. B. Todd (textual ed.), Indianapolis: Liberty Classics, 1981.

Tang, Renwu (2014). 'A Comparison between Confucian and Daoist Economic Philosophies in the Pre-Qin era'. In Cheng Lin, Terry Peach and Wang Fang (eds.), *The History of Ancient Chinese Economic Thought* (106–139), London: Routledge.

Torrens, R. (2019). *An Essay on the Production of Wealth*, Delhi: Facsimile Publisher. First published 1821.

Vaggi, Gianni (1987). *The Economics of François Quesnay*, Durham: Duke University Press.

Viner, Jacob (1937). *Studies in the Theory of International Trade*, New York: Harper and Brothers Publishers.

Waldauer, Charles, William J. Zahka and Surendra Pal (1996). 'Kautilya's Arthashastra: A Neglected Precursor to Classical Economics', *Indian Economic Review*, 31(1): 101–8.

Walker, Paul (2016). *The Theory of the Firm: An Overview of the Economic Mainstream*, London: Routledge.

Whittaker, Edmund (1940). *A History of Economic Ideas*, New York: Longmans, Green and Co.

Williams, Philip L. (1978). *The Emergence of the Theory of the Firm: From Adam Smith to Alfred Marshall*, London: The Macmillan Press.

Wood, Diana (2002). *Medieval Economic Thought*, Cambridge: Cambridge University Press.

3 The division of labour and the theory of the firm

Introduction

George Stigler argues that the division of labour should be seen as integral to the theory of the firm.

> The division of labor is not a quaint practice of eighteenth-century pin factories; it is a fundamental principle of economic organization.
>
> (Stigler 1951: 193)

But while the division of labour is an ancient idea in economics, it did not spark discussion about the firm until relatively recently.

This chapter examines the influence (or lack of influence) that the analysis of the division of labour has had on mainstream economic thinking to do with the theory of the firm/theory of production.[1] It will be shown that despite the division of labour being a very old idea in economics, dating from at least the ancient Indians, Greeks and Chinese, it took more than two thousand years for it to give rise to a theory of the firm. Following on from the ancient scholars, in the medieval period both Islamic and Christian theologians and philosophers analysed the concept and consequences of the division of labour. The pre-classical, classical and neoclassical economists continued and expanded the enquiry, but all without applying the division of labour to the theory of the firm.

It was not until the twentieth century that a division of labour based theory of the firm finally appeared. In the 1920s Lawrence Frank saw an increasing division of labour as giving rise to the vertically integrated firm. In the 1930s E. A. G. Robinson argued that the division of labour affected the size of the firm due to its effects on production technology and management. By the 1950s George Stigler was arguing that the size of the firm was limited by the division of labour due to the division of labour being limited by the extent of the market. In the 1990s Gary Becker and Kevin Murphy saw the size of the firm as being limited not just by the size of the market but also, more often, by coordination costs. In 2018 Michael Rauh showed that the division of labour, which translates to the size of the firm, can be, depending on circumstances, limited by the extent of the labour market, moral hazard or an 'O-ring' property. In this paper

Rauh utilises a stochastic or 'O-ring' production function. Importantly, with an O-ring production function, if one part of the production process fails, the whole process fails.

But despite this belated interest in the division of labour, within the contemporary mainstream economics literature, the division of labour is still very much a minority approach to the analysis of the firm.[2]

Ancient philosophers

Trade economist Douglas Irwin argues that

> [p]erhaps Plato's (1930, 153) greatest contribution to economics was his early discussion (dating from about 380 B.C.) of the advantages of the division of labor in the *Republic*: "The result [of such a division], then, is that more things are produced, and better and more easily when one man performs one task according to his nature, at the right moment, and at leisure from other occupations".
>
> (Irwin 1996: 13)

The historian of economic thought James Bonar emphasises the point that for Plato the division of labour drives the social organisation of production. Bonar gives us a sense of Plato's view when he writes,

> Plato's conception of Production is in close connection with this view of Wealth. It is important not that men should have as many wants as possible, and satisfy them all, but that they should find out what their special work is in the world and do it. He illustrates this doctrine in various passages of the Republic, and especially in the clearest of his economic analyses, the account of division of labour in the Second Book. A State, he there says, is formed because the individual is not able to supply all his wants by himself, but only when he makes common cause with other men, and devotes himself to one single industry for the common good, on the understanding that the rest are doing the same. Thus arise the separate trades of farming, building, weaving, and shoemaking; and this division of labour is best for the following reasons: Men and women are not all born alike, but with special powers fitting them for special work. Second, by attention to one occupation alone men will do much better work than when attempting several. Third, because time is saved and opportunities (of season, etc.) are more promptly utilized. In this way articles are made in greater number, of better quality, and with greater ease, than when each man is a Jack-of-all-trades.
>
> (Bonar 1992: 14–15)

As this Bonar quote highlights, Plato's discussion was about the social division of labour, that is, the separation of employments and professions within a society, rather than the division of labour within a factory or within the limits of a single industry, that is, the manufacturing division of labour. Bonar (1992: 34–5) also argues that while on the issue of production Aristotle was clearer than Plato, he did not deviate much from Plato's earlier analysis of the division of labour. Xenophon saw that larger cities provided a larger market for individual products, which resulted in a greater division of labour and an increased level of skill among workers.

> In small towns, the same man makes a couch, a door, a plough, and a table; and frequently the same person is a builder too, and is very well content if he can thus find customers enough to maintain him; and it is impossible for a man who works at many things to do them all well; but, in great cities, because there are numbers that want each particular thing, one art alone suffices for the maintenance of each individual; and frequently indeed, not an entire art, but one man makes shoes for men, and another for women; sometimes it happens, that one gets a maintenance merely by stitching shoes, another by cutting them out, another by cutting out upper-leathers only, and another by doing none of these things, but simply putting together the pieces. He, therefore, that is employed in a work of the smallest compass, must, of necessity, do it best.
>
> (Xenophon 1876: 244)

Xenophon also, much like al-Ghazali (see page 35) and Adam Smith (see page 39) after him, hints at the manufacturing division of labour with an example of the organisation of cooking for King Cyrus.

> but where there is employment enough for one man to boil meat, for another to roast it, for one to boil fish, for another to broil it, and for another to make bread, (and that not of every sort either, but it is enough for him to furnish one sort of good,) each man, in my opinion, must of necessity bring the things that are thus made to very great perfection. Cyrus therefore, by such means, greatly exceeded all other people in making presents of dishes from his table.
>
> (Xenophon 1876: 245)

But, also like al-Ghazali and Smith, Xenophon doesn't utilise this insight to develop a theory of production or the firm.[3]

With regard to Chinese writers in the 'period of philosophers', which ran from the time of Confucius (551 BCE–479 BCE) to about 100 BCE, Sun (2016: 103) writes,

> [o]ver such a long "period of philosophers", a number of Chinese thinkers wrote extensively on the division of labour. In particular, Kuan Chung (Kuan Tzu, Guan Zhong, d. 645 BC), Mencius (c. 372–289 BC) and Hsün Tzu (Xunzi, Xun Kuang, c. 312–238 BC) explicitly discussed the division of labour and indeed carried out rather sophisticated analyses of the subject.

> The necessity of the division of labour and the division of employment into what is termed the "main genera" of social production (agriculture, manufacturing and services) posited in the classical political economy of the eighteenth-nineteenth centuries (see, e.g., Marx 1867/1976, p. 471, and the citations therein) had been recognised in the writings of those authors – as has long been known in the literature on the history of Chinese philosophy and political thought (see, e.g., Fung 1937; Hsiao 1979).

In ancient India there was also an appreciation of the division of labour. Deodhar (2018: 12) gives the example of Rig-Veda,[4] an important religious text from around 1500 BCE:

> [t]he recognition of division of labour and specialization seems to have emerged towards the last phase of Rig-Veda. What we know as 'caste' system today emerged in its original form as the Varna system (Nadkarni, 2012). The sacred text Gita referred to in the earlier subsection, has a clear reference to what varna means. In Hymns 4.13 and 18.41 to 18.44, one finds the following description, where Krishna, the speaker, says:
>
> > "I created the four divisions of human society based on aptitude and vocation. The division of human labour is based on the qualities inherent in peoples' nature or their make-up."
>
> Clearly, the division of people among four varnas; *brahmin, kshatriya, vaishaya, and shudra;* i.e., knowledge seeker, warrior, tradesman, and artisan/cultivator, was based on guna-karma (aptitude driven vocation) and not birth.

As with the Greeks, we see an emphasis on the social division of labour in the work of the Chinese and Indian philosophers.

Medieval period

When discussing the contribution to the literature on the division of labour of the Persian-speaking medieval Muslim scholars, Hosseini (1998: 656–7) writes,

> [t]his explicit discussion concerning division of labor is found in the works of various Persian-speaking medieval Muslim writers including Farabi (873–950), Kai Kavus (eleventh century), Ibn Miskaway (d. 1030), Ibn Sina (980–1037), Ghazali [1058–1111], Nasir Tusi (12011274), and Asaad Davani (b. 1444).

Sun (2012: 27–35) also examines the treatment of the division of labour in medieval Islamic thought, and he explains that the social division of labour was discussed by al-Fārābi, trade and the international and interregional division of labour was discussed by al-Fārābi, al-Ghazali and Kai Kavus, and the sexual division of labour by Ibn Sīna, Nasir al-Din Tui and al-Ghazali. Sun also notes that al-Ghazali gave an example of the manufacturing division of labour strikingly similar to Adam Smith's famous pin factory example:

> al Ghazali used needle production as an example, writing that "even the small needle becomes useful only after passing through the hands of needle-makers about twenty-five times, each time going through a different process" (*Ihya*, 4:119, [quoted in Ghazanfar and Islahi 1990:] 390).
>
> (Sun 2012: 29)

In addition, Sun (2012: 28) contends that the Islamic scholarship on the division of labour was incorporated into the Latin scholastics' system of thought, largely without acknowledgement, and therefore become available to later writers such as the mercantilists and the classical economists, including Adam Smith.

Turning to the medieval Latin scholastics Sun (2012: 35) explains that much of the medieval Latin schoolmen's contribution does not relate directly to the division of labour but rather to providing a framework for study of the institutions underlying the social division of labour. In particular the schoolmen discussed private property, private ownership and market exchange, without which the division of labour could not develop and function. As Koehler (2016: 59) puts it,

> [i]f private property is the personal responsibility of its owner, then by implication it brings in its wake division of labour and, moreover, a rightful claim to the fruits of that labour.

But there were some scholastics who wrote directly on the division of labour. McGee (1990: 472) notes that Thomas Aquinas was one scholastic who clearly recognised the need for, and the benefits of, the division of labour:

> Smith advanced this idea in 1776, based on his observations of Scottish industry on the eve of the industrial revolution. But Aquinas anticipated Smith's division of labor theory by 500 years.
>
> > One man does not suffice to perform all those acts demanded by society, and therefore it is necessary that different persons be occupied in different pursuits. The diversification of men for diverse tasks is the result, primarily, of divine providence, which details the various compartments of man's life in such a way that nothing necessary to human existence is ever lacking; secondarily, this diversification proceeds from natural causes which bring it about that different men are born with aptitudes and tendencies for the different functions and the various ways of living.

Groenewegen (2008) points out that,

> [b]y the end of the Middle Ages, social division of labour was extensively practiced; manufacturing division of labour, generally speaking, came with the industrial revolution.

Importantly for our purposes, the practice of the social division of labour did not generate a need for the development of a theory of production and/or the firm. It had to wait for later developments centred around the manufacturing division of labour before such theories were to emerge.

Pre-classical economics period

Groenewegen (2008) contends that the English economics literature rediscovered the division of labour in the late seventeenth century, and it was only then that the manufacturing version of it was developed in any detail. The manufacturing form was linked to productivity growth, cost reduction and increased international competitiveness. The relationship between an increased manufacturing division of labour and the greater extent of markets that arose due to urbanisation was also highlighted. Authors such as William Petty saw benefits from the division of labour in industries as varied as textiles and shipping,

> for as Cloth must be cheaper made, when one Cards, another Spins, another Weaves, another Draws, another Dresses, another Presses and Packs; than when all the Operations above-mentioned, were clumsily performed by the same hand; so those who command the Trade of Shipping, can build long slight Ships for carrying Masts, FirTimber, Boards, Balks, &c. And short ones for Lead, Iron, Stones &c. One sort of Vessels to Trade at Ports where they need never lie a ground, others where they must jump upon the Sand | | twice every twelve hours; One sort of Vessels, and way of manning in time of Peace, and cheap gross Goods, another for War and precious Commodities; One sort of Vessels for the turbulent Sea, another for Inland Waters and Rivers; One sort of Vessels, and Rigging, where haste is requisite for the Maidenhead of a Market, another where $\frac{1}{5}$ or $\frac{1}{4}$ part of the time makes no matter. One sort of Masting and Rigging for long Voyages, another for Coasting. One sort of Vessels for Fishing, another for Trade. One sort for War for this or that Country, another for Burthen only. Some for Oars, some for Poles, some for Sails, and some for draught by Men or Horses, some for the Northern Navigations amongst Ice, and some for the South against Worms, & c. And this I take to be the chief of several Reasons, why the Hollanders can go at less Freight than their Neighbours, viz. because they can afford a particular sort of Vessels for each particular Trade.
>
> (Petty 1690: 260–1)

Petty was also aware of the advantages for the division of labour that follow from the increased size of markets in large cities,

> [b]ut the Gain which is made by *Manufactures*, will be greater, as the Manufacture it self is greater and better. For in so vast a City *Manufactures* will beget one another, and each *Manufacture* will be divided into as many parts as possible, whereby the Work of each *Artisan* will be simple and easie; As

> for Example. In the making of a *Watch*, If one Man shall make the *Wheels*, another the *Spring*, another shall Engrave the *Dial-plate*, and another shall make the *Cases*, then the *Watch* will be better and cheaper, than if the whole Work be put upon any one Man. And we also see that in *Towns*, and in the *Streets* of a great *Town*, where all the *Inhabitants* are almost of one Trade the Commodity peculiar to those places is made better and cheaper than elsewhere.
>
> (Petty 1683: 473)

Groenewegen (2008) notes that during eighteenth century an increasing range of authors discussed the advantages of the division of labour.

> Practical writers like Patrick Lindsay (1733), Richard Campbell (1747) and Joseph Harris (1757) tended to concentrate on manufacturing division of labour using examples from linen and pin production as well as from the familiar watch making. Those writing from the position of moral or political philosophy, like Mandeville (1729), Hutcheson (1755), Ferguson (1767) and Josiah Tucker (1755; 1774) concentrated more on aspects of the social division of labour.

Groenewegen (2008) also points out that consideration of the division of labour took place outside of England as well. The German Ernst Ludwig Carl saw benefits from an international division of labour driven by differences in climate, resource availability and locational advantages. The gains from this international division of labour could be exploited through free trade among countries. In France, François Quesnay and A. R. J. Turgot wrote on the idea. Turgot discusses the division of labour in his *Reflections on the Production and Distribution of Wealth*. He explains the development of the division of labour in terms of the fact that if everyone had to produce whatever he needed, starting from an equal distribution of natural resources, almost no one would be able to secure his needs. To develop the division of labour and stages of production, it is necessary to accumulate large sums of capital and to undertake extensive exchanges, none of which is possible without money. For Turgot the division of labour results in inequality, but this is the price of progress. Quesnay, the leader of the physiocrats, examined, albeit only briefly, the social aspects of the division of labour in a 1765 essay entitled 'Natural Right'. Quesnay wrote

> the system of co-operation in which each person contributes to the welfare of the society according to his ability. Everybody makes his contribution to it in a different way, but the services performed by one lessen the services which have to be performed by another; as a result of this distribution of services, each person can perform his own more thoroughly; and as a result of this mutual supplementation each person contributes almost equally to the welfare of the society.
>
> (Quesnay 1765: 51)

Two further contributions of note are those of the Italian criminologist and economist Cesare Beccaria and the French *Encyclopédie, ou dictionnaire raisonné des sciences, des arts et des métiers* (Encyclopaedia, or a Systematic Dictionary of the Sciences, Arts and Crafts) edited by Denis Diderot and Jean le Rond d'Alembert. In his work *Elementi di economia publica* Beccaria shows that he was aware of the benefits of the division of labour insofar as it results in greater skills and dexterity of workers. As for the *Encyclopédie* of Diderot and d'Alembert, there are two articles worthy of attention. The article on "Art" discussed the manufacturing division of labour, pointing out its benefits, including improvements in skill, improved quality of products, the saving of time and of materials and creating an incentive for the invention of a new machinery or the discovery of a better ways of working. In the second article on pins ("Epingle"), a clear example of the manufacturing division of labour is described, during which it is explained that the manufacture of pins is separated into eighteen different operations.

An additional reference should be made to Bernard de Mandeville (1670–1733), who also discussed the division of labour and is often accorded the credit of inventing the phrase.[5] For example, F. B. Kaye wrote in the introduction to Mandeville (1988),

> [t]he celebrated phrase, too – "division of labour" – was anticipated by Mandeville, and, apparently, by no one else.
>
> (Mandeville 1988: v1, cxxxv)

Sun (2012: 49) writes,

> [a]s is widely known, it was Bernard Mandeville (1714–1729)[6] who coined the term "division of labour".

and Mandeville did write about dividing and subdividing tasks

> [t]here are many Sets of Hands in the Nation, that, not wanting proper Materials, would be able in less than half a Year to produce, fit out, and navigate a First-Rate: yet it is certain, that this Task would be impracticable, if it was not divided and subdivided into a great Variety of different Labours; and it is as certain, that none of these Labours require any other, than working Men of ordinary Capacities.
>
> (Mandeville 1988: v2, p. 142)

and

> [n]o number of Men, when once they enjoy Quiet, and no Man needs to fear his Neighbour, will be long without learning to divide and subdivide their Labour.
>
> (Mandeville 1988: v2, p. 284)

and

> [b]y dividing the Employments in a great Office, and subdividing them into many parts, every Man's Business may be made so plain and certain, that, when he is a little used to it, it is hardly possible for him to make Mistakes. (Mandeville 1988: v2, p. 325)

Adam Smith

Perhaps the most famous analysis of the division of labour is that of Adam Smith. Smith opens his magnum opus, *An Inquiry into the Nature and Causes of the Wealth of Nations*, with a discussion of the division of labour at the micro-economic level, the justly famous pin factory example,[7]

> [t]o take an example, therefore, from a very trifling manufacture; but one in which the division of labour has been very often taken notice of, the trade of the pin-maker; a workman not educated to this business (which the division of labour has rendered a distinct trade), nor acquainted with the use of the machinery employed in it (to the invention of which the same division of labour has probably given occasion), could scarce, perhaps, with his utmost industry, make one pin in a day, and certainly could not make twenty. But in the way in which this business is now carried on, not only the whole work is a peculiar trade, but it is divided into a number of branches, of which the greater part are likewise peculiar trades. One man draws out the wire, another straights it, a third cuts it, a fourth points it, a fifth grinds it at the top for receiving the head; to make the head requires two or three distinct operations; to put it on, is a peculiar business, to whiten the pins is another; it is even a trade by itself to put them into the paper; and the important business of making a pin is, in this manner, divided into about eighteen distinct operations, which, in some manufactories, are all performed by distinct hands, though in others the same man will sometimes perform two or three of them. I have seen a small manufactory of this kind where ten men only were employed, and where some of them consequently performed two or three distinct operations. But though they were very poor, and therefore but indifferently accommodated with the necessary machinery, they could, when they exerted themselves, make among them about twelve pounds of pins in a day. There are in a pound upwards of four thousand pins of a middling size. Those ten persons, therefore, could make among them upwards of forty-eight thousand pins in a day. Each person, therefore, making a tenth part of forty-eight thousand pins, might be considered as making four thousand eight hundred pins in a day. But if they had all wrought separately and independently, and without any of them having been educated to this peculiar business, they certainly could not each of them have made twenty, perhaps not one pin in a day; that is, certainly, not the two hundred and fortieth, perhaps not

> the four thousand eight hundredth part of what they are at present capable of performing, in consequence of a proper division and combination of their different operations.
>
> (Smith 1776: Book 1, Chapter 1, pp. 14–5)

Importantly, Smith emphasises the increase in production brought about by the division of labour. Compare this is to the Xenophon quote on page 33 which highlights the quality improvements brought about by the division of labour.

According to Smith, this division of labour has three advantages: (1) the improved dexterity of men wholly concentrated on single tasks; (2) the savings of time in not having to pass from one task to another; and (3) the encouragement which it provides to the invention of 'labour-abridging machinery'.

But Smith does not, however, develop a theory of the firm, or production, based on this analysis. Best (2012: 29) states simply that "Adam Smith did not elaborate a theory of the firm", while Williams (1978: 11) argues that

> [t]he firm was disembodied and became a unit in which resources congeal in the productive process. When we come to examine the equilibrium/value theory of *The Wealth of Nations* it will be shown that, in that context, the firm is little more than a passive conduit which assists in the movement of resources between alternative activities.

Smith, in fact, quickly moves the analysis away from the level of the firm to the level of the market. When discussing Smith's approach to the division of labour, McNulty (1984: 237–8) comments,

> [h]aving conceptualized division of labor in terms of the organization of work within the enterprise, however, Smith subsequently failed to develop or even to pursue systematically that line of analysis. His ideas on the division of labor could, for example, have led him toward an analysis of task assignment, management, or organization. Such an intra-firm approach would have foreshadowed the much later – indeed, quite recent – efforts in this direction by Herbert Simon, Oliver Williamson, Harvey Leibenstein, and others, a body of work which Leibenstein calls "micro-microeconomics". . . . But, instead, Smith quickly turned his attention away from the internal organization of the enterprise, and outward toward the market and the realm of exchange, perhaps because he found therein both the source of division of labor, in the "propensity in human nature . . . to truck, barter and exchange" and its effective limits.

A contrary view is taken in Zouboulakis (2015). Michel S. Zouboulakis argues that Smith's discussion of the division of labour does offer an elementary explanation for the existence of firms. In Zouboulakis's view of Smith, the existence of firms is explained through division of labour dynamics. As the market grows, more firms are created and they become larger, thereby employing more labour and capital, and thus there is an increase in specialisation and the division of labour. This in turn increases efficiency and productivity, which increases general economic well-being. One possible issue[8] with Zouboulakis's argument is that while large firms which were able to take advantage of the division of labour did exist in Smith's time, they were not the norm. Most firms were small, with many larger firms being partnerships and thus restricted in their ability expand, and they would cooperate in production via long supply chains in which each firm would specialise in making a small contribution to the overall production process. An example of such a process is given by Smith in this description of the making of the woollen coat for a day-labourer.

> Observe the accommodation of the most common artificer or day-labourer in a civilized and thriving country, and you will perceive that the number of people of whose industry a part, though but a small part, has been employed in procuring him this accommodation, exceeds all computation. The woollen coat, for example, which covers the day-labourer, as coarse and rough as it may appear, is the produce of the joint labour of a great multitude of workmen. The shepherd, the sorter of the wool, the wool-comber or carder, the dyer, the scribbler, the spinner, the weaver, the fuller, the dresser, with many others, must all join their different arts in order to complete even this homely production.
>
> (Smith 1776: Book 1, Chapter 1, p. 13)

For all this increasingly detailed work on the division of labour, there was still no development of a theory of the firm or a micro-level theory of production. In the classical period, the classical economists furthered the discussion of the division of labour, but again without creating a theory of the firm. The approach to the firm taken by the classical economists was described by historian of economic thought Mark Blaug as being that the classical economists simply "had no theory of the firm" (Blaug 1958: 226). Bowen (1955: 5–6) argues in a similar fashion:

> economists of the classical tradition had usually assumed that the level and distribution of income and the allocation of resources were determined by forces that could be understood without a detailed theory of the firm. . . . Everything else would be settled by the impersonal forces of the market, and there would be no need to consider in detail the decisions and actions of the individual firm.

The standard theory of (micro-level) production that did eventually develop (post-1930) did not rely on the division of labour; rather, it followed the (macro) classical economics approach of thinking about production as being the result of inputs being transformed into outputs via a production function.

Nineteenth century

Following on from Adam Smith, a number of writers in the nineteenth century expanded the analysis of the division of labour even more, especially with regard to the manufacturing form of it. Among these authors, Charles Babbage was one of the most prominent. For Babbage, "[p]erhaps the most important principle on which the economy of a manufacture depends, is the division of labour amongst the persons who perform the work" (Babbage 1832: 121). Babbage extended the advantages that Smith had set forth. Babbage (1832: 122–6) listed four main advantages that flow from the manufacturing division of labour: (1) Of the time required for learning. The smaller the number of operations that have to be learned, the less time it takes to learn them. (2) Time is always lost from changing from one occupation to another. The fewer changes a worker has to make, the less time is lost. Also, the fewer changes in occupation, the less time is lost in adjusting machinery. (3) Skill acquired by frequent repetition of the same process. The more a worker carries out a task, the better they become at it. (4) The division of labour suggest the contrivance of tools and machinery to execute its processes. The more a worker carries out a task, the more likely it is that they will think of improvements in their machinery or methods of using the machines. Although all these four advantages are important, Babbage believed that a fifth principle needed to be added.

> *That the master manufacturer, by dividing the work to be executed into different processes, each requiring different degrees of skill and force, can purchase exactly that precise quantity of both which is necessary for each process; whereas, if the whole work were executed by one workman, that person must possess sufficient skill to perform the most difficult, and sufficient strength to execute the most laborious, of the operations into which the art is divided.*
>
> (Babbage 1832: 127; emphasis in the original)

Another important discussion of the manufacturing division of labour is Andrew Ure (1835). Ure saw the expanded use of machinery in manufacturing as a method for superseding skilled labour. Ure pointed out what he saw as a limitation in Smith's "old principle of the division of labour". Ure argued that under Smith's division of labour, the assignment of tasks to workers is done with reference to the skills of the worker. But the factory system calls for a new principle of the division of labour, one where machines were replacing the most skilled of workers. It was the most difficult tasks, those which required the most sophisticated skills in the workmen, that were being taken over by machinery.

> The principle of the factory system then is, to substitute mechanical science for hand skill, and the partition of a process into its essential constituents, for the division or graduation of labour among artisans. On the handicraft plan, labour more-or-less skilled, was usually the most expensive element of production – Materiam superabat opus [The workmanship was better than

> the subject matter]; but on the automatic plan, skilled labour gets progressively superseded, and will, eventually, be replaced by mere overlookers of machines.
>
> By the infirmity of human nature it happens, that the more skilful the workman, the more self-willed and intractable he is apt to become, and, of course, the less fit a component of a mechanical system, in which, by occasional irregularities, he may do great damage to the whole. The grand object therefore of the modern manufacturer is, through the union of capital and science, to reduce the task of his work-people to the exercise of vigilance and dexterity, – faculties, when concentred to one process, speedily brought to perfection in the young. In the infancy of mechanical engineering, a machine-factory displayed the division of labour in manifold gradations – the file, the drill, the lathe, having each its different workmen in the order of skill: but the dexterous hands of the filer and driller are now superseded by the planing, the key-groove cutting, and the drilling-machines; and those of the iron and brass turners, by the self-acting slide-lathe.
>
> (Ure 1835: 20–1)

For Ure, the advantages due to this new system of manufacturing included improvements in the quality of products, savings in time and costs workmen would otherwise pay in terms of an apprenticeship, the creation of new products that could not be made without the machinery and improvements in the well-being of workers.

> It was indeed a subject of regret to observe how frequently the workman's eminence, in any craft, had to be purchased by the sacrifice of his health and comfort. To one unvaried operation, which required unremitting dexterity and diligence, his hand and eye were constantly on the strain, or if they were suffered to swerve from their task for a time, considerable loss ensued, either to the employer, or the operative, according as the work was done by the day or by the piece. But on the equalization plan of self-acting machines, the operative needs to call his faculties only into agreeable exercise; he is seldom harassed with anxiety or fatigue, and may find many leisure moments for either amusement or meditation, without detriment to his master's interests or his own. As his business consists in tending the work of a well regulated mechanism, he can learn it in a short period; and when he transfers his services from one machine to another, he varies his task, and enlarges his views, by thinking on those general combinations which result from his and his companions' labours. Thus, that cramping of the faculties, that narrowing of the mind, that stunting of the frame, which were ascribed, and not unjustly, by moral writers, to the division of labour, cannot, in common circumstances, occur under the equable distribution of industry.
>
> (Ure 1835: 22–3)

Nassau W. Senior argued that one advantage of the division of labour omitted by Adam Smith occurs in situations in which "the same exertions which are necessary to produce a single given result are often sufficient to produce many hundreds or many thousands similar results". Senior used the Post Office as an example.

> The same exertions which are necessary to send a single letter from Falmouth to New York are sufficient to forward fifty, and nearly the same exertions will forward ten thousand. If every man were to effect the transmission of his own correspondence, the whole life of an eminent merchant might be passed in travelling, without his being able to deliver all the letters which the Post Office forwards for him in a single evening. The labour of a few individuals, devoted exclusively to the forwarding of letters, produces results which all the exertions of all the inhabitants of Europe could not effect, each person acting independently.
>
> (Senior 1836: 74)

Senior goes on to state that "[a]dditional Labour when employed in manufactures is MORE, when employed in Agriculture is LESS, efficient in proportion" (Senior 1836: 81–6). Here Senior implicitly sees manufacturing as satisfying increasing returns to scale while agriculture does not. Senior writes,

> [t]he proposition that, in agriculture, additional labour generally produces a less proportionate result, or, in other words, that the labour of twenty men employed on the land within a given district, though it will certainly produce more than that of ten men, will seldom produce twice as much.
>
> (Senior 1836: 84)

and

> [o]n the other hand, every increase in the number of manufacturing labourers is accompanied not merely by a corresponding, but by an increased productive power. If three hundred thousand families are now employed in Great Britain to manufacture and transport two hundred and forty millions of pounds of cotton, it is absolutely certain that six hundred thousand families could manufacture and transport four hundred and eighty millions of pounds of cotton. It is, in fact, certain that they could do much more. It is not improbable that they could manufacture and transport seven hundred and twenty millions.
>
> (Senior 1836: 86)

One reason for this is the division of labour:

> [e]very increase in the quantity manufactured has been accompanied by improvements in machinery, and an increased division of labour, and

> their effects have much more than balanced any increase which may have taken place in the proportionate labour necessary to produce the raw material.
>
> (Senior 1836: 84)

Interestingly, in the modern literature Allen and Lueck (1998) argue that because of seasonal forces farms cannot take advantage of specialisation and the division of labour.

With regard to the work of John Stuart Mill Groenewegen (2008) states,

> Mill (1848) treated division of labour as an important aspect of cooperation, arguing that irrespective of its well known productivity advantages, without this complex cooperation in the modern division of labour "few things would be produced at all" (Mill, 1848, p. 118) In discussing the productivity advantages, Mill cited the modification and additional advantages provided by Babbage (1832) and Rae (1834), adding little to their discussion. However, in Chapter 9 dealing with large scale and small scale production, he highlighted the point, so "ably illustrated by Mr Babbage . . . [that] the larger the enterprise, the farther the division of labour may be carried . . . as one of the principal causes of large manufactories" (Mill, 1848, p. 131), thereby bringing the argument firmly into the corpus of economics.

Groenewegen also points out that Mill's discussion of the division of labour was largely followed by other late-nineteenth-century authors such as Fawcett (1863) and Nicholson (1893).

We owe the distinction between the social division of labour and the manufacturing division of labour to Karl Marx. For Marx (1867), the difference between the two forms of the division of labour lies in the mechanisms by which the two versions are coordinated. For the social division of labour it is the decentralised market exchange of commodities that coordinates, while for the manufacturing division of labour coordination take place through the exploitation of the authority inherent in the employment relationship. Marx also recognised that the manufacturing division of labour originated from developments in the social division of labour and that the manufacturing form then exerted an influence on the social division of labour.

> Since the production and the circulation of commodities are the general prerequisites of the capitalist mode of production, division of labour in manufacture requires that a division of labour within society should have already attained a certain degree of development. Inversely, the division of labour in manufacture reacts back upon that society, developing and multiplying it further.
>
> (Marx 1867: 473)

The manufacturing division of labour is what differentiates capitalism from other modes of production.

> While the division of labour in society at large, whether mediated through the exchange of commodities or not, can exist in the most diverse economic formations of society, the division of labour in the workshop, as practised by the manufacture, is an entirely specific creation of the capitalist mode of production.
>
> (Marx 1867: 480)

To understand Alfred Marshall's ideas on the division of labour, an examination of Book IV of his *Principles of Economics* is necessary. In Book IV Marshall sees four factors as contributing to production: land, labour, capital and organisation. Marshall regards organisation as increasing the efficiency of labour, and its introduction begins his discussion of the division of labour (Marshall 2009: 200).

Marshall (2009: 201) introduces two new concepts, firstly "differentiation" and secondly "integration". By the first Marshall means "the division of labour, and the development of specialized skill, knowledge and machinery"; by the second he refers to

> a growing intimacy and firmness of the connections between the separate parts of the industrial organism, shows itself in such forms as the increase of security of commercial credit, and of the means and habits of communication by sea and road, by railway and telegraph, by post and printing-press.

In the following chapters Marshall discusses four variants of the division of labour: (i) the division of labour among operatives and its relation with the use of machinery; (ii) the reciprocal effects of the division of labour and the localisation of industry; (iii) the advantages of the division of labour in relation to large-scale production; (iv) the emergence of specialised business management (Marshall 2009: 208).

With regard to point (i), Marshall (2009: 208) notes that the division of labour simplifies workers' tasks and increases their productivity. But at a certain degree of simplification labour is replaced by machinery (Marshall 2009: 212). There is, however, a counterbalancing effect in that the introduction of machinery allows us "to increase the scale of manufactures and to make them more complex; and therefore to increase the opportunities for division of labour of all kinds, and especially in the matter of business management" (Marshall 2009: 213). As an example, consider printing and watchmaking:

> In the printing trades, as in the watch trade, we see mechanical and scientific appliances attaining results that would be impossible without them; at the same time that they persistently take over work that used to

> require manual skill and dexterity, but not much judgment; while they leave for man's hand all those parts which do require the use of judgment, and open up all sorts of new occupations in which there is a great demand for it.
>
> (Marshall 2009: 216–7)

The advantages of localisation of industry, as in point (ii), include the interactions among people following the same skilled trade that are possible only because they are in near proximity to each other. Also, subsidiary trades can develop because there is a market for their outputs. Firms providing access to specialised machines, too expensive for any single firm to own, can develop since there are enough small firms to keep the machine is constant use. The concentration of firms also provides a market for highly skilled and specialised workers, and thus such workers are drawn to this location in a way that they would not be if there was only one, or a few, firms.

As to point (iii), the major advantages of large-scale production that Marshall sees are to do with the economising on skill and machinery and savings of materials. Marshall argues that large-scale production allows firms to use specialised machines since the large firm can keep the machine in 'constant employment' which a smaller firm cannot (Marshall 2009: 233). In addition, the large firm is better able to afford the fixed cost involved with the invention and development of new machinery.

Marshall divides the economies that arise from an increase in the scale of production of any kind of goods into two general groups: points (i) and (iii) refer to what Marshall calls internal economies, that is, "those dependent on the resources of the individual houses of business engaged in it, on their organization and the efficiency of their management" while point (ii) refers to external economies, that is, "those dependent on the general development of the industry" (Marshall 2009: 221).

Such economies lead Marshall into a discussion of increasing returns:

> The general argument of the present Book shows that an increase in the aggregate volume of production of anything will generally increase the size, and therefore the internal economies possessed by such a *representative firm*; that it will always increase the external economies to which the firm has access; and thus will enable it to manufacture at a less proportionate cost of labour and sacrifice than before.
>
> (Marshall 2009: 265; emphasis added)

Or more precisely, "[t]he law of increasing return may be worded thus:- An increase of labour and capital leads generally to improved organization, which increases the efficiency of the work of labour and capital" (Marshall 2009: 265). A point to note about Marshall's argument is that it links the division of labour to economies of scale. The larger a firm is, the better able it is to take advantage of specialisation, and thus grow even larger. This point was also made in an earlier book, *The Economics of Industry* (Marshall and Marshall 1879):

> §10. It will be useful to refer to the **Law of division of labour**, which may be stated thus: –
>
> > When the demand for a commodity becomes very large, the· process of making it is generally divided among several distinct classes of workers, each with its proper appliances, and each aided by Subsidiary industries; for such a division diminishes the difficulty of making the commodity.
>
> Anticipating a term which will be defined later on, we may say: – The Cost of production of a manufactured commodity is diminished whenever an increase in the demand for it leads to an increased division of labour in making it.
>
> The Law of division of labour implies that an increase in the amount of capital and labour which is applied to any process of manufacture is likely to cause a more than proportionately increased return. It is therefore sometimes called the **Law of Increasing Return**, so as to bring out the contrast in which it stands to the Law of Diminishing Return which applies to agriculture.
>
> (Marshall and Marshall 1879: 57; emphasis in the original)

For our purposes, the critical point here is that for the first time in our discussion we see a 'theory of the firm' (more correctly a theory of micro-level production) being offered. In his discussion of increasing and diminishing returns, Marshall introduced his concept of the 'representative firm' (see Chapter 5 for more detail).

Marshall wrote,

> [w]e shall have to analyse carefully the normal cost of producing a commodity, relatively to a given aggregate volume of production; and for this purpose we shall have to study the expenses of a representative producer for that aggregate volume. On the one hand we shall not want to select some new producer just struggling into business, who works under many disadvantages, and has to be content for a time with little or no profits, but who is satisfied with the fact that he is establishing a connection and taking the first steps towards building up a successful business; nor on the other hand shall we want to take a firm which by exceptionally long-sustained ability and good fortune has got together a vast business, and huge well-ordered workshops that give it a superiority over almost all its rivals. But our representative firm must be one which has had a fairly long life, and fair success, which is managed with normal ability, and which has normal access to the economies, external and internal, which belong to that aggregate

> volume of production; account being taken of the class of goods produced, the conditions of marketing them and the economic environment generally
>
> Thus a representative firm is in a sense an average firm. But there are many ways in which the term "average" might be interpreted in connection with a business. And a Representative firm is that particular sort of average firm, at which we need to look in order to see how far the economies, *internal and external*, of production on a large scale have extended generally in the industry and country in question. We cannot see this by looking at one or two firms taken at random: but we can see it fairly well by selecting, after a broad survey, a firm, whether in private or joint-stock management (or better still, more than one), that represents, to the best of our judgment, this particular average.
>
> (Marshall 2009: 264–5)

Unfortunately, the representative firm was a nebulous concept, mired in controversy, before being replaced in the economics literature during the 1920s and '30s.

> The representative firm has been a much-criticized concept, subject to conflicting interpretations with respect to both its configuration and its intended role in Marshall's Principles (the Principles). The concept found itself a focal point of much of the debate during the significant cost controversies of the 1920s; however, it has appeared infrequently in subsequent economic analysis. In its place, the equilibrium firm has taken centre stage in the microeconomic textbooks, sometimes being mistaken for its vanquished predecessor.
>
> (Hart 2003: 158)

Importantly, however, the controversy surrounding the representative firm did lead to the development of the neoclassical (now textbook) theory of micro-level production.[9]

Twentieth century

Up to this point in more than two thousand years of discussion starting with the ancient Greeks, Indian and Chinese the division of labour has played little part in the development of a theory of production/the firm, but in the twentieth century the manufacturing division of labour does, finally, play such a role.

An early analysis of the relationship between the division of labour and the firm was Frank (1925). Frank argued that the development of machinery to carry out production tasks, an advancement greatly accelerated by the industrial revolution, lead to the production process being split into a growing number of separate stages. That is, there was an increasing division of labour.

> It is customary, in commenting upon the industrial revolution, to emphasize the increase in production consequent upon the adoption of machines

> in place of hand tools. But it is equally important to notice, at least for our present purpose, that the machine process split up production into an ever growing number of separate processes, separate because of the invention of new techniques and new machines for performing each step in the formerly unified handicraft operations.
>
> (Frank 1925: 180)

This expanded division of labour bought about a significant change in the organisation of production. Single firms no longer controlled the entire manufacturing process; now they just undertook one or two steps.

> Under the handicraft scheme the single individual, or partnership, undertook the direction and management of the complete process of production from raw materials to finished goods. It now became necessary for each of them to confine his operations to the conduct of one or perhaps two steps in this total industrial process, because the small capital of each limited the number and variety of the new machines which he could purchase.
>
> (Frank 1925: 180)

Given that multiple firms made up the total productive process, these firms needed to be coordinated to ensure the final product was successfully produced. At first, Frank contends, this coordination was provided by simple contracts between the different firms at each stage of production.

> But as the industrial equipment became more complex and more widely distributed among separate owners and geographical districts, there was a more or less concomitant development in the elaboration of pecuniary devices and operations and the organization of markets, as shown especially in loan credit, negotiable instruments and similar instrumentalities for facilitating buying and selling, speculating in commodities, and the like. Only a cursory glance at present-day litigation is needed to discover how these pecuniary activities are working and how difficult it has become to observe all the necessary rules and limitations upon the use of pecuniary methods.
>
> (Frank 1925: 181–2)

That is, the use of these 'pecuniary devices' was not without its costs and problems. Frank saw vertical integration as a response to such issues.

> For undoubtedly vertical integration is an attempt to bring together under one management the separate stages of the industrial process which technically require unified direction and control. Since this technical requirement cannot effectively nor continuously be met through buying and selling of goods between separately owned stages, however ingeniously and elaborately those pecuniary operations be conducted, it has become both feasible

> and desirable to bring a number of consecutive stages of production under one managerial control.
>
> (Frank 1925: 185–6)

Thus an expanded division of labour has led to an integrated firm.

Frank maintained that the coordination of the whole production process by one firm was more efficient than controlling the process by the use of contracts between multiple independent firms. He argues that the development of new techniques of management, such as cost accounting, administrative statistics, planning and control, and industrial engineering, enabled the managers of the integrated firm to direct and control the multiple process now part of their business in a more efficient manner, and at a lower cost, than was possible when coordination was achieved via contracts between separate firms.

> With the several stages of the total industrial process brought under one managerial control, with each plant put upon a budget of performance and costs and the whole process directed to the production of the finished product, it becomes possible to achieve that technical co-ordination of process which the pecuniary operations of buying and selling could rarely approximate, except perhaps for brief intervals and then only with undesirable "booms".
>
> (Frank 1925: 187)

While Frank is clear as to the benefits of vertical integration, he seemed oblivious any disadvantages or costs associated with it. There are, for example, no costs of any kind attributed to management or bureaucracy. There are no information or incentive problems in the integrated firm. In fact with regard to the advantages of integration he goes so far as to write,

> The great advantages accruing to an integrated industry, *which grow cumulatively with the extension of the integration*, are found in the assurance of an adequate and dependable source of supplies, on the one hand, and a certain "market" for its product, on the other, for each stage in the industrial process.
>
> (Frank 1925: 189; emphasis added)

The problem this gives rise to is that without any costs to integration and with its benefits seemingly growing without bound, there is no way to determine the boundaries of a firm. If integration only has advantages it will, presumably, continue until there is one firm producing everything![10] Also, Frank does not analyse the internal organisation of the integrated firm. Thus, Frank's analysis does not provide a basis for a theory of the firm, at least not if we consider the theory of the firm in its modern formulation.

Another early attempt to relate the division of labour to the structure of firms was Robinson (1931). In *The Structure of Competitive Industry*, Robinson offered an analysis of the factors that determined the optimum size for a firm. For Robinson, the interaction of five factors determined the size of the firm: technique, management, finance, marketing and risk of fluctuations. The theoretical optima associated with each of these factors must be reconciled to give the size or constitution of a real firm, after allowing for the difficulties and anomalies of growth. The division of labour has a role to play with regard to technique and management. Because of this we will concentrate on these two factors here.

For Robinson, the optimum firm is that firm which, given the existing conditions of technique and organising ability, produces at the minimum of long-run average costs. Under the conditions of perfect competition, we would expect to see the optimum firm emerge, but under conditions of imperfect competition it may not materialise. Consider, for example, the case of monopolistic competition in which a firm will be in equilibrium at an output quantity which is less than the average cost minimising quantity.[11]

The first application of the division of labour to the size of the firm that Robinson considers is the relationship between the division of labour and the optimum technical unit. Robinson follows Adam Smith in seeing three different reasons for the division of labour giving rise to more efficient production. First is the increase in dexterity of workmen; second, the saving of time which is commonly lost in passing from one type of work to another; and third, the invention of a great number of machines which facilitate and abridge labour and thus enable one person to do the work of many.

With regard to the issue of dexterity, Robinson notes Smith's observation that a person who works at a given task for some time is likely to develop a skill or knack for doing that task. In addition, the division of labour can allow those people with a natural skill for carrying out a given task to specialise in that task.

Adam Smith (and Robinson) saw another advantage of the division of labour in the fact that specialisation at a task saved the time that would otherwise be spent on passing from one task to another. Time could be saved because workers do not have to move between machines or processes. Also time would be lost if machines had to be reset to perform a different function. The division of labour saves time by concentrating both workers and machine upon a given function, and a larger factory enjoys an advantage over a smaller one insofar as it makes this concentration possible.

The third economy Smith saw is due to the development of specialised equipment to carry out the tasks that the manufacture of an item is divided into. Separation of a process into its constituent parts makes development of machines to carry out those parts easier.

It is important to keep in mind when considering the size of a firm that the principle of the division of labour requires a firm of sufficient size to obtain the maximum profitable division of labour. This size will differ across industries depending on the nature of the production process for that industry and how detailed a division of labour can be implemented for that particular process.

Larger firms will, often, have the capacity to implement a greater division of labour than a smaller firm, giving the larger firm an advantage in terms of efficiency.

The next issue discussed by Robinson is what he calls 'the integration of process'. Robinson explains that often a large firm has fewer rather than more processes of manufacture. They can utilise a large machine which has been designed to take over what would otherwise be a series of manual, or at least less completely mechanical, operations. A complicated machine can perform two or three or more consecutive processes, and it can thereby eliminate the labour and time which would be required to set up the work on each of the successive earlier machines. Only large firms can keep such a machine running at its full capacity, and this fact gives the large firm an advantage over the smaller, and less mechanised, firm. But this difficulty can be overcome by the small firm as long as the size of the market for the process is large enough. If a given process requires a scale of production too great for a smaller firm, the small firm can outsource the process to a specialist firm. But such outsourcing is only possible if the extent of the market for a particular process is large enough to allow the division of labour to develop to the point where a specialist firm is viable. Robinson refers to this outsourcing as 'vertical disintegration'.

The second of the areas for which Robinson sees the division of labour having a role to play is with regard to management. A manager in a small firm will have multiple tasks to preform, some of which he will be good at, others that he will not be so good at. In a larger firm a division of labour can develop which allows managers to specialise on those functions for which they are best suited. The larger firm gains in two ways from its division of managerial labour: (1) special abilities can be utilised to their fullest extent. Talents are not wasted by having managers carry out functions which could be better assigned to another manager with a particular ability at that function. (2) A manager who specialises in a given task will increase their knowledge of that task.

A potential downside of the managerial division of labour is the problem of coordination. As the division of labour becomes greater the problems associated with the coordination of the different parts of the production process also increases. As new tasks are created by dividing up the production process, new administrative functions are also created to coordinate the ever more disjoint production process. The advantage that a larger firm has over the smaller depends, in a large part, on how well it solves this coordination problem.

Stigler (1951) also utilises the division of labour to explain the functions of the firm. Stigler begins his argument by saying that the division of labour, and its limit due to the extent of the market, lies at the core of a theory of the functions, and thus the boundaries, of a firm. Stigler outlines this theory in the second section of his paper.

In this theory a firm is seen as engaging in a series of distinct operations leading to the production of a final product. That is, the firm is partitioned not among its input markets but among the functions or processes that determine the scope of its activities and thus determine the firm's boundaries.

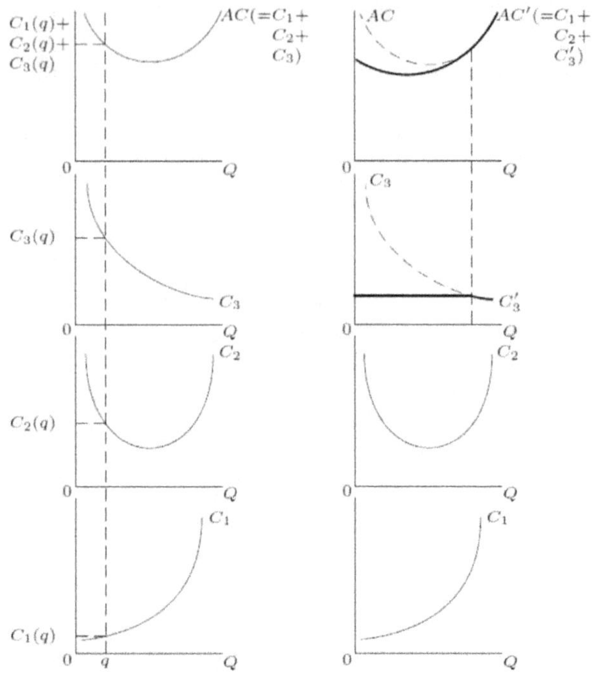

Figure 3.1 The firm's costs of production

To allow the graphical representation of the firm's costs of production, we will assume that the average costs of each activity depends only on the rate of output of the firm. In addition, if we assume that there is a constant proportion between the rate of output of each activity and the rate of output of the final product, then all the cost functions can be drawn on the same diagram, and the vertical sum of these costs will be the conventional average cost curve for the firm. With reference to the left-hand column of Figure 3.1, to produce q units of final output requires a given number of units of activity 1, with an average cost of $C_1(q)$, a number of units of activity 2, with an average cost of $C_2(q)$, and a number of units of activity 3, with an average cost of $C_3(q)$. These costs can be (vertically) summed to give the average cost of production for q units of output, $C_1(q) + C_2(q) + C_3(q)$.

With respect to the shape of the average cost curves for the various activities, some are increasing continuously (C_1, in the left-hand column of Figure 3.1), some are falling continuously (C_3, in the left-hand column of Figure 3.1) and some are conventionally U-shaped (C_2, in the left-hand column of Figure 3.1).

Now consider Adam Smith's idea that the division of labour is limited by the extent of the market. First take the activities for which there are increasing returns. Why doesn't the firm exploit the returns more fully and in the process become a monopoly in the output market? Because as the firm expands output production, activities also have to be increased and some of these are subject to diminishing returns, and these cost increases are such that they overwhelm the cost advantages of the increasing returns and increase the average cost of the final product. So why then does the firm not abandon these C_3-like activities and let some other firm (and thus industry) specialise in them to exploit the increasing returns fully? At a given time, the market for these activities may be too small to support specialised firms.[12] Given this, firms must perform these activities for themselves.

But with an expansion of the market for the increasing returns, activity firms specialising in that activity would develop. The firms currently carrying out this activity for their own consumption would forgo this activity and let it be taken over by a new (monopoly) firm. This monopoly could not fully exploit its market power, however, since it has to charge a price which is less than the average cost of production for the firm abandoning the activity. As the market for this activity grows even larger, the number of firms specialising in it grows. That is, the industry becomes increasingly competitive.

The abandonment of this activity by the original firms will change the cost function for each firm. The cost curve, C_3, will be replaced by a horizontal line (the horizonal section of C_3' in the righthand column of Figure 3.1) in the affected region. This also changes the average cost curve for the final product, with the new curve (the black solid curve, AC', in the righthand column of Figure 3.1) being lower than the current curve. Here we have assumed that average costs C_1 and C_2 are unchanged.

What about the increasing cost case? Why not abandon or reduce use of those activities with increasing cost? Much of the previous discussion carries over to this case, with the exception that as the market and the industry grows, the original firm does not have to stop utilising that activity completely. Part of the needed use of that activity can still be produced in-house without high average (and marginal) cost, with the rest being purchased via the market.

A third, and more modern, approach to specialisation and the division of labour is Becker and Murphy (1992). This paper starts with the idea that productivity is increased by a more extensive division of labour, since the returns to any time spent on a task are normally greater for workers who concentrate on a narrow range of skills. As seen with Stigler (1951) the stated argument is that the division of labour is limited by the extent of the market. Becker and Murphy argue that the degree of specialisation is often determined not by the size of the market but by other factors, such as the costs involved in 'coordinating' specialised workers who perform complementary tasks, and by the amount of general knowledge available.

Assume a continuum of tasks, s, along a unit interval which must be performed to produce a good Y. The Becker and Murphy model 'must be performed' by the production function

$$Y = \min_{0 \le s \le 1} Y(s) \tag{3.1}$$

The rate of production from the *s*th task ($Y(s)$) is the product of the working time devoted to task *s* ($T_w(s)$) and the productivity of each hour ($E(s)$)

$$Y(s) = E(s)T_w(s) \tag{3.2}$$

For Becker and Murphy, a 'team' is a group of workers who cooperate, by carrying out different tasks and functions, to produce the good *Y*. Note that a team can be either part of one firm, or they can engage in transactions across a number of firms. Perhaps the obvious interpretation of the team is a firm or a division, factory or group within a firm. It is assumed that all workers are intrinsically identical and that all tasks are equally difficult. Each of the intrinsically identical members of an efficient team concentrates on an equal set of tasks of width $w = \frac{1}{n}$, where the team size is denoted by *n*. The output for each task depends on the size of the task set and on the general knowledge (*H*) available:

$$Y = Y(H, w) \text{ where } Y_h > 0,\ Y_w < 0 \tag{3.3}$$

Importantly, $Y_w < 0$ implies that there are increasing returns to specialisation.

In some cases, as examined earlier in the paper by Stigler, the division of labour is limited by the extent of the market. Under other situations it is limited by other factors. Conflict among members of the team grows as the team grows. Principal agent conflicts, hold-up problems and breakdowns in supply and communications all tend to increase as the degree of specialisation grows. Becker and Murphy call such problems part of the costs of 'coordinating' specialists and assume that the total coordination costs per team member (*C*) depends on *n* (or *w*).

$$C = C(n),\ C_n > 0. \tag{3.4}$$

Net output per member *y* is the difference between benefits and costs,

$$y = B - C = B(H, n) - C(n),\ B_n > 0,\ C_n > 0 \tag{3.5}$$

If $B_n > C_n$ for all $n \leq N$, then the division of labour is only limited by the extent of the market. Consider, by way of an illustration, the case where *B* and *C* are linear with $B_n > C_n$, then the optimal $n^\star = N$, the extent of the market. See Figure 3.2.

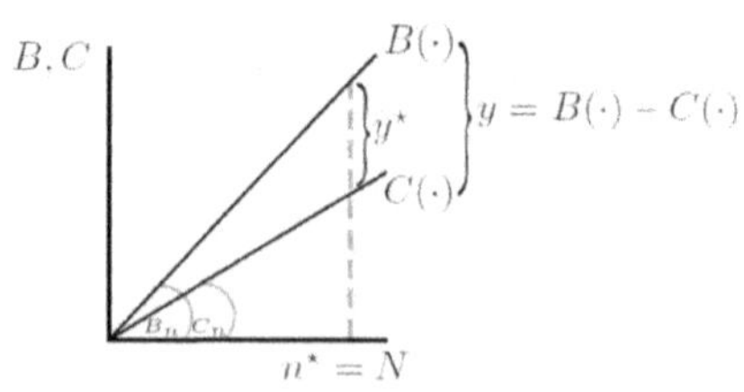

Figure 3.2 The division of labour is limited by the extent of the market

If $B_n \not> C_n$ for all $n \leq N$ then the optimal $n^\star < N$ is found where $B_n = C_n$. That is, the difference between $B(H,n)$ and $C(n)$ is maximised at a point where $n^\star$ is not determined by the size of the market but by the costs of coordination. See Figure 3.3.

In these situations the division of labour is, therefore, limited not by the size of the market but rather by coordination costs.

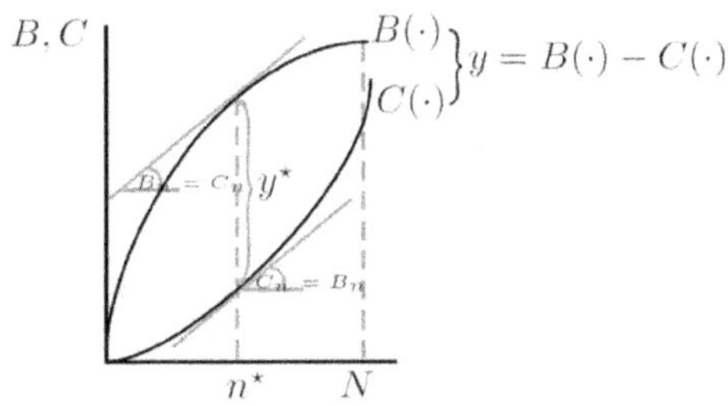

Figure 3.3 The division of labour is limited by coordination costs

Note that if B did not depend on n, then one-member teams would be efficient just as long as C increases in n. If C were independent of n, the division of labour would be limited only by N, the extent of the market assuming that B increases in n. In situations where both $B_n > 0$ and $C_n > 0$, any efficient team would have more than one member but fewer members than all workers in the market. The efficient amount of specialisation can be found formally by differentiating equation 3.5 with respect to n. This gives

$$B_n \geq C_n \tag{3.6}$$

The second order condition is $B_{nn} - C_{nn} < 0$, and it is assumed that $B_n > C_n$ for small n.

At this point Becker and Murphy take advantage of a particular example:

$$E(s) = dH^\gamma T_h^\theta (s) \tag{3.7}$$

where $\theta > 0$ determines the productivity of T_h – the time devoted to acquiring task specific skills. H is general knowledge and is assumed to increase the productivity of time spent on investing in skills, $\gamma > 0$. The total time spent on the sth skill is denoted $T(s)$ and thus

$$T(s) = T_h(s) + T_w(s) \tag{3.8}$$

That is, time is either devoted to 'investing', T_h, or 'working', T_w, so that output is maximised. This implies,[13]

$$Y(s) = A(\theta)H^\gamma T(s)^{1+\theta} \tag{3.9}$$

where $A = d\theta^\theta(1 + \theta)^{-(1+\theta)}$

Note that if a worker allocates one unit of working time uniformly between a set $w = \frac{1}{n}$ of tasks, then $T(s)w = T(s)\frac{1}{n} = 1$, i.e. $T(s) = n$. Substituting this into equation 3.9 gives the output on each task as a function of the team size:

$$Y = AH^{\gamma}n^{1+\theta} \tag{3.10}$$

Output per worker is given by

$$y = \frac{Y}{n} = B(H,N) = AH^{\gamma}n^{\theta}. \tag{3.11}$$

From this equation it is clear that B rises as the size of the team increases as long as $\theta > 0$, that is, just as long as investments in task-specific skills have a positive marginal productivity.

Becker and Murphy assume that in equation 3.11 an increase in human capital not only increases the average product per team but also the marginal product of a bigger team.

$$\frac{\partial}{\partial H}\left(\frac{\partial B}{\partial n}\right) = B_{nh} > 0 \tag{3.12}$$

Remember that the first-order condition given by equation 3.6 gives us the maximum income per worker, if we differentiate this with respect to H we get[14]

$$\frac{dn\star}{dH} = \frac{B_{nh}}{C_{nn} - B_{nn}} > 0 \tag{3.13}$$

where $B_{nn} - C_{nn} < 0$ is the second-order condition. Equation 3.13 tells us that teams get larger and workers become specialised as human capital and technological knowledge grows.

Equation 3.12 determines how workers with different knowledge get allocated to different areas of a team. The costs of 'coordinating' specialists differ among the areas within a team. An efficient allocation allocates workers whose productivity is least affected by coordination costs to the high cost sectors. This implies that those workers who have lower human capital would be allocated to the high cost sectors if greater coordination costs lower the marginal product of human capital. The first-order condition for n and the envelope theorem[15] gives this result.[16]

$$\frac{\partial^2 y}{\partial H \partial \lambda} = \frac{\partial(B_h)}{\partial \lambda} = B_{hn}\frac{\partial n\star}{\partial \lambda} < 0 \tag{3.14}$$

where λ is a coordination-cost-raising parameter, with $C_{n\lambda} > 0$, $B_{hn} > 0$ by an application of Young's Theorem[17] to equation 3.12 and $\frac{\partial n\star}{\partial \lambda} < 0$.

The paper now turns to the question of the division of labour being limited by the extent of the market. It is noted that Adam Smith offers the most famous statement of the idea. While Becker and Murphy mostly argue against the notion, they do admit that there are some situations where the result does hold. In their model, for example, it is true when n^*, the optimal number of team members, is greater than or equal to N, the number of workers in the market. In this case, each worker can specialise in different tasks so that each will have some monopoly power ex post. However, it is not true when there are many workers with essentially the same specialised skills and they compete in the same market.

Becker and Murphy claim that the division of labour is not, in these cases, limited by the extent of the market but by the costs of coordinating workers with different specialties. Thus, the size of a firm may depend on coordination costs rather than the extent of the market. Becker and Murphy argue that this can even be seen in Smith's famous pin factory example.[18]

> There even seems to be a problem with Smith's justly famous example of a pin factory, where workers specialize in various functions, including drawing out, straightening, and cutting the wire. Why didn't the several factories that made pins in Smith's England combine their activities, get a larger scale and market, and specialize more within each factory? If the answer is that the cost of combining these factories exceeded the gain from a greater division of labor, then specialization was limited by these costs of "coordination," not by the extent of the market.
>
> (Becker and Murphy 1992: 1147–8)

An even more recent paper that develops a theory, incorporating the division of labour and specialisation and a stochastic ('O-ring')[19] production function to explain the incentive structure and size of the firm, is Rauh (2018).

Rauh assumes a production process that can be divided into a number of distinct tasks. This makes it possible for the tasks to be allocated across workers (the division of labour) and for workers to make investments in task-specific human capital (specialisation). This is the kind of situation just discussed in the Becker and Murphy paper. We saw that an increase in employment gave rise to a greater division of labour, that is, fewer tasks assigned to each worker and greater specialisation, and thus higher productivity. Importantly, Rauh postulates an additional feature of the production process: a breakdown at any point in production, which could be due to shirking, poor decision-making or a negative shock, will have serious adverse consequences for the successful manufacturing of the product – this is the 'O-ring' type production function.

This second condition has important implications for the moral hazard problems that arise within a firm. In the first best case, the principal can directly monitor individual worker effort and thus will be able to identify and respond to any shirking by workers with probability one. In the second best case, individual output can be monitored, and, again, shirking can be punished with probability one. Note that in this case a worker who experiences a negative shock will also be punished. In the third best case all workers will be punished, with probability one, if any single worker shirks. In each of the three cases there will be no free rider issues, since shirkers cannot hide behind the efforts of their co-workers.

Rauh considers a production process where the set of tasks is the unit interval. The principal chooses the number of workers, and the set of tasks to be performed is divided equally across all workers. Each of the workers is able to choose their production effort and their level of investment in task-specific human capital for each task they are assigned. To produce one unit of output requires one unit of output of each task. This means that you get zero output if any of the workers shirks or suffers an adverse shock in any of their assigned tasks. In line with Becker and Murphy (1992), having greater levels of employment implies fewer tasks being assigned to each worker, which in turn means the workers can increase their investments in human capital for each of their reduced set of assigned tasks. This results in greater productivity and thus increasing returns to employment.

The stochastic (O-ring) nature of the production function is thought about in the following way.

> In addition to production effort and investments in human capital, each agent monitors his assigned tasks and makes decisions about whether or not a problem has arisen, whether or not to halt production to fix it, whether he can fix it himself, and which potential solution is appropriate. When there is only one agent, there is a high probability that at least some of these decisions will be faulty because he has limited cognitive resources and performs all the tasks himself. When there are two agents, the probability that either one will make a mistake should be lower because each performs only half the set of tasks and can therefore devote more care and attention to each of them. On the other hand, we now have two probabilities instead of one, so the effect of an increase in employment is ambiguous.
>
> (Rauh 2018: 83)

More formally, the probability that a worker suffers a negative shock to at least one of the tasks they have been allocated is an increasing function of the proportion of tasks being performed by that worker. Under an assumption of independence, the probability of a product defect is the product of the individual probabilities. If the number of workers is increased, this results in two effects. Firstly, it will decrease the probability that each worker will suffer a negative shock. Secondly, it will increase the number of points in the production process at which a negative shock can occur. Rauh then defines a production process as satisfying the O-ring property if the probability of a defect occurring is increasing in the number of workers and converges to one as the number of workers goes to infinity.

Given this background, the main question for the paper is then considered: What limits the size of a firm? For Rauh the answer has to do with the effects (or lack of effects) of moral hazard. Since there is a one-to-one relationship between the division of labour and the level of employment in the paper, the question can be rephrased as what limits the division of labour? As has been noted earlier, Becker and Murphy (1992) see this limit as being determined not by the extent of the market, as Adam Smith argued, but rather by coordination costs, including agency costs.

When determining the relationship between moral hazard and the size of the firm,

> the optimal employment level balances the following considerations: (i) the increasing returns to employment due to specialization and division of labor, (ii) the O-ring property of the production technology, where the probability of team failure increases with the size of the team, and (iii) the marginal cost of employment (the cost of hiring another agent).
>
> (Rauh 2018: 83)

In the first best case of no moral hazard, Rauh shows that the standard zero incentive, full insurance contract is employed. Effectively, the firm is behaving as if it were a perfectly competitive wage-taker despite it being a monopolist. Since, in this case, each worker's payment is fixed, the firm's labour costs (the number of workers times the expected payment to each worker) are linear in workers, and the marginal cost of a worker is constant. Importantly, however, given increasing returns to employment, which arises from specialisation and the division of labour, but only linearly increasing costs to employment, these costs cannot limit the extent of employment. Thus, in this case, the extent of the market for labour or the O-ring property must be limiting employment and thus the size of the firm. If it were not for these constraints, the first best firm would be of infinite size, since there are increasing returns to employment.

Next Rauh considers the second best contract. Here effort cannot be observed, but individual output can. Rauh shows that the optimal (second best) contract involves awarding a bonus to a worker when their individual output is high, that is, when the worker's effort is first best and there is a positive shock, and replacing the worker otherwise. Rauh shows that the worker's bonus is decreasing in employment. This follows from the fact that as employment increases, the proportion of tasks carried out by each worker falls, which increases the likelihood of a positive shock. This increases the expected value of the worker's payment if the worker selects the first best effect level. This means the principal can reduce the bonus paid to the worker. It is also shown that this reduction in the bonus reduces the expected payment to the worker, and this implies that the payment is decreasing in employment as well. If this type of effect is large enough, then the marginal cost of an extra worker can decline with employment and could even be negative. In this situation, the second best cost of employment could be less than the first best (constant) marginal cost of employment. This would mean the second best firm could be larger than the first best firm. Thus, the second best firm would have weak incentives (low bonus), low expected pay (small worker payment) and an excessive division of labour (and an excessive amount of specialisation). Motivation is provided by the fact that shirking workers will be identified and fired rather than through the use of incentive schemes.

As before, as the level of employment increases, fewer tasks are carried out by each worker and the probability of a positive shock converges to one. This means that the second best expected payment to a worker converges to the first best payment. In turn, this means that the second best cost function tends towards the (linear) first best cost function. Thus, as with the first best case, the increasing returns to employment resulting from the division of labour and specialisation cannot be contained by an asymptotically linear cost of employment. Rauh concludes from this that when the principal can monitor individual output, even if not effort, the size of the firm under moral hazard is again limited by either the total number of workers available or the O-ring property.

Lastly, Rauh looks at the third best situation where the principal can observe only team output. Here the results are the opposite of the second best case. This is because the third best incentive relies on the probability that all workers experience a positive shock rather than depending on the probabilities that individual workers experience a positive shock. Given the O-ring property, an increase in workers increases the probability that an individual worker experiences a positive shock but reduces the probability that all workers experience a positive shock. In this case, increasing the number of workers decreases the team probability of success, and this decreases the expected payments made to workers when they put in the first best level of effort. This means that the principal will increase the third best bonus, which increases the third best expected payment to workers and the marginal cost of employment. From this it is clear that all of the third best bonus, expected payments and the marginal cost of a worker are increasing in the number of workers. This is the opposite of the second best case.

As the number of workers employed continues to increase, the third best bonus, expected payments and the marginal cost of employment all explode. This is contrary to the second best case, where all these variables tended to their first best levels. The third best marginal cost of employment is shown to always exceed the first and second best marginal costs of employment. This means the third best firm is usually smaller than either the first or second best firms.

Thus, for Rauh's model, moral hazard concerns only limit the division of labour and the size of the firm, when the principal can monitor just the output of the whole team. When either worker's effort or individual output can be observed, either the extent of the labour market or the O-ring property limit the extent of the division of labour or the size of the firm.

Discussion and conclusion

One point to note about all the models considered here is that they are, implicitly, complete contracts models. But as the modern mainstream literature on the theory of the firm highlights, this means that the division of labour approach can give us models of (market-mediated) production, but they cannot give us theories of the firm. The contemporary literature on the theory of the firm is, for the most part, an incomplete contracts literature.[20] In a world of complete contracts, it is not clear why a firm is needed to carry out production at all. As Coase (1937) first highlighted, in such a world, any organisational form can mimic any other, meaning that production could be carried out via the market just as efficiently as within a firm. Thus, incomplete contracts are needed to explain the existence and boundaries of the firm.

The discussion so far does raise the question as to why the division of labour took so long to be utilised as the foundation for a theory of production. One possible reason for the delay is that while the division of labour approach to production is based around the manufacturing division of labour, which was not exploited until the mid-nineteenth century, for most of its history the emphasis in the division of labour literature was on the social division of labour.

A number of the reasons which have been put forward to explain why the theory of the firm, in general, was ignored for so long also apply to the particular case of the division of labour approach.[21] Firstly, Foss and Klein (2006: 67) argue that there is the possibility of an empirical reason for the firm being overlooked; the relative unimportance of the (large, vertically integrated, often diversified) firm. Until relatively recently, firms were simply not a large part of the economy. Thus, analysing anonymous 'firms' may not have been a bad approximation to the empirical realities of the time.

It has also been argued that during the neoclassical period, firms were ignored simply because many economists of the era did not see economic theory as being relevant to business or saw the internal workings of the firm as being outside the competence of economists. Arthur Pigou, for example, wrote

> it is not the business of economists to teach woollen manufacturers to make and sell wool, or brewers how to make and sell beer, or any other business men how to do their job. If that was what we were out for, we should, I imagine, immediately quit our desks and get somebody doubtless at a heavy premium, for we should be thoroughly inefficient to take us into his woollen mill or his brewery.
>
> (Pigou 1922: 463–4)

Another reason given for the lack of emphasis on the theory of the firm was a more general lack of emphasis on positive economics for much of the history of economic analysis. Thinking on economic matters began and developed with a more normative/moral orientation than is common today, and so there was no stimulus to develop a positive theory of what firms are and what they do.

Also, there was a concentration on macroeconomic issues rather than microeconomic concerns for much of the history of the development of economics. It was not until the 1870s, with the advent of neoclassical economics, that microeconomic questions began to come to the fore. Less emphasis on microeconomics in general lessened the probability of a microeconomic-based theory developing in the particular case of the theory of production or the firm.

Foss (1997: 176) puts forward an additional reason:

> [i]n fact, some 25 years ago Ronald Coase (1972, p. 63) observed tartly that his 1937 essay "The Nature of the Firm" had been "much cited and little used," and – it is fair to say – economists did in general neglect the firm. The reason? The conviction – brilliantly articulated by Fritz Machlup (1967) – that the purpose of economic theory primarily is to explain market-level phenomena, and that the firm is therefore, at most, an intermediate step in the price theoretic logic.

Lastly, it has been argued that the rise in formalism in economics resulted in the firm being ignored. Foss and Klein (2006) write

> while these advances in tooled knowledge are partly the result of the increased use of formal methods in economics, it was the rise of formalism in economic theory that was largely responsible for the neglect of the firm's characteristics in the first place. In other words, if the purpose of economic theory is prediction, not explanation, then treating the firm as a production function or a price taker is perfectly acceptable, as long as it generates accurate predictions (Friedman 1953: 150).
>
> (Foss and Klein 2006: 2, footnote 2)

While discussions of the division of labour go back at least as far as ancient India, the European tradition developed from the works of the ancient Greek philosophers such as Democritus, Xenophon, Plato and Aristotle. At around the same time as Plato and Aristotle were writing, Chinese philosophers, such as Kuan Chung, Lao Tzu, Confucius and Mencius, were also investigating the division of labour. During the medieval period, both Islamic and Christian theologians and philosophers considered its consequences. Works by al-Ghazali, Nasir al-Din Tusi, Thomas Aquinas and Ibn Khaldün all treated aspects of the division of labour. The pre-classical, classical and neoclassical economists continued and expanded the enquiry, but all without applying the division of labour to the theory of the firm. Finally, in the twentieth century, theories of the firm based around the division of labour started to appear.

So it took more than two thousand years of discussion of the division of labour, in its various forms, before, starting in the twentieth century, a small amount of work utilising the manufacturing division of labour to construct a theory of the firm finally emerged. But this belated work on a division of labour approach to the firm has been work to no avail, since the economic mainstream has, for the most part, ignored this approach when developing a theory of the firm. The contemporary mainstream literature has, largely, taken a contractual approach to the firm, based on the pioneering work of Coase (1937).[22]

Notes

1 Colander, Holt and Rosser (2004: 490) argue that the

> [m]ainstream consists of the ideas that are held by those individuals who are dominant in the leading academic institutions, organizations, and journals at any given time, especially the leading graduate research institutions. Mainstream economics consists of the ideas that the elite in the profession finds acceptable, where by elite we mean the leading economists in the top graduate schools. It is not a term describing a historically determined school, but is instead a term describing the beliefs that are seen by the top schools and institutions in the profession as intellectually sound and worth working on.

The concentration of the mainstream of economic thought does mean some non-mainstream ideas will be ignored.

2 It is also a minority approach within the non-mainstream literature. Bylund (2016) is one of the few non-mainstream works (Bylund writes within the Austrian school of economics) that utilises the division of labour in a theory of the firm. The non-mainstream (or 'heterodox') grouping includes dissenting schools of economic thought such as the Austrians, the evolutionary approach, the (old) institutionalists, Marxists and post-Keynesians, among others.

3 There is a debate over the exact significance of Xenophon's discussion of the division of labour. Some see it as a significant economic contribution, while others see it as a few commonplace observations. See Lowry (1987: 69–73) for more on this point.

4 Deodhar (2018) says of Rig-Veda that

> Rig-Veda, one of the premier religious texts originating in India dates back at least to 1500 BCE (Violatti, 2013). For want of good writing materials and its durability in those times, such texts were composed using terse metrical verses and passed-on to future generations through memorization. In fact, there are four different kinds of Vedas and most were orally composed in the third millennia BCE (Vinod, 2012), before being written down between 1500 BCE to 600 BCE.
>
> (Deodhar 2018: 4)

and

> Rig-Veda, composed within its 1028 hymns, 10,600 verses, and ten books (mandalas) is the world's oldest religious text in continuous use till date (Klostermaier, 1984; Kurtz, 2015). There are many hymns which relate to matters on material prosperity, prices, bargaining, and taxes.
>
> (Deodhar 2018: 8)

5 Backhouse (2002: 130) credits Francis Hutchinson with the phrase: "The phrase 'division of labour' was coined by Hutcheson, and the concept was widely understood in Xenophon's day". But he gives no reference.

6 These dates refer to the publication dates of volumes 1 and 2 of the 'Fable of the Bees'.

7 For a discussion of the origins of Smith's pin making example, see Peaucelle (2006) and Peaucelle and Guthrie (2011).

8 I am grateful to Gavin Kennedy for pointing this out to me.

9 Walker (2018) discusses these developments.

10 Murray Rothbard argues that vertical integration of a firm is limited for much the same reason that a socialist economy cannot function, as the firm takes over more and more input and output markets rational economic calculation becomes increasingly difficult, ultimately impossible (Rothbard 2004: 609–16).

11

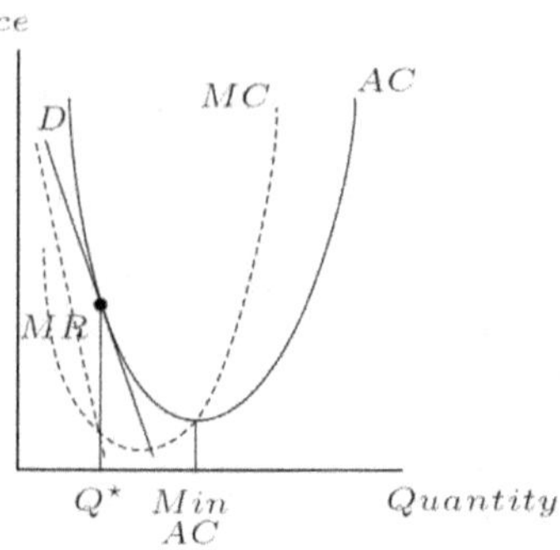

Monopolistic competition equilibrium, Q*

12 Becker and Murphy (1992: footnote 3, p. 1149) argue against this:

> a firm need not specialize *only* in these functions. Each firm could be the sole provider of some functions subject to increasing returns and one of several providers of functions subject to decreasing returns.

13 Using equation 3.2

$$Y(s) = E(s)T_w(s)$$

$$\Rightarrow dH^{\gamma}T_h^{\theta}(s)\left(T(s) - T_h(s)\right) \quad \text{using equations 3.7 and 3.8}$$

$$\Rightarrow dH^{\gamma}T_h^{\theta}(s)T(s) - dH^{\gamma}T_h^{\theta+1}(s)$$

$$\frac{\partial Y(s)}{\partial T_h(s)} = \theta dH^{\gamma}T_h^{\theta-1}(s)T(s) - (1+\theta)dH^{\gamma}T_h^{\theta}(s) = 0$$

$$\Rightarrow \theta dH^{\gamma}T_h^{\theta-1}(s)T(s) = (1+\theta)dH^{\gamma}T_h^{\theta}(s)$$

$$\Rightarrow T(s)T_h^{\theta-1} = \frac{(1+\theta)}{\theta}T_h^{\theta}(s)$$

$$\Rightarrow T_h(s) = \frac{\theta}{(1+\theta)}T(s)$$

$$Y(s) = dH^{\gamma}T_h^{\theta}(s)\left(T(s) - T_h(s)\right)$$

using equations 3.2, 3.7 and 3.8

$$= dH^{\gamma}\left(\frac{\theta}{1+\theta}\right)^{\theta}T^{\theta}(s)\left[T(s) - \left(\frac{\theta}{1+\theta}\right)T(s)\right]$$

Using the $T_h(s)$ term

$$= dH^{\gamma}\left(\frac{\theta}{1+\theta}\right)^{\theta}T^{\theta}(s)\left(\frac{1}{1+\theta}T(s)\right)$$

$$= dH^{\gamma}\theta^{\theta}(1+\theta) - (1+\theta)T^{1+\theta}(s)$$

$$= A(\theta)H^{\gamma}T^{1+\theta}(s)$$

where $A(\theta) = d\theta^{\theta}(1+\theta)^{-(1+\theta)}$

14 Equation 3.6 gives $B_n(H, n) - C_n(n) \geq 0$. Remember that n is a function of H.

$$\frac{\partial}{\partial H}(B_n(H,n) - C_n(n)) = \frac{\partial B_n}{\partial H} + \frac{\partial B_n}{\partial n}\frac{dn}{dH} - \frac{\partial C_n}{\partial n}\frac{dn}{dH} = 0$$

$$\Rightarrow \frac{\partial B_n}{\partial H} = \frac{dn}{dH}\left(\frac{\partial C_n}{\partial n} - \frac{\partial B_n}{\partial n}\right)$$

$$\Rightarrow \frac{dn}{dH} = \frac{B_{nh}}{C_{nn} - B_{nn}}$$

This result involves taking a total derivative:

If $y = f(x,w)$ where $x = g(w)$ then $\frac{dy}{dw} = f_x\frac{dx}{dw} + f_w = \frac{dy}{dx}\frac{dx}{dw} + \frac{dy}{dw}$, see Chiang and Wainwright (2005: 189–93)

and use of the sum-difference rule:

$\frac{d}{dx}[f(x) \pm g(x)] = \frac{d}{dx}f(x) \pm \frac{d}{dx}g(x) = f'(x) \pm g'(x)$, see Chiang and Wainwright (2005: 152–3)

and the chain rule:

If $z = f(y)$ and $y = g(x)$, then $\frac{dz}{dx} = \frac{dz}{dy}\frac{dy}{dx} = f'(y)g'(x)$, see Chiang and Wainwright (2005: 161–3) for details.

15 Consider the unconstrained optimisation problem: Maximise $U = f(x, y, \lambda)$, where λ is a parameter and x and y are variables. The first-order conditions are: $f_x(x, y, \lambda) = f_y(x, y, \lambda) = 0$. These implicitly determine the optimal levels of x and y: $x^\star = x^\star(\lambda)$ and $y^\star = y^\star(\lambda)$. These in turn determine the maximum-value function. Substitute $x^\star$ and $y^\star$ into the objective function, $f(x, y, \lambda)$, to get $V(\lambda) = f(x^\star(\lambda), y^\star(\lambda), \lambda)$. The maximum-value function gives the value of the objective function, $f(x^\star, y^\star, \lambda)$, when the values of the variables, x and y, are set to their optimal values. Differentiating the maximum-value function, $V(\lambda)$, with respect to λ gives, $\frac{dV}{d\lambda} = f_x\frac{\partial x^*}{\partial \lambda} + f_y\frac{\partial y^*}{\partial \lambda} + f_\lambda$. But from the first-order conditions we know that $f_x = f_y = 0$, so $\frac{dV}{d\lambda} = f_\lambda$. This means that, at the optimum, when $x^\star$ and $y^\star$ are allowed to adjust, the derivative $dV/d\lambda$, gives the same outcome as if we treated $x^\star$ and $y^\star$ as constants. Thus, the essence of the envelope theorem is that only the direct effects of a change in a parameter need be considered, even though the parameter may also enter the maximum-value function indirectly via the solution to the problem of the optimal values of the variables.

For a much more complete discussion of the envelope theorem see Carter (2001: 603–9), Chiang and Wainwright (2005: section 13.5) or Varian (1992: 490–2).

16 Thanks to Professor Ulrich Schwalbe for providing this derivation of the result. Using equation 3.6 we get $n^\star$. Equation 3.6 implies that $n^\star$ is parameterised by λ and H, denoted $n^\star(H, \lambda)$. Substituting $n^\star(H, \lambda)$ into equation 3.5 gives,

$y^\star(H, n^\star(H, \lambda)) = B(H, n^\star(H, \lambda)) - C(n^\star(H, \lambda))$ (the maximum-value function)

We want to know $\frac{\partial y^*}{\partial H}$, that is, the change in the maximum value of output per worker, $y^\star$, for a change in general knowledge, parameter H. But note that by the envelope theorem $\frac{\partial y^*}{\partial H} = \frac{\partial y(H, n^*(H,\lambda))}{\partial H}$, so we only need to calculate $\frac{\partial y}{\partial H}$.

Differentiating $y(H, n^\star(H, \lambda))$ (or $y^\star$) with respect to H, i.e., finding $\frac{\partial y}{\partial H}$, gives the marginal product of human capital. Differentiating that result by λ, i.e., finding $\frac{\partial^2 y}{\partial H \partial \lambda}$, gives the effect of coordination costs on the marginal product of human capital.

$$\frac{\partial y}{\partial H} = \frac{\partial B\left(H, n^*(H, \lambda)\right)}{\partial H} + \frac{\partial B\left(H, n^*(H, \lambda)\right)}{\partial n^*}\frac{\partial n^*(H, \lambda)}{\partial H} - \frac{\partial C\left(\lambda, n^*(H, \lambda)\right)}{\partial n^*}\frac{\partial n^*(H, \lambda)}{\partial H}$$

$$= \frac{\partial B\left(H, n^*(H, \lambda)\right)}{\partial H} + \left(\frac{\partial B\left(H, n^*(H, \lambda)\right)}{\partial n^*} - \frac{\partial C\left(\lambda, n^*(H, \lambda)\right)}{\partial n^*}\right)\frac{\partial n^*(H, \lambda)}{\partial H}$$

but from the first order condition $B_n - C_n = 0$, i.e. $n^\star < N$, so we are left with

$$\frac{\partial y}{\partial H} = \frac{\partial B\left(H, n^*(H, \lambda)\right)}{\partial H}, \text{ and thus,}$$

$$\frac{\partial^2 y}{\partial H \partial \lambda} = \frac{\partial\left(\frac{\partial B\left(H, n^*(H, \lambda)\right)}{\partial H}\right)}{\partial \lambda} = \frac{\partial^2 B\left(H, n^*(H, \lambda)\right)}{\partial H \partial n^*}\frac{\partial n^*(H, \lambda)}{\partial \lambda} < 0$$

$$\text{since } \frac{\partial^2 B\left(H, n^*(H, \lambda)\right)}{\partial H \partial n^*} > 0 \text{ and } \frac{\partial n^*(H, \lambda)}{\partial \lambda} < 0.$$

17 Young's theorem: Let $f\colon U \to R$ be a function where $U \subset R^n$ is open and assume that the second-order partial derivatives of f are continuous, then $\frac{\partial^2 f}{\partial x_j \partial x_i} = \frac{\partial^2 f}{\partial x_i \partial x_j}\, i, j = 1, 2, \ldots, n.$

18 The rest of the Becker and Murphy paper deals with economic growth and the relationship between workers who produce for current consumption and teachers who, indirectly, contribute to future consumption by raising the human capital of others. Such issues are outside our concerns with the division of labour and firms.

19 The O-ring production function was introduced by Kremer (1993). The name comes from the fact that it was an O-ring failure that caused the space shuttle *Challenger* disaster. The basic idea is that the failure of a small component can have large adverse consequences for the enterprise as a whole. Here one part of the production process failing causes the whole process to fail.

20 See Foss, Lando and Thomsen (2000) and Walker (2016) for more on this. It is standard practice to include (complete contract) agency theory as part of the theory of the firm, although strictly speaking such theories are not about the main questions of the contemporary theory of the firm, that is, the existence and boundaries of firms. "Principal-agent theory enriches neoclassical theory significantly, but still fails to answer the vital questions of what defines a firm and where the boundaries of its structure are located" (Hart 1989: 1759).

21 See Walker (2018: chapter 4) for an expanded discussion of the following points.

22 See Ricketts (2019) and Walker (2016) for introductions to this literature.

References

Allen, Douglas W. and Dean Lueck (1998). 'The Nature of the Farm', *Journal of Law and Economics*, 41(2) October: 343–86.

Babbage, Charles (1832). *On the Economy of Machinery and Manufacturers*, Philadelphia: Carey & Lea.

Backhouse, Roger E. (2002). *The Ordinary Business of Life: A History of Economics From the Ancient World to the Twenty-First Century*, Princeton, NJ: Princeton University Press.

Becker, Gary and Kevin M. Murphy (1992). 'The Division of Labor, Coordination Costs, and Knowledge', *Quarterly Journal of Economics*, 107(4) November: 1137–60.

Best, Michael H. (2012). 'The Obscure Firm in the Wealth of Nations'. In Michael Dietrich and Jackie Kraff (eds.), *Handbook on the Economics and Theory of the Firm* (29–41), Cheltenham, UK: Edward Elgar Publishing Ltd.

Blaug, Mark (1958). 'The Classical Economists and the Factory Acts – A ReExamination', *Quarterly Journal of Economics*, 72(2) May: 211–26.

Bonar, James (1992). *Philosophy and Political Economy*, New Brunswick: Transaction Publishers. First published 1893.

Bowen, Howard R. (1955). *The Business Enterprise as a Subject for Research: Prepared for the Committee on Business Enterprise Research*, Social Science Research Council, Pamphlet No. 11, New York: Social Science Research Council.

Bylund, Per L. (2016). *The Problem of Production: A New Theory of the Firm*, London: Routledge.

Carter, Michael (2001). *Foundations of Mathematical Economics*, Cambridge, MA: MIT Press.

Chiang, Alpha C. and Kevin Wainwright (2005). *Fundamental Methods of Mathematical Economics*, 4th edn., New York: McGraw-Hill/Irwin.

Coase, Ronald Harry (1937). 'The Nature of the Firm', *Economica*, n.s. 4(16) November: 386–405.

Colander, David, Richard Holt and J. Barkley Rosser Jr. (2004). 'The Changing Face of Mainstream Economics', *Review of Political Economy*, 16(4): 485–99.

Deodhar, Satish (2018). 'Indian Antecedents to Modern Economic Thought', W.P. No. 2018–01–02 January, Indian Institute of Management, Ahmedabad.

Fawcett, H. (1863). *Manual of Political Economy*, London and Cambridge: Macmillan & Co.

Foss, Nicolai J. (1997). 'Austrian Insights and the Theory of the Firm'. In *Advances in Austrian Economics* (Advances in Austrian Economics, vol. 4, pp. 175–98), Bingley: Emerald Group Publishing Limited.

Foss, Nicolai J. and Peter G. Klein (2006). 'The Emergence of the Modern Theory of the Firm', Center for Strategic Management and Globalization, Copenhagen Business School, SMG Working Paper 1/2006, January.

Foss, Nicolai J., Henrik Lando and Steen Thomsen (2000). 'The Theory of the Firm'. In Boudewijn Bouckaert and Gerrit De Geest (eds.), *Encyclopedia of Law and Economics* (vol. III, pp. 631–58), Cheltenham, UK: Edward Elgar Publishing Ltd.

Frank, Lawrence K. (1925). 'The Significance of Industrial Integration', *Journal of Political Economy*, 33(2) April: 179–95.

Ghazanfar S. M. and A. Azim Islahi (1990). 'Economic Thought of an Arab Scholastic: Abu Hamid al-Ghazali (A.H. 450–505/A.D. 1058–1111)', *History of Political Economy*, 22(2) Summer: 381–403.

Groenewegen, Peter (2008). 'Division of Labour'. In Steven N. Durlauf and Lawrence E. Blume (eds.), *The New Palgrave Dictionary of Economics*, 2nd edn., Basingstoke, Hampshire and New York: Palgrave Macmillan. The New Palgrave Dictionary of Economics Online. Palgrave Macmillan. 30 December 2016. Available at: www.dictionaryofeconomics.\-com/article?id=pde2008D000176.

Hart, Neil (2003). 'From the Representative to the Equilibrium Firm: Why Marshall Was Not a Marshallian'. In Richard Arena and Michel Quéré (eds.), *The Economics of Alfred Marshall: Revisiting Marshall's Legacy* (158–81), Houndmills, Basingstoke, Hampshire: Palgrave Macmillan.

Hart, Oliver D. (1989). 'An Economist's Perspective on the Theory of the Firm', *Columbia Law Review*, 89(7) November: 1757–74.

Hosseini, Hamid (1998). 'Seeking the Roots of Adam Smith's Division of Labor in Medieval Persia', *History of Political Economy*, 30(4) Winter: 653–81.

Irwin, Douglas A. (1996). *Against the Tide: An Intellectual History of Free Trade*, Princeton: Princeton University Press.

Koehler, Benedikt (2016). 'The Thirteenth-Century Economics of Thomas Aquinas', *Economic Affairs*, 36(1) February: 56–63.

Kremer, M. (1993). 'The O-Ring Theory of Economic Development', *Quarterly Journal of Economics*, 108(3) August: 551–75.

Lowry, S. Todd (1987). *The Archaeology of Economic Ideas: The Classical Greek Tradition*, Durham: Duke University Press.

Mandeville, Bernard (1988). *The Fable of the Bees or Private Vices, Publick Benefits*, 2 vols., with a commentary, critical, historical, and explanatory by F. B. Kaye, Indianapolis: Liberty Fund.

Marshall, Alfred (2009). *Principles of Economics*, Unabridged 8th edn., New York: Cosimo, Inc. Eighth edition first published 1920. First edition 1890.

Marshall, Alfred and Mary Paley Marshall (1879). *The Economics of Industry*, London: Macmillan and Co., Limited.

Marx, K. (1867). *Capital*, vol. 1, Moscow: Foreign Languages Publishing House, 1959.

McGee, Robert W. (1990). 'The Work of Thomas Aquinas: A Pioneer in the Field of Law & Economics', *Western State University Law Review*, 18(1) Fall: 471–84.

McNulty, Paul J. (1984). 'On the Nature and Theory of Economic Organization: The Role of the Firm Reconsidered', *History of Political Economy*, 16(2) Summer: 233–53.

Nicholson, J. S. (1893). *Principles of Political Economy*, 2nd edn., London: A. & C. Black.

Peaucelle, Jean-Louis (2006). 'Adam Smith's Use of Multiple References for His Pin Making Example', *European Journal of the History of Economic Thought*, 13(4) December: 489–512.

Peaucelle, Jean-Louis and Cameron Guthrie (2011). 'How Adam Smith Found Inspiration in French Texts on Pin Making in the Eighteenth Century', *History of Economic Ideas*, 19(3): 41–67.

Petty, William (1683). 'Another Essay in Political Arithmetick Concerning the Growth of the City of London'. In Charles Henry Hull (ed.), *The Economic Writings of Sir William Petty, Together with The Observations Upon Bills of Mortality, More Probably by Captain John Graunt* (vol. II, pp. 451–78), Cambridge: Cambridge University Press, 1899.

Petty, William (1690). 'Political Arithmetick'. In Charles Henry Hull (ed.), *The Economic Writings of Sir William Petty, Together with The Observations Upon Bills of Mortality, More Probably by Captain John Graunt* (vol. I, pp. 233–313), Cambridge: Cambridge University Press, 1899.

Pigou, A. C. (1922). 'Empty Economic Boxes: A Reply', *Economic Journal*, 32(128) December: 458–65.

Quesnay, François (1765). 'Natural Right'. In Ronald L. Meek (ed.), *The Economics of Physiocracy: Essays and Translations* (43–56), London: Routledge, 2003.

Rauh, Michael T. (2018). 'The O-ring Theory of the Firm', *Journal of Economics & Management Strategy*, 27(1) Spring: 82–101.

Ricketts, Martin (2019). *The Economics of Business Enterprise: An Introduction to Economic Organisation and the Theory of the Firm*, 4th edn., Cheltenham, UK: Edward Elgar.

Robinson, E. A. G. (1931). *The Structure of Competitive Industry*, Cambridge: Cambridge University Press.

Rothbard, Murray N. (2004). *Man, Economy, and State: A Treatise on Economic Principles with Power and Market: Government and the Economy*, Scholar's Edition, Auburn: Ludwig von Mises Institute.

Senior, Nassau W. (1836). *An Outline of the Science of Political Economy*, New York: Augustus M. Kelly, Inc., 1938.

Smith, Adam (1776). *An Inquiry into the Nature and Causes of the Wealth of Nations*, 2 vols., R. H. Campbell and A. S. Skinner (general eds.), W. B. Todd (textual ed.), Indianapolis: Liberty Classics, 1981.

Stigler, George J. (1951). 'The Division of Labor is Limited by the Extent of the Market', *Journal of Political Economy*, 59(3) June: 185–93.

Sun, Guang-Zhen (2012). *The Division of Labour in Economics: A History*, London: Routledge.

Sun, Guang-Zhen (2016). 'The Economics of the Division of Labour in Early Chinese Literature: With Particular Comparison to the Ancient Greek Thought', *The European Journal of the History of Economic Thought*, 23(1) February: 102–26.

Ure, Andrew (1835). *The Philosophy of Manufactures: Or, an Exposition of The Scientific, Moral, and Commercial Economy of the Factory System of Great Britain*, London: Charles Knight.

Varian, Hal R. (1992). *Microeconomic Analysis*, 3rd edn., New York: W.W. Norton & Company.

Walker, Paul (2016). *The Theory of the Firm: An Overview of the Economic Mainstream*, London: Routledge.

Walker, Paul (2018). *A Brief Prehistory of the Theory of the Firm*, London: Routledge.

Williams, Philip L. (1978). *The Emergence of the Theory of the Firm: From Adam Smith to Alfred Marshall*, London: The Macmillan Press.

Xenophon (1876). *The Cyropædia, or Institution of Cyrus, and The Hellenics, or Grecian History*. Translated by J. S. Watson and Henry Dale, London: George Bell and Sons.

Zouboulakis, Michel S. (2015). 'Elements of a Theory of the Firm in Adam Smith and John Stuart Mill'. In George C. Bitros and Nicholas C. Kyriazis (eds.), *Essays in Contemporary Economics: A Festschrift in Memory of A. D. Karayiannis* (45–52), Heidelberg: Springer Cham.

4 Proto-neoclassicals and the theory of production

Introduction

It has been suggested by Robert Ekelund and Robert Hébert that part of the commonly believed folk law regarding the development of neoclassical economics may need to be revised.

> A genuine, functioning toolkit for neoclassical microeconomics existed long before Marshall's Principles in 1890 and well before the legendary triumvirate of Menger, Jevons and Walras circa 1870.
>
> (Ekelund and Hébert 2002: 212)

Many, if not most, economists believe that the division between classical and neoclassical economics occurred in the 1870s with the advent of the 'neoclassical revolution'.[1] It was then, so the standard story goes, that the three co-founders of neoclassical economics published their works: William Stanley Jevons, *The Theory of Political Economy*, in 1871; Carl Menger, *Principles of Economics*, in 1871; and Léon Walras, *Elements of Pure Economics*, in 1874. Following them, Alfred Marshall then codified these new ideas for modern economists with the publication of his hugely influential book *Principles of Economics* in 1890.[2]

> In the 1870s there was a qualitative change in some economists' approach to doing economics. During this time utilitarianism and marginalism rose in importance, and deductive models with utilitarian foundations became more fashionable. To capture this change, it was helpful to develop a new classicization to distinguish that approach from the earlier Classical approaches based on the labor, or cost, theories of value. The term that developed was neoclassical.
>
> The term neoclassical was initially coined by Thorstein Veblen (1900) in his "Preconceptions of Economic Science." As Veblen used the term, it was a negative description of Alfred Marshall's economics, which itself was a type of synthesis of the marginalism found in Menger and W.S. Jevons with broader Classical themes in Smith, Ricardo, and J.S. Mill. . . .

> Hicks (1932, 1934) and Stigler (1941) extended the meaning of neoclassical to encompass all marginalist writers, including Menger, Jevons, and J.B. Clark. Most writers after John Hicks and George Stigler used the term inclusively. Thus it lost most of its initial meaning. Instead of describing Marshallian economics, it became associated with the use of calculus, the use of marginal productivity theory, and a focus on relative prices.
>
> (Colander 2000: 131)

Colander (2000: 134–5) goes on to list six primary attributes of neoclassical economics:[3]

1. Neoclassical economics focuses on allocation of resources at a given moment in time
2. Neoclassical economics accepts some variation of utilitarianism as playing a central role in understanding the economy
3. Neoclassical economics focuses on marginal tradeoffs. Colander comments here that neoclassical economics came into existence just as calculus was introduced into economics and the initial neoclassical endeavours were centered upon the marginal tradeoffs that calculus emphasised
4. Neoclassical economics assumes farsighted rationality
5. Neoclassical economics accepts methodological individualism. Assumptions 3, 4 and 5 are all tied to the use of a constrained maximisation approach to the analysis. Someone must be carrying out the optimisation procedure and in the neoclassical approach that someone is the individual
6. Neoclassical economics is structured around a general equilibrium conception of the economy

The neoclassical approach changed the way economists perceived of and did economics. Classical and neoclassical economics were substantially different schools of thought. Simpson (2013: 1) remarks that "[m]any people might suppose from the similarity of the terms 'classical' and 'neoclassical' that one school of economic thought is closely related to the other. In fact . . ., they are more nearly exact opposites". The two schools differed fundamentally in the way they viewed the central propositions of economics. A major division between the two centred around a macroeconomic versus a microeconomic view of economic analysis.

The classical economists were, by and large, preoccupied with macroeconomic issues. O'Brien (2003: 112) remarks that

> [c]lassical economics ruled economic thought for about 100 years [approximately 1770–1870]. It focused on macroeconomic issues and economic growth. Because the growth was taking place in an open economy, with a currency that (except during 1797–1819) was convertible into gold, the classical writers were necessarily concerned with the balance of payments,

the money supply, and the price level. Monetary theory occupied a central place, and their achievements in this area were substantial and – with their trade theory – are still with us today.

Simpson (2013: 1, emphasis added) writes that

> [t]he hallmarks of the classical tradition are principally three. *The first is the brief that the growth of the economy, rather than relative prices, should be the principal object of analysis*. Coupled with that belief is an understanding of the market economy as a collection of process of continuing change rather than as a structure, and that the nature of this change is self-organising and evolutionary. Finally there is a conviction that economic activity is rooted in human nature and the interaction of individual human beings.

While classical economists did develop a theory of production, it was primarily a theory of macro production aimed at explaining the production of an entire economy rather than being a microeconomic theory of firm production. Lionel Robbins remarked that the classical theories of production and distribution were about determining the total wealth, or 'total product', of the nation:

> The traditional approach to Economics, at any rate among English-speaking economists, has been by way of an enquiry into the causes determining the production and distribution of wealth. Economics has been divided into two main divisions, the theory of production and the theory of distribution, and the task of these theories has been to explain the causes determining the size of the "total product" and the causes determining the proportions in which it is distributed between different factors of production and different persons.
>
> (Robbins 1935: 64)

O'Brien emphasises that one important change that occurred during the evolution from classical to neoclassical economics was the change from macro to microlevel analysis:

> [t]he core of neo-classical economics is the theory of microeconomic allocation, to which students are introduced in their first year in an elementary and largely intuitive form, and which receives increasingly sophisticated statements during succeeding years of study. On top of this, as a sort of icing on the cake, comes the macroeconomics theory of income determination, with, in little attached boxes so to speak, theories of growth and trade appended. But the approach of the classical economists was the very reverse of this. For them the central propositions of economics concerned macroeconomic problems. Their focus above all was on the problem of growth, and the macroeconomic distribution conclusions which followed from their view of growth. On the one hand, international trade, at least for

> Smith was inextricably bound up with all this: on the other, the microeconomic problems of value and microdistribution took their place as subsets of the greater whole.
>
> (O'Brien 2004: 63)

Given this shift towards microeconomics, relative prices became the principle object of analysis.

But while this characterisation is largely true, there were some writers in the classical period who were developing neoclassical-like analysis, including inquiries into what at the time was referred to as the theory of the 'firm'. But importantly, what went under the heading of the theory of the firm then is more likely to be designated a theory of markets today. These pre-1870 writers are part of a group that Ekelund and Hébert (2002) have referred to as "proto-neoclassicals".

In this chapter we will look at five proto-neoclassical economists who anticipated aspects of the neoclassical theory of the 'firm': Dionysius Lardner, Johann von Thünen, John Stuart Mill, Charles Ellet, Jr., and Antoine Augustin Cournot.

Each of their contributions will be briefly outlined. Lardner, Ellet and Cournot analysed monopoly, oligopoly and, in Cournot's case, perfectly competitive product markets, while von Thünen looked at the firm's input markets, all using neoclassical-type tools and all working before 1870. Mill wrote on the economics of the firm, even if not strictly on the theory of the firm in the sense of the other writers. He introduced the notion of the entrepreneur to the English-speaking economics literature, considered the effects of wealth on the number of firms and discussed joint production and the scale of production. He also scrutinised the advantages and disadvantages of the joint-stock company.

It will be argued that even without the founders of the neoclassical revolution it is likely that the marginalist theory of the 'firm' still would have developed, given that the theory had largely been created before 1870. The effects of the proto-neoclassical on the neoclassicals will be evaluated, and the long-term contributions of the proto-neoclassical writers to the economics of the firm will be considered. Today, Lardner and Ellet are largely forgotten, while von Thünen and Mill are remembered for contributions other than those to the theory of the firm. Of the five, only Cournot is well known today, and his influence is to do with market structure rather than the theory of the firm in the modern sense.

Dionysius Lardner

One person who made a contribution to the theory of the 'firm' during the later classical era, albeit a contribution largely forgotten now, was Dionysius Lardner. Ekelund and Hébert (2002) summarise Lardner's contribution made in his 1850 book *Railway Economy* as he "[a]nalyzed railroad pricing structures; developed simple and discriminating monopoly analysis; analyzed monopoly firm in terms of total cost and total revenue, both mathematically and graphically (with an implicit demand curve)" (Ekelund and Hébert 2002: Table 1, p. 199).

This suggests that Lardner foreshadowed a number of aspects of the neoclassical theory of the firm. Lardner modelled a profit maximising monopoly firm (Lardner assumed the firm has the power to set its price) and analysed its choice of price (and thus implicitly quantity) using revenue and cost curves, and implicitly a demand curve.[4] He effectively showed that a profit maximum would occur when "marginal revenue" equals "marginal cost".

To understand Lardner's reasoning, consider Figure 4.1.

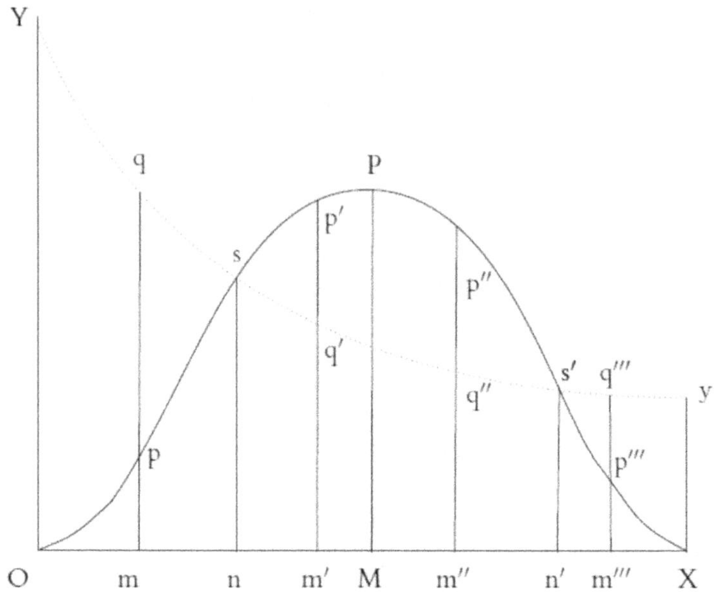

Figure 4.1 Lardner's cost and revenue curves

Source: Lardner (1850: 288)

In Figure 4.1, the solid bell-shaped curve is what we would refer to today as a total revenue curve, but where the curve is graphed in revenue/output-price space rather than the standard revenue/quantity space, that is, the horizontal axis measures the price of output. At low prices, revenue is also low, but as demand is inelastic, revenue increases as price increases. It reaches a maximum, point P in Figure 4.1, and then as demand becomes more elastic, revenue falls as price continues to increase.[5]

The negatively sloped dotted line, Yy, is the total cost curve, again where the curve is graphed in cost/output-price space rather than cost/quantity space. This explains why the curve is negatively sloped. As the price of output increases, the quantity demanded falls; that is, Lardner is implicitly using a demand curve here, and as quantity falls the variable costs of production fall. Fixed costs, the vertical distance Xy, still needed to be paid. Lardner's cost curve shows total costs, fixed plus variable, declining due to the reduction in variable costs.

Lardner notes that the profit maximising point is to be found somewhere between P and s′ in Figure 4.1. Between s and s′, total revenues are greater than total costs, and so profits are positive. As we move from s to P, total revenues are increasing while total costs are falling and thus profits are increasing. As we move from P towards s′, Lardner argues that, initially, total costs will fall more than total revenue, and thus profit will increase. This keeps occurring up until the point at which the fall in revenue equals the fall in costs. At this point profits are maximised. Fortunately for the modern reader, Lardner then clarifies this by stating,

> [t]his may be geometrically expressed by stating it to be the point at which the two curves become parallel to each other.
>
> (Lardner 1850: 292)

This observation would be expressed today by saying that 'marginal revenue' equals 'marginal cost'. Note however that for Lardner both 'marginal revenue' and 'marginal cost' would be defined in terms of the derivative with respect to output-price rather than quantity.

Lardner's explanation also shows that the profit maximising price is greater than the revenue maximising price, point P, that is, the profit maximising quantity is less than the revenue maximising quantity.

Lardner also hints at the advantages of price discrimination, insofar as he sees an advantage to having a lower tariff (price per mile per ton) on longer distances (think, larger quantities of 'railway services'). For example, he writes,

> [i]t is clear, therefore, that every reduction which can be made on the tariff affecting the larger class of distances, will have the effect of increasing the area over which the producer can carry on a profitable business, and will proportionally increase the available traffic of the railway. For lesser distances, the reduction of the tariff will only have the effect of augmenting the quantity of the articles transmitted, and this can only be effected in the proportion in which the reduction of the tariff can effect a diminution of price in the market.
>
> A due consideration of these circumstances will easily demonstrate the advantage which must result to the railways from such a graduated tariff as would favour transport to greater distances,
>
> (Lardner 1850: 299)

and he also said,

> [i]t follows, therefore, that for traffic generally, but more especially for every description of merchandise and of live stock, a tariff graduated upon the principle of diminishing as the distance transported increases, must be the source of largely augmented profits.
>
> (Lardner 1850: 301)

This justifies Mark Blaug's comment that *Railway Economy* is "a book containing the first exposition in English of what approximates to the modern [neoclassical] theory of the firm" (Blaug 1997: 293).

Johann Heinrich von Thünen

A second proto-neoclassical who made a contribution to the theory of the 'firm' is Johann von Thünen. While Lardner analysed the firm's output market, von Thünen looked at the firm's input markets. He argued that the firm should use inputs up to the point where the value of the marginal product of the input equals the price of that input. His treatment of the issue has become known as the marginal productivity theory of distribution.

Von Thünen began by looking at the effects of adding additional workers to the production process, holding capital constant, in agricultural production and explaining that the marginal productivity of labour diminishes with each additional worker.

> It is in the nature of agriculture – and this is a circumstance that must be stressed – that the additional yield is not in direct proportion to the number of additional laborers, but every additional laborer brings an additional product lower than the preceding, the 22nd worker less than the 21st, the 23rd less than the 22nd, and so forth.
>
> (Dempsey 1960: 203)

The question then asked is, At what point will the landowner stop adding workers? "Unquestionably at that point where the value of the additional product obtained compensates for the work which has been applied" (Dempsey 1960: 307).

What emerges from von Thünen's analysis is what today is referred to as the marginal productivity analysis of wages.

> "*The value of the labor of the last worker employed is also his wage.*" . . . As in the example of the large estate complex which we have set up, so in reality the striving of entrepreneurs to increase the number of their workers until no more advantage comes to them through a further increase – that is, when the wage for the work reaches the value of the work – is universal because this is founded in the nature of the case and in the advantage of the entrepreneur. But the wage that the last employed worker receives must be the norm for all workers of the same skill and proficiency *because for the same effort there cannot be paid an unequal wage.*
>
> (Dempsey 1960: 312, emphasis in the original)

Von Thünen's applies the same analysis to variations in capital, holding labour constant, and obtains analogous results.

This means, according to Schumpeter (2006: 441), that von Thünen developed the marginal productivity theory of distribution, "which he correctly puts, in words, in terms of partial differential coefficients".

In addition, in Volume II, Part 2, Chapter 3 of *The Isolated State* (see Dempsey 1960: 340–54), von Thünen gives the first algebraic formula for a production function.[6]

> Von Thünen's clear realization of the substitutability of factors was a necessary prelude to the concept of a production function. Furthermore, his definition of product as that part of gross output attributable to capital and labor was unquestionably a fortuitous aid, leading him to regard the product explicitly as a function of the two variables, inputs of capital and labor.
>
> To put his discovery of the production function beyond dispute, we need only note that Von Thünen gives the equation of the production function which he believed described the actual output of his Tellow estate. This is probably the first algebraic formula for a particular production function. The general equation (Dempsey translation, p. 347) is
>
> $$p = h(g + k)^n, \tag{4.1}$$
>
> where p is the product of a unit of labor, k is the quantity of capital per laborer, g is a positive constant, and n is a constant whose value Von Thünen always took to be less than unity. Capital may be measured in terms of the worker's means of subsistence, or it may be measured in terms of labor, since in Von Thünen's model capital is itself stored-up labor. (When capital is measured in terms of labor, Von Thünen uses the symbol g to represent capital per worker. Thus g has two different meanings in Volume II, Part 2, of *The Isolated State*.) The parameter h is also a constant. (Lloyd 1969: 31)

To illustrate von Thünen's argument, we will look at the simplest possible model. We will assume a central marketplace which is surrounded by agricultural land, all of which is of equal fertility. There will be one good, which we call wheat. The landowners hire a single input to production, labour. L units of labour produces $W(L)$ units of wheat. The price of wheat in the marketplace is p, while the costs of transporting the wheat to the market is \$$t$ per mile per ton. Thus the earnings generated from wheat grown m miles away from the marketplace is $p - t \cdot m$ per ton. Total revenue from the wheat will be $W(L) \cdot (p - t \cdot m)$. Assume that the landowner pays workers a wage of w resulting in a total wage bill of $w \cdot L$. This means that the landowner's profit from producing wheat m miles from the marketplace will be $W(L) \cdot (p - t \cdot m) - w \cdot L$.

Further assume that the landowner selects L to maximise profits. This results in a problem we can represent mathematically as

$$\max_L W(L) \cdot (p - t \cdot m) - w \cdot L$$

Maximising this objective function with respect to L gives the first order condition,

$$\frac{\partial W(L^{*})}{\partial L}(p - t \cdot m) - w = 0$$

$$\Rightarrow \frac{\partial W(L^{*})}{\partial L}(p - t \cdot m) = w \tag{4.2}$$

where $\frac{\partial W(L)}{\partial L}$ is the marginal product of labour and $\frac{\partial W(L)}{\partial L}(p - t \cdot m)$ is the value of the marginal product of labour. Equation 4.2 tells the firm it wants to select the level of labour such that the value of the marginal product of labour equals the marginal cost of labour, the wage rate.

Put more generally, a profit maximising firm will choose the level of an input so that the value of the marginal product of the input equals the price of that input. Therefore, from the point of view of a firm, the theory indicates how many units of a factor it should demand.

Blaug (1985: 17–18) sums up von Thünen's analysis by saying,

> [h]is analysis culminates in the perfectly modern statement that net revenue is maximized when each factor is employed to the point at which its marginal value product (*Wert des Mehrertrags*) is equalized to its marginal factor cost (*Mehraufwand*). Although the discussion proceeds in verbal terms, illustrated by numerical examples, von Thünen correctly points out that the marginal product of a factor is a partial differential coefficient of a multivariable production function. Moreover, apart from clearly recognizing the distinction between fixed and variable factors, and between the average and the marginal returns of a factor, he took great care to define the inputs of capital, labor, and land in strictly homogeneous units, observing that this condition was rarely obtained in practice – this too was literally more than sixty years ahead of his time.

John Stuart Mill

A third, possible, proto-neoclassical, who wrote on the economics of the firm, if not strictly on the theory of the firm, was John Stuart Mill. While Mill is most often thought of as a classical economist, Ekelund and Hébert (2002: 198) argue he can be considered as a proto-neoclassical.

According to Schumpeter (2006: 530) Mill introduced the concept of the entrepreneur to the English speaking economics literature.[7] The influence of J. B. Say helped Mill go beyond just analysing the role of the owner of the factors of production and begin focusing on the role of the entrepreneur and on the internal organization of the firm (Zouboulakis 2015: 49).

For Mill, the number of collective organisations, including firms – both investor controlled and cooperatives, would increase as wealth increases,

> [a]s wealth increases and business capacity improves, we may look forward to a great extension of establishments, both for industrial and other purposes, formed by the collective contributions of large numbers; establishments like those called by the technical name of joint-stock companies, or the associations less formally constituted, which are so numerous in England, to raise funds for public or philanthropic objects, or, lastly, those associations of workpeople either for production, or to buy goods for their common consumption, which are now specially known by the name of co-operative societies.
>
> (Mill 1848: 699)

Mill gave the first discussion of joint production and of the importance of the scale of production. With regard to joint production George Stigler writes,

> Mill clearly formulated the problem of joint production, i.e., production of two or more products in fixed proportions. He gave the complete and correct solution: the sum of the prices of the products must equal their joint cost, and the price of each product is determined by the equality in equilibrium of quantity supplied and quantity demanded.
>
> (Stigler 1955: 297)

As to the significance of the scale of production Stigler adds that,

> Mill's chapter (Bk.I, c.IX), "Of production on a large, and production on small, scale", is the first systematic discussion of the economies of scale of the firm to be found in a general economic treatise. It would take us afield to analyse this chapter in detail, but we may point out that Mill was the first economist to notice that one can deduce information on the costs of firms of different sizes from their varying fortunes through time.
>
> (Stigler 1955: 298)

Zouboulakis (2015: 50) writes that

> [a]mong the advantages of production on a large scale, he [Mill] mentions the more advanced division of labour, the less than proportionate increase of "the expenses of a business", the greater possibility of investment to "expensive machinery" and "the saving in the labour of the capitalists themselves" (1848: 132–6).

Mill also scrutinised the advantages and disadvantages of the joint stock company.

> On the one hand, only such a company can afford the amount of capital necessary to build important projects such as a railway, and to guarantee the continuity of such costly and risky business operations such as banking and

> insurance. On the other hand, he recognizes that "joint stock or associated management" has some disadvantages over "individual management".
>
> (Zouboulakis 2015: 50)

Mill, like Adam Smith, saw the potential for, what today we would call, principal-agent problems in the relationship between the owners and the managers of joint-stock companies. The interests of the managers may not be aligned with the interests of the owners. When discussing methods to the alleviate such problems, Mill makes the observation that

> [i]n the case of the managers of joint stock companies, and of the superintending and controlling officers in many private establishments, it is a common enough practice to connect their pecuniary interest with the interest of their employers, by giving them part of their remuneration in the form of a percentage on the profits. The personal interest thus given to hired servants is not comparable in intensity to that of the owner of the capital; but it is sufficient to be a very material stimulus to zeal and carefulness, and, when added to the advantage of superior intelligence, often raises the quality of the service much above that which the generality of masters are capable of rendering to themselves.
>
> (Mill 1848: 141)

Interestingly, such observations give Mill more of a proto-modern feel than a proto-neoclassical feel. But, again, like Smith, Mill did not develop his insights into a full-blown theory of the firm.

Charles Ellet, Jr.

Thus far we have considered European proto-neoclassicals, but the United States has representatives in this group as well. For our purposes, the major US exponent of proto-neoclassical economics is Charles Ellet, Jr.

Ellet (1839), like Lardner (1850), is concerned with the pricing policies of a monopoly railway. For Ellet the problem is one about selecting the cost of freight, on an "improvement" (railway line), for commodities brought to it by lateral connecting road branches (Figure 4.2). The monopoly railway must decide what the charge per ton-mile for profit, or a toll, is to be set at.

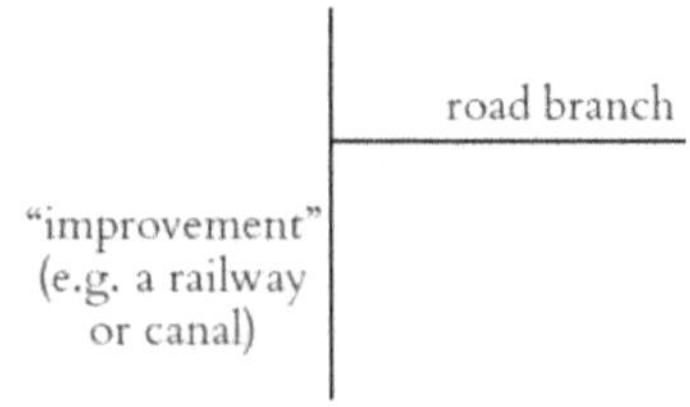

Figure 4.2 Ellet's monopoly model

Ellet assumes that the railway is a profit maximiser. His notation is:

π = the transport charge the commodity will bear (any charge greater than π results in zero demand)
C = the transport charge per ton-mile on the improvement, including profit
c = the charge per ton-mile for profit or toll
δ = the charge per ton-mile for freight
β = the charge on the feeder road
h = the distance the article is carried on the improvement

Given this, $C = \delta + c$, hC is the expenditure on movement of the article along the improvement, $(\pi - hC)$ is the maximin remaining expenditure to cover movement along the feeder road and

$$\frac{(\pi - hC)}{\beta} \tag{4.3}$$

is the distance the article can be carried along the feeder road.

Multiply equation 4.3 by c to get the profit along the feeder road,[8]

$$\begin{aligned} r &= \frac{(\pi - hC)}{\beta} c \\ &= \frac{\pi c - h\delta c - hc^2}{\beta} \end{aligned} \tag{4.4}$$

To maximise profit, we differentiate 4.4 with respect to c. This results in,[9]

$$\begin{aligned} \frac{\partial r}{\partial c} &= \frac{\pi - h\delta - 2hc}{\beta} = 0 \\ \Rightarrow c &= \frac{\pi - h\delta}{2h} \end{aligned} \tag{4.5}$$

Equation 4.5 is:

> *the proper charge per ton per mile toll, on articles which do not excite competition of other lines, . . . is equal to the difference between the whole charge which the article will bear, and the actual cost of transporting it on the improvement, divided by twice the distance it is carried on the improvement.*
>
> (Ellet 1839: 63, emphasis in the original)

Ellet was not just concerned with simple monopoly; he also examined the pricing policies of a discriminating monopolist. In Ellet (1840), he considered the problem of charging different groups of passengers different prices.

To begin, his notation is

ζ = gross charge per mile of railroad
δ = expense per passenger mile on the railroad
c = toll (or charge in excess of costs) per passenger mile on railroad
h = distance from assumed origin to tributary
T = number of passengers on the railroad when price is zero

Assume that for each one unit increase in the charge, c, the number of passengers declines by t. Ekelund and Hooks (1973: 45) comment that "t represents a constant coefficient or slope of the travel demand curve" (see the following equations).

Also note that,[10]

$$\zeta = \delta + c$$

$$\text{Gross charge between two places} = \zeta h$$

$$\text{Number of passengers} = T - t\zeta h \text{ (the travel demand curve)}$$

$$\begin{aligned}\text{Net revenue} &= (T - \zeta ht)ch \\ &= Tch - \delta h^2tc - c^2h^2t \qquad (4.6)\end{aligned}$$

Maximising 4.6 with respect to c gives the first order condition[11]

$$Th - h^2\delta t - 2ch^2t = 0$$

$$\Rightarrow ch = \frac{1}{2}\left(\frac{T}{t} - h\delta\right) \qquad (4.7)$$

If to this expression we add actual expenses, δh, we get the gross charge,[12]

$$\begin{aligned}\delta h + ch = \zeta h &= \delta h + \frac{1}{2}\left(\frac{T}{t} - h\delta\right) \\ &= \frac{1}{2}\left(\frac{T}{t} + \delta h\right)\end{aligned} \qquad (4.8)$$

> From which we conclude that under the circumstances assumed, the gross charge which will yield the highest revenue on all the travelers who pass between the two cities, at which they reside, will be obtained by *adding half the actual expenses to a certain constant quantity.*
>
> (Ellet 1840: 10, emphasis in the original)

Passengers can be classified into different groups and each of these groups will have its own constant term, $\frac{1}{2}\frac{T}{t}$, and thus its own version of equation 4.8. But Ellet thinks it likely that for the United States, only two groups are important

> the first consisting of those who regard cheapness as more important than the superior comforts and more select society offered in the best class of

cars, and the second, of those who are willing to pay something for these considerations.

(Ellet 1840: 15)

Ellet also considers a model where railways compete (a duopoly). Here we follow the discussion of the Ellet (1839) model given in Calsoyas (1950). To under understand his model, see Figure 4.3. There are two lines of improvement, one ending at *A* and the other at *B*. Which improvement will be used depends not just on the costs involved with transporting goods on each of the lines but also with the relative advantages of the markets at *A* and *B*.

Let h be the distance along the improvement which ends at *A*, from the junction of the connecting road *RR*. X is the length of the lateral road, *RR*, and h' is the distance *BR* along the rival improvement from the junction of the connecting road to the ending at *B*. x is the distance *Ra* from the improvement *A* to the point *a*, where the trade is divided. β is the charge on the connecting road. ζ is the charge per ton per mile for conveyance on the improvement terminating at *A*. ζ' is the charge on the rival improvement. M is the value of the superiority of the market at *A* over that at *B*. c is the charge per ton-mile for profit, or the toll, and δ is the charge per ton-mile for freight. Therefore $\zeta = \delta + c$.

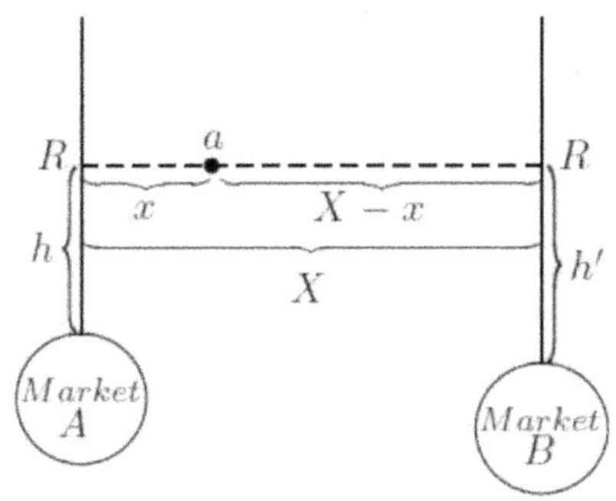

Figure 4.3 Ellet's first duopoly model

The division of trade will be given by the point *a* at which the costs of using improvement *A* equals those of using *B*, i.e. $h\zeta + x\beta - M = h'\zeta' + (X - x)\beta$. $h\zeta + x\beta$ is the total cost of using the improvement *A*, while $x\beta$ is the cost of using the lateral road up to point *a*. M equalises the attractiveness of the two markets *A* and *B*. Here, *A* is superior to *B* by an amount M. $h'\zeta'$ is the cost of using improvement *B*, while $(X - x)\beta$ is the cost for *B* of using the lateral road up to point *a*.[13]

$$h\zeta + x\beta - M = h'\zeta' + (X - x)\beta$$

$$\Rightarrow x = \frac{h'\zeta' - h\zeta + X\beta + M}{2\beta} \tag{4.9}$$

$$\Rightarrow x = \frac{h'\zeta' - h\delta - hc + X\beta + M}{2\beta} \tag{4.10}$$

If we multiply 4.10 by c we get profits per mile for the firm, which operates the improvement ending at A; that is,

$$\begin{aligned} xc &= \frac{h'\zeta' - h\delta - hc + X\beta + M}{2\beta} c \\ &= \frac{h'\zeta' c - h\delta c - hc^2 + X\beta c + Mc}{2\beta} \end{aligned} \tag{4.11}$$

To maximise profits, we differentiate 4.11 with respect to c, since c is the variable under the control of the firm.[14]

$$\begin{aligned} \frac{\partial xc}{\partial c} &= \frac{X\beta + h'\zeta' - h\delta - \ 2hc + M}{2\beta} = 0 \\ \Rightarrow c &= \frac{X\beta + h'\zeta' - h\delta + M}{2h} \end{aligned} \tag{4.12}$$

c is the profit maximising toll. Ellet writes

> [w]e learn from the above equation that, when the markets offer equal attractions, the toll *corresponding with the maximum revenue is equal to the cost of sending the commodity from the point where it comes on the work to the rival port, less the cost of freight on the improvement, divided by twice the distance it is transported on the improvement.*
>
> (Ellet 1839: 74, emphasis in the original)

The total charge, $\zeta = \delta + c$, is obtained by adding δ to equation 4.12.[15]

$$\begin{aligned} c + \delta = \zeta &= \frac{X\beta + h'\zeta' - h\delta + M}{2h} + \delta \\ &= \frac{X\beta + h'\zeta' + h\delta + M}{2h} \end{aligned} \tag{4.13}$$

What we have happening here is that the firms determine x by equalising the (given) costs of using each of the improvements A and B, and then, when maximising profits, each firm acts as a monopolist in their share of the market.

If we make $x = 0$ in equation 4.9 we get the value of ζ that would exclude the firm controlling improvement A from the market.[16] The firm controlling improvement B would then be a monopoly for the total market.

$$\begin{aligned} 0 &= \frac{h'\zeta' - h\zeta + X\beta + M}{2\beta} \\ \Rightarrow \zeta &= \frac{h'\zeta' + X\beta + M}{h} \end{aligned} \tag{4.14}$$

Given that $\zeta = \delta + c$ equation 4.14 gives,[17]

$$\begin{aligned} \delta + c &= \frac{h'\zeta' + X\beta + M}{h} \\ c &= \frac{h'\zeta' - h\delta + X\beta + M}{h} \end{aligned} \tag{4.15}$$

This value of c would shut out A from the trade, which leaves B as the monopolist for the whole market.

Notice that equation 4.12 is half the size of equation 4.15. In other words, the toll per ton per mile at the profit maximum is half the toll per ton per mile that would exclude A from the trade.

This has important implications for Ellet's second model of duopoly. Within a given area, let there be a single line of improvement that is divided into two (sub)lines of unequal length and let each (sub)line be controlled by a monopolist; see Figure 4.4.

The following notion will be used.

- P is the greatest toll that could be exacted without entirely excluding the trade
- h is the length of the longer of the two lines
- h' is the length of the shorter line
- c is the toll per ton per mile on the longer line
- c' is the toll on the shorter line

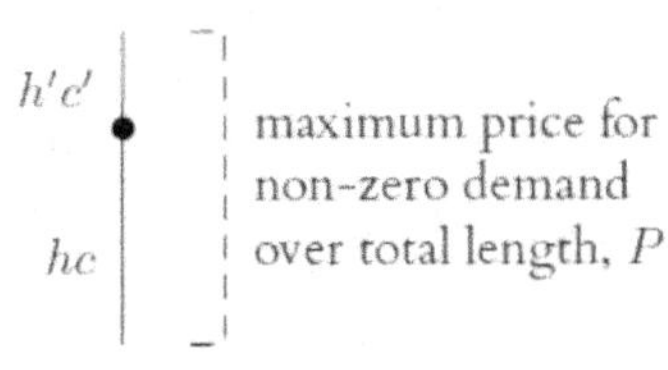

Figure 4.4 Ellet's second duopoly model

The toll for one ton of merchandise to be carried the entire length of the longer railway line is hc, and thus the toll for the shorter line would be $h'c' = \frac{P-hc}{2}$. Charging anything greater than $P - hc$ on the shorter line would mean that the trade would be excluded from the line, since the total charge would be greater than P. We know from the previous analysis that the profit maximising toll is half of the zero trade toll, or in this instance $h'c' = \frac{P-hc}{2}$.

But the toll levied on the longer line must depend on the toll on the shorter line, $h'c'$, just worked out. So, $hc = \frac{P-h'c'}{2}$.

If we use the two equations to eliminate $h'c'$, we get,[18]

$$hc = \frac{P - h'c'}{2}$$

$$= \frac{1}{3}P$$

This tells us that the charge on the longer of the two lines will be one-third of the charge that would stop trade from taking place. Substituting this into $h'c' = \frac{P-hc}{2}$ gives[19]

$$h'c' = \frac{P - \frac{1}{3}P}{2}$$

$$= \frac{1}{3}P$$

If we add hc and $h'c'$ together, we get the total charge for the toll,

$$hc + h'c' = \frac{2}{3}P$$

So a monopolist who controls both sections of the improvement would set a total charge of half the maximin possible rate, that is, $\frac{1}{2}P$, while the independent duopolists set a charge of $\frac{2}{3}P$.

Thus, when compared to the situation of a single profit-maximising monopolist, the duopolists charge a higher toll, and the volume of trade will be lower for the duopolists.

Thus, Ellet has showed that a unified monopoly that controls all the different parts of a network (upstream/downstream parts) would price in such a way as to ensure higher profits and permit a higher level of service than if individual monopolies controlled each individual part of the network and maximised their own individual profits. To put this in more modern and general terms, in a vertically-related industry with an upstream and a downstream monopolist in which each firm maintains the price-setting power of its product, the retail price is above the monopoly price set by a vertically integrated firm. Thus, Ellet anticipated the idea of 'double marginalisation'. This puts Ellet 110 years ahead of Spengler.[20]

Calsoyas (1950: 170) makes an important point about Ellet's influence on economics, namely that "Ellet did not affect the course of economic inquiry". Significantly for the theory of the firm, such an observation could be made about all, with perhaps one exception, of the proto-neoclassicals.

Antoine Augustin Cournot

> The [neoclassical] theory of the firm as we know it today originates historically in the work of Cournot (1838).
>
> (Boulding 1960: 1)

This Boulding quote suggests that the one exception to the 'dismal' assessment given at the end of the previous section is Antoine Augustin Cournot. He is the one proto-neoclassical who has influenced economic analysis, albeit only after more than a 100 year lag, and who is known to every economics student today. Any undergraduate microeconomics textbook will cover his analysis.

Cournot's major economics work was *Researches into the Mathematical Principles of the Theory of Wealth* (Cournot 1838). In chapter 5 of the book, Cournot gives his analysis of monopoly. He assumes a profit-maximising producer. He begins his analysis by positing a cost function $\phi(D)$ where $D = F(p)$ is the demand curve.

He writes the producer's profits function as,

$$pF(p) - \phi(D)$$

where $pF(p)$ is revenue. This profit function can be rewritten as

$$pD - \phi(D). \tag{4.16}$$

Maximising this version of the profit function gives,

$$D + p\frac{dD}{dp} - \frac{d\phi}{dD}\frac{dD}{dp} = 0$$
$$\Rightarrow D + \frac{dD}{dp}\left[p - \frac{d\phi}{dD}\right] = 0.$$

This was Cournot's way of saying that marginal revenue equals marginal cost, since in his notation $D + p\frac{dD}{dp}$ is "marginal revenue" and $\frac{d\phi}{dD}\frac{dD}{dp}$ is "marginal cost".[21]

In chapter 7, Cournot presents his famous duopoly model. He starts by assuming that there are two rival producers of a homogeneous product (two mineral springs), for each of whom the costs of production are zero. Again we have a demand function $D = F(p)$, but here $D = D_1 + D_2$. D_1 are the sales for producer 1 and D_2 the sales for producer 2. Revenues for each producer are given by pD_1 and pD_2 respectively.

Cournot then switches to working with the inverse demand function, $p = f(D)$. This allows him to rewrite the profits of each of the producers as

$$D_1 \times f(D_1 + D_2) \tag{4.17}$$

and

$$D_2 \times f(D_1 + D_2). \tag{4.18}$$

Maximising these two equations, with respect to D_1 and D_2 respectively, gives the first order conditions,

$$f(D_1 + D_2) + D_1 f'(D_1 + D_2) = 0 \tag{4.19}$$

$$f(D_1 + D_2) + D_2 f'(D_1 + D_2) = 0 \tag{4.20}$$

Solving equations 4.19 and 4.20 gives[22]

$$f(D_1 + D_2) + D_1 f'(D_1 + D_2) = f(D_1 + D_2) + D_2 f'(D_1 + D_2)$$
$$\Rightarrow D_1 = D_2$$

This result is not surprising, since the two producers are identical.

If we add 4.19 to 4.20 we get $2f(D) + Df'(D) = 0$, using $D = D_1 + D_2$. Cournot rewrites this equation.[23]

$$2f(D) + Df'(D) = 0$$
$$\Rightarrow 2p\frac{dD}{dp} + D = 0 \tag{4.21}$$

Note that if both firms where divisions of a monopolist, the profit maximisation problem would be $\max_D D \times f(D)$. The first order condition for this problem is,[24]

$$f(D) + Df'(D) = 0$$
$$\Rightarrow p\frac{dD}{dp} + D = 0 \tag{4.22}$$

Cournot notes that the monopoly solution of equation 4.22 would give each of the producers a greater income than that obtained from the duopoly equation 4.21. This does raise the question as to why the producers do not set the value of p to that given by 4.22. Cournot writes

> The reason is that, producer (1) having fixed his production at what it should be according to equation (4) [4.22] and the condition $D_1 = D_2$, the other will be able to fix his own production at a higher or lower rate with a *temporary benefit*. To be sure, he will soon be punished for his mistake, because he will force the first producer to adopt a new scale of production which will react unfavourably on producer (2) himself. But these successive reactions, far from bringing both producers nearer to the original condition [of monopoly], will separate them further and further from it. In other words, this condition is not one of stable equilibrium; and, although the most favourable for both producers, it can only be maintained by means of a formal engagement.
>
> (Cournot 1838: 83)

It is then shown that the price under monopoly is greater than that under duopoly, or as Cournot puts it, "[i]n consequence the root of equation (3) [4.21] is always smaller than that of equation (4) [4.22]; or (as every one believes without any analysis) the result of competition is to reduce prices"

(Cournot 1838: 84). He goes on to say, more generally, that the price will decrease as the number of firms increases,

> "[i]f there were 3,4, . . . , *n* producers in competition, all their conditions being the same, equation (3) [4.21] would be successively replaced by the following:
>
> $$D+3p\frac{dD}{dp}=0, D+4p\frac{dD}{dp}=0, \ldots D+np\frac{dD}{dp}=0;$$
>
> and the value of *p* which results would diminish indefinitely with the indefinite increase of the number *n*"
>
> (Cournot 1838: 84).

Friedman (2000) highlights the (often ignored) point that Cournot moved beyond the simple model just presented.

> Antoine Augustin Cournot is most remembered for duopoly theory; in particular for homogeneous goods duopoly with output as the choice variable of each firm in a model with a linear demand function and zero costs. Some economists are aware that Cournot actually analyzed *n*-firm oligopoly, for arbitrary *n*, using both a fairly general demand function and general cost functions that differ from one firm to another. His oligopoly solution concept has been seen in recent years as an early manifestation of the non-cooperative equilibrium concept of game theory due to Nash (1951).
>
> (Friedman 2000: 31)

On page 85 of the *Researches* Cournot gives the first order conditions for an *n*-firm oligopoly with cost functions $\phi_i(D_i)$, $i = 1, \ldots, n$:

$$\begin{aligned} f(D) + D_1 f'(D) - \phi'_1(D_1) &= 0 \\ f(D) + D_2 f'(D) - \phi'_2(D_2) &= 0 \\ &\vdots \\ f(D) + D_n f'(D) - \phi'_n(D_n) &= 0 \end{aligned}$$

He then shows that production at one firm will be greater than at a second firm if expanding output at the second firm is more expensive than at the first firm, that is, $D_1 > D_2$ if $\phi'_2 > \phi'_1$. Next, Cournot demonstrates that the costs under oligopoly are greater than those under monopoly. A monopolist will produce at the least cost plant, leaving others idle, whereas a high cost oligopolist will produce as long as he can make any positive profit. He then shows that the monopoly price is greater than the oligopoly price.

In chapter 8, Cournot deals with the case of 'unlimited competition'. It is this chapter that first argued that perfect competition is the limiting case of the entire spectrum of market structures defined in terms of the number of sellers.[25] As the number of sellers increases the output of the industry converges in the limit to the output of what we now refer to as a perfectly competitive industry. Cournot shows that in equilibrium the price will equal marginal cost.

> In Chapter VII, he shows that the market price decreases as the number of competitors increases. In the next Chapter, he describes a competitive (partial) equilibrium with great precision. Such a state of the market arises under what he calls the *hypothesis of unlimited competition*, and leads to equality of market price with the 'differential coefficient' of the cost function [marginal cost].
>
> (Gary-Bobo 1989: 519, emphasis in the original)

Thus

> [i]t was Auguste Cournot who in 1838 first invented the idea of perfect competition as a market structure in which business firms are so numerous that each firm must take price as given, being free only to adjust the quantity it produced.
>
> (Blaug 2001: 153)

(The Appendix to this chapter very briefly outlines the development of the theory of perfect competition beginning with Cournot and ending with Frank Knight.)

While Cournot is well known in economics today, it required something of a rediscovery in the 1960s for him to become a standard part of the economics curriculum. It was only after the usefulness of game theory become recognised and it was realised that the Cournot equilibrium is just a form of Nash equilibrium that Cournot become established as an economic innovator.

At the time of its publication, the *Researches* was not well received. "The lack of response of the economics profession to Augustin Cournot's *Recherches sur les principes mathématiques de la théorie des richesses* is a widely cited example of failure to appreciate ideas that are ahead of their time" (Dimand 1988: 610). J. W. Friedman has written,

> [f]or many years Cournot's work was ignored and, by the time of his death in 1877, he was apparently unaware of any influence on economists.
>
> (Friedman 2000: 32)

and

> [h]e was not a mainstream economist; his career was primarily outside of economics and the economists of his time paid little attention to him.
>
> (Friedman 2000: 34)

and

> [a]lthough Cournot had a generally successful career, his economic writings brought him virtually no recognition in his lifetime.
>
> (Friedman 2000: 37)

In fact, it took until 1883 for the book's (second[26] and) most famous review to appear, and it wasn't kind.

> In a scathing review that reviled Cournot (1838), he [Bertrand] singled out the oligopoly chapter, the most original gem of a strikingly original and deep monograph, for special contempt. He says oligopolists will collude and, supposing they do not collude, then Cournot got the equilibrium wrong due to having erred in switching from price to quantity as the choice variable. Next he proceeds to an analysis of the linear demand, zero cost duopoly example using prices. Cournot clearly makes a conscious choice in Chapter VII to switch to outputs. He writes (page 59)[27] "Au lieu de poser, comme précédemment, $D = F(p)$, il nous sera commode d'employer ici la notation inverse $p = f(D)$"[28] which sounds very purposeful and which follows an earlier statement that there can be only one price in the market. This switch of variables is justified by Cournot only for convenience and, later on he speaks of changing output (i.e., sales) by changing price; a contradiction of the notion of output as the choice variable. He does this in the context of an illegitimate pseudo-dynamic argument.
>
> (Friedman 2000: 40)

After that Cournot did get favourable mentions from a number of authors who were influenced by the mathematical approach to economics. Alfred Marshal, for example, in the Preface to the first edition of his *Principles* wrote, "Cournot's genius must give a new mental activity to everyone who passes through his hands" (Marshall 1890: xi). "The first mainstream 'mathematical economists,' Marshall, Jevons, Walras, and Edgeworth, read Cournot and surely recognized that he was expressing economic theory mostly correctly and with a crystalline clarity that had not previously been seen" (Friedman 2000: 37). Cournot also had his detractors among the early mathematical economists, F. Y. Edgeworth, for example, wrote in 1897,

> He [Cournot] concludes that a determinate proposition of equilibrium defined by certain quantities of the articles will be reached. Cournot's conclusion has been shown to be erroneous by Bertrand for the case in which there is no cost of production; by Professor Marshall for the case in which the cost follows the law of increasing returns; and by the present writer for the case in which the cost follows the law of.
>
> (Edgeworth 1925: 117–8)

Some of Cournot's ideas were rediscovered in later time periods, "the concept of marginal revenue had to be rediscovered in 1920s when the case of imperfect competition drew the theorists' attention to the possibility of a downward sloping demand curve confronting the individual firm" (Blaug 1997: 302). G. L. S. Shackle notes that around 1930 "this tool [marginal revenue] suddenly and simultaneously appeared in many hands, in the published or unpublished work of authors who had discovered it independently of each other" (Shackle 1967: 22).

While Cournot's ideas were debated among a small group of mathematically inclined economists after 1870 it had to wait until the 1960s, when the interest in game theory renewed interest in Cournot, for him to become part of the standard training of all economists.

> As mathematics was not generally integrated into the mainstream language and analysis of economics until the second half of the twentieth century, he [Cournot] was not widely known among economists, except for the prominence of his oligopoly theory in the 1920's and 1930's when much attention was being given to imperfectly competitive markets.
>
> (Friedman 2000: 32)

But Cournot's most famous contributions can be seen more as theories of industries or markets, rather than as theories of the firm per se.

Discussion

One thing that was missing from the discussion of the pre-1870 development of the marginal productivity theory of distribution given in the previous section on Johann Heinrich von Thünen is mention of Mountifort Longfield. Longfield (1834) is sometimes accorded the honour of the first statement of a marginal productivity theory of distribution.

> [H]e presented a reasonably complete and reasonably correct theory of distribution based upon the marginal productivity principle, not only the marginal cost principle. That is to say, he explained both 'profits' (return upon physical capital) and wages in terms of the contributions to total product that result from the addition to the productive set-up of the last element of capital (tools) or labor. Thus at least it seems fair to interpret him, though in details his argument is open to many criticisms (among other things he failed, as did many writers even after 1900, to distinguish clearly between the last laborer added and the least efficient laborer). The argument is still worth reading because it shows nicely the operations by which economists' minds paved their way toward the use of the general marginal principle.
>
> (Schumpeter 2006: 439–40)

But not all writers agree with Schumpeter, Moss (2010) is one who does not.

> The details of the Longfieldian system belong most properly to another study. Here our main conclusion has been to show how in the context of a discussion about the division of output between the workers and the capitalists, Longfield was one of the first to employ the technique of varying the amount of one factor (while holding the other constant) in order to determine its contribution to total output. However, Longfield used this technique only in this one instance and did not realize that it provides a general conceptual technique for determining the contribution of one factor when used in combination with several others, when the proportions in which they are combined can be varied. This concept is also capable of providing an answer to the question left unanswered by Say, namely, how the utility of a final product can be imputed back to the agents that participated in its production. Longfield, though no doubt familiar with Say's writings, did not contribute directly to the development of this line of reasoning.
>
> (Moss 2010: 219)

Pullen (2009) is another: "[a]lthough Longfield's argument could be described as a marginal productivity theory of capital, it cannot readily be interpreted as a productivity theory of labour" (Pullen 2009: 13).

Thus, Longfield got close to the marginal productivity theory of distribution but not all the way, and so "[t]he first truly marginal productivity theory of distribution appears to have come from J. H. von Thünen" (Pullen 2009: 14).

When we consider the behaviour of a firm in its output market rather than its input markets, Cournot, Lardner and Ellet offer a homogeneity in method of analysis and results. First of all, each of these authors assume that the firm's objective is to maximise profits. All three, in their own ways, imply that a firm will maximise profits when marginal revenue equals marginal cost, although in most cases marginal revenue and cost are defined with respect to price rather than the now more standard quantity.

For monopoly, what differs among the three is how they formulate the profit objective. Cournot has the most general formulation; see equation 4.16. Ellet is concerned with the particular case of a railway and his maximisation objective, equation 4.4, reflects this. Lardner does not give a general profit expression,

> [t]o determine this point of maximum profits rigorously, it would be necessary to express the strict arithmetical relation between the tariff and the traffic. [But] the strict arithmetical connection between the tariff and the traffic does not admit any general expression.
>
> (Lardner 1850: 292)

However, he does give a mathematical statement of a profit objective for the case of the movement of goods (Lardner 1850: 293–4). His notation is,

r is the tariff per mile per ton
D is the average number of miles each ton of goods is carried

N is the of tons of goods to be transported
R gross revenue e is the cost per ton per mile
E′ are the fixed costs of the railway
E are the total costs
P is profit

From this we can see that the average revenue gained by each ton of goods carried is D × r and total revenue is R = N × D × r. The cost of moving each ton of goods is D × e (average variable costs) and the total cost of moving the goods (total variable costs) is N × D × e. This means that total costs are E = E′ + N × D × e.

The total cost per ton is therefore given by $\frac{E}{N} = \frac{E'}{N} + D \times e$.

Finally, profits are given by P = R – E = N D(r – e) – E′ and profits per ton are $\frac{P}{N} = D(r - e) - \frac{E'}{N}$

With regard to this last equation, Lardner writes,

> [t]his is equivalent to stating that the profit realised on each ton booked is found by multiplying the difference between the tariff and the expenses of transport per mile by the average distance to which the ton is carried, and subtracting from the product the expenses which are independent of the distance.
>
> (Lardner 1850: 294)

Thus all three authors maximise the difference between revenue and costs, albeit writing the profit objective in different ways, and they all take price as the variable under the control of the firm.

In the case of duopoly, Ellet continues to use price as the firm's choice variable, whereas Cournot switches to now standard quantity.

Another difference between Cournot's model of duopoly and Ellet's first approach is that Ellet formulates his model in a spatial framework; the basic problem concerns determining the position of *a* along the roadway rather than a mutual best-response framework for the two competing firms, that is, determining the optimal levels of output for the firms. Ellet examines the equilibrium for one line of improvement, while Cournot examined the conditions for an equilibrium for both lines simultaneously.

To get equation 4.13, Ellet has assumed that each owner of a railway line makes their own pricing decision on the assumption that the other owner will not change their pricing decision. But if the owner of line A changes their pricing decision, this will affect B's profit and thus induce a change in B's pricing, which will in turn affect A's profits, and so on. Put in more modern terms, Ellet's solution may not be a Nash equilibrium, while Cournot's is.

The Cournot approach and Ellet's second approach to duopoly are also different. Cournot used the now standard approach of two firms competing in the same market, a horizontal relationship, while "Ellet had a peculiar theory of monopolistic duopoly in which a single line of improvement is divided between two monopolists" (Calsoyas 1950: 169), more of a vertical relationship; see page 87.

The horizontal versus vertical relationship difference gives the two models a different emphasis. It was the vertical nature of the Ellet model that allowed Ellet to, effectively, discover the notion of 'double marginalisation'. This was not an issue within the Cournot framework. Cournot sought an equilibrium in the output market which determined the outputs of the two competing firms.

Ellet is not as well-known as Cournot, and his models are different from that of Cournot, "but Ellet's ability to conceptualize and mathematize the duopoly problem was, at base, as sophisticated as Cournot's" (Ekelund and Hébert 1999: 175).

Only Cournot went the next step and the let the number of firms in an oligopoly go to infinity. By doing so, Cournot started the development of the theory of perfect competition.

Conclusion

What this chapter has shown is that there were pre-1870 authors who developed neoclassical ideas, under the heading of the 'theory of the firm', to do with producer behaviour in input and output markets, even if not to do with the theory of the firm in the modern sense. Lardner, Ellet and Cournot analysed monopoly, oligopoly and, in Cournot's case, perfectly competitive product markets while von Thünen looked at the firm's input markets, all using neoclassical type tools and all working before 1870. If we think in terms of Colander's list of neoclassical attributes given on page 73, these proto-neoclasscials satisfy points 1, 2, 3, 4 and 5. As to 6, it should be noted that the proto-neoclassical models are partial equilibrium models. But Colander (2000: 135) points out that the 'general equilibrium conception of the economy' attribute '. . . is more debatable than the others' and that '. . . if it were absolutely central it would eliminate Marshall from the neoclassical school'. Our modern, introductory, models of markets are still the proto-neoclassical models, in particular those of Cournot.

The (proto-)neoclassical models were, implicitly, zero transaction cost models, and thus they can be interpreted as models with production – but production without firms. Given that transaction costs are zero, there is no need for firms to act as intermediates between the owners of the factors of production and the consumers, where the firm's function is to organize and carry out the process of production. With perfect and costless contracting, consumers could contract directly with owners of the means of production to get what they want produced.

The move from a theory of 'markets with production but without firms' to a 'theory of the firm' is the major change that has taken place within the mainstream approach to the theory of the firm over the theory's history, but this change did not commence until around 1970, when work based on the ideas articulated in Coase (1937) started to develop. What we have seen since the

1970s is a movement away from the theory of the firm being seen as developing a component of price theory, namely the component which asks "How does a 'producer' act in its factor and product markets?" to the theory being concerned with the firm as an important institution in its own right (Walker 2018). The proto-neoclassical writers contributed to the 'theory of markets with production but without firms' approach by providing models of market structure, that is, theories of monopoly, oligopoly and perfect competition.

But history has not been kind to some of them. Lardner and Ellet are long forgotten, while von Thünen and J. S. Mill are mainly known today for contributions other than those to do with the theory of the firm. Cournot is the only one of the five who is commonly referred to in modern economics teaching and in microeconomics textbooks, but it is usually in the context of discussions to do with market organisation rather than the theory of the firm per se.

Mark Blaug highlights Cournot's contribution to the theory of market structures by noting that

> Cournot did more than invent the theory of pure monopoly Conclusion and the theory of duopoly: he also planted the idea that perfect competition is the limiting case of the entire spectrum of market structures defined in terms of the number of sellers.
>
> (Blaug 1997: 303)

As the number of sellers increases "the output of the industry converges in the limit on the output of a perfectly competitive industry. Here, in embryo, is the later popular notion of perfect competition as the standard for judging the outcome of non-competitive market structures" (Blaug 1997: 303).

But Paul McNulty contends that Cournot's approach to 'unlimited competition' started a process that actually led, over time, to the producer playing an increasingly passive role as an economic agent:

> [t]he "perfection" of the concept of competition, beginning with the work of A. A. Cournot and ending with that of Frank Knight, which was at the heart of the development of economics as a science during the nineteenth and early twentieth centuries, led on the one hand to an increasingly rigorous analytical treatment of market processes and on the other hand to an increasingly passive role for the firm.
>
> (McNulty 1984: 240)

A passive role for the firm is not surprising given the zero transaction cost nature of the model.

Those who neglected the firm included the founders of neoclassical economics. Hutchison (1953: 307) summarised the early neoclassical contributions to the theory of the firm as "Jevons has little on the firm. . . . Walras's assumptions of perfect competition (maintained virtually throughout) and of fixed technical 'coefficients', limited his contribution to the analysis of firms and markets". When discussing the early Austrian School, which includes Menger, Hutchison (1953: 308) comments "[t]he Austrian School, with the exception of Auspitz and Lieben, did not concern themselves much with the analysis of markets and firms, except in respect to their general principle of imputation". Foss (1994: 32) goes so far as to state that "Austrian analysis of market phenomena has even manifested a tendency to dispose of the concept of the firm". He adds in a footnote that "[t]he words 'firm,' 'business enterprise' or substitute terms do not figure in the indexes to Menger (1871)".

But not everyone saw the firm as passive; Alfred Marshall was one who did not. For Marshall firms were dynamic, heterogeneous, in disequilibrium; they progressed through a life cycle in much the same way as people. "They began young and vigorous, but after a period of maturity they became old and were displaced by newer more efficient firms" (Backhouse 2002: 179). Marshall gave us the famous metaphor of an industry being like a forest – while it might appear uncharged if considered as a whole, the individual trees that make it up are constantly changing (Backhouse 2002: 179–80). Marshall's approach to the firm was what he referred to as the 'representative firm'.

The problem Marshall was grappling with was how could he construct an industry supply which would show the quantity supplied for the industry at any given price. Clearly the supply of commodities is dependent on the costs a firm faces when producing the good. Marshall knew that, even within a given industry, there were firms of many different sizes who would be able to access different levels of internal economies and thus be able to produce at different levels of costs. The problem this gives rise to is which of these costs determined the market price of the good? Textbook microeconomics states that the supply price is that of the marginal firm; firms who cannot supply at or below the marginal firms' costs would not produce. But Marshall's investigations of industries told him that in any given industry there would be firms who had just entered the market and would be willing, in the short term, to make a loss in the hope of gaining a foothold in the market and making profits later on. On the other hand there would also be firms who are well established and would be making profits now. The industry supply price would be higher than the established firm's costs but lower than the new firm's costs. For Marshall the 'representative firm' is a firm whose costs of production are equal to the industry supply price.

Marshall aside, the process of 'perfection' meant that an emphasis on the firm as a separate, important economic entirety never developed, and by the 1930s, the firm was being treated as little more than a calculus problem ("max profit"), with no real boundaries, internal structure or even a reason to exist. There are no decisions that have to be made, no problems for management or workers to solve, there is no organisational structure to facilitate decision making or problem solving, and it's not clear what determines the boundaries between firms or between firms and markets. Being, implicitly, a zero transaction cost environment, there is no need for a real firm of any substance in the (proto-)neoclassical model.

> In many economics textbooks the "firm" is portrayed as a production function or production possibilities set, a black box that transforms inputs into outputs.

> The firm is modeled as a single actor, solving a maximization problem completely analogous to the problem facing the utility-maximizing consumer. How production is organized – for example, whether inputs x_1, x_2, and x_3 are combined into output y within a single firm, between partners, across a network of independent contractors, or by some other means – is treated as secondary, even trivial, issue with little consequence for resource allocation.
>
> (Foss, Klein and Linder 2015: 274)

The neoclassical model of the 'firm' developed out of the cost controversy of the 1920s in a process that expunged Marshall's representative firm from the economics literature.[29] Marshall's critics used the proto-neoclassical initiated idea of perfect competition as a framework in which to attack the representative firm.

> It was generally agreed that the theory of the representative firm applied to conditions of what Marshall called "free competition" and "long-run equilibrium." The meaning of these terms was the pivot upon which, it can now be seen, criticism has turned. Those who attacked Marshall assumed that he had in mind what we would now call perfect competition and static equilibrium.
>
> (Wolf 1954: 338)

The neoclassical replacement for the representative firm was based on Pigou's equilibrium firm. Moss (1984) argues that there were three steps in the development of the neoclassical firm based on the equilibrium firm, and the last of these steps was taken by Robinson (1933) and Chamberlin (1933) (for more on this process see Walker 2018):

> [w]ithout Pigou's analytical use of the industry [step one] and his invention of the equilibrium firm [step two], we could not have had the "firm" of the neoclassical theory. None the less, the now-conventional conception of the firm was left incomplete by Pigou in two respects.
>
> First, Pigou himself did not assume that the industry was comprised entirely of equilibrium firms, but only that an equilibrium firm could be constructed from the law of returns (increasing, constant or diminishing) obeyed by any industry. Second, Pigou did not assume the firm *qua* production function to be facing household preference functions. It was the inclusion of these two elements that constituted the third step in the creation of the firm analysed in the neoclassical theory of the firm.
>
> Although there were some preliminaries, notably Roy Harrod's, this final step was completed by Joan Robinson (1933) and Edward Chamberlin (1933) .
>
> (Moss 1984: 313)

Thus, by the mid-1930s the neoclassical 'firm' had largely developed. Puu (1970: 230), for example, writes, "the theory of the firm had, in substance, been developed to its present state by 1940". This model is still the only model of the 'firm' found in most modern introductory microeconomic textbooks. The proto-neoclassicals helped create the environment in which this debate took place.

This lack of substance to the firm is a characteristic not just of the perfect competition model; it applies to the neoclassical 'firm' in all market structures, in both the general and partial equilibrium versions of the neoclassical model. For example, in the archetypal statement of the neoclassical general equilibrium model, Debreu (1959), there are no substantive firms, there are just 'producers':

> when one abstracts from legal forms of organization (corporations, sole proprietorships, partnerships, . . .) and types of activity (Agriculture, Mining, Construction, Manufacturing, Transportation, Services, . . .) one obtains the concept of a producer, i.e., an economic agent whose role is to choose (and carry out) a production plan.
>
> (Debreu 1959: 37)

One obvious question to ask is what level of influence did the proto-neoclassicals have on the neoclassicals, and the answer can differ depending on the domain over which we choose to ask the question. In terms of the neoclassical theory of production/the 'firm', the proto-classicals had little influence. As just noted, the development of the neoclassical theory of the firm took place in the 1920s–1930s and was driven by the assault on Marshall's representative firm. Apart from the fact that much of the debate took place in an environment of perfect competition, this assault was largely independent of the work of the proto-neoclassicals.

If, however, we consider the analysis of input markets or the theories of monopoly, oligopoly and perfect competition, then the influence of the proto-neoclassicals is great; the neoclassical theories are essentially the proto-neoclassical theories. But these theories are theories of markets, and it is here we begin to see the difference between the (proto-)neoclassical theory of the 'firm' and the modern, Coaseian inspired, theory of the firm come to light. The (proto-)neoclassical theory of the 'firm' (supply side of the market) that underlies the (proto-)neoclassical theories of markets is a theory of production rather than a true theory of the firm. In the (proto-)neoclassical model the questions asked are about how the firm acts in its various markets, how it prices its outputs or how it combines its inputs; in the contemporary literature on the firm the questions are very different. The modern questions have to do with the reasons for the firm's existence, what determines the firm's boundaries and what determines the firm's internal organisation. From this perspective the (proto-)neoclassical model isn't a 'theory of the firm' in any meaningful sense, since it cannot answer the modern questions. The output side of the neoclassical model is a theory of supply or production rather than a true theory of the firm.

In summary, this chapter shows, on a positive note, that as Blaug (1997: 301) has argued, "even if Jevons, Menger and Walras had never lived, all the ingredients of marginalism were available in the writings of these lesser known [proto-neoclassical] figures". This includes the work on the theory of markets.

On a more negative note, the proto-neoclassical contributions to the theory of markets, avant-garde as they were, have either resulted in their developers being forgotten or, even if remembered, they helped create an environment that led to a theory of production, but it is a theory of production without firms.

Notes

1 For a discussion of the question, Was There a Marginal Revolution? see Blaug (1972).

2 Ekelund and Hébert (2002) argue that Marshall's contribution to neoclassical economics is under appreciated. "As it stands, the legend undervalues the key contribution of Alfred Marshall, who put an indelible stamp on neoclassical economics by defining the appropriate method of economic inquiry. When we refer to neoclassical economics today, we usually mean the collection of tools of economic knowledge available to (and invented by) Marshall, channeled and directed into uses dictated by Marshall's view of economic science. To be sure, not every contemporary neoclassical economist follows Marshall's path. Some "highbrow" theorists prefer to adopt Cournot's view of economics as rational mechanics. Others maintain that connection to the real world is unimportant in theoretical research. But the bulk of the profession walks in Marshall's footsteps".

(Ekelund and Hébert 2002: 198)

3 That there is no generally accepted characterisation of neoclassical economics is noted by Ekelund and Hébert (2002: 198).

> The essence of neoclassical economics is far from settled in the history of economic thought. Some writers emphasize the increasingly mathematical character of economics after 1870. Others point to marginalism as the hallmark of neoclassical economics (as in Hutchison, 1953, p. 16, or the papers in a special 1972 issue of History of Political Economy). Others emphasize the roots of neoclassical economics in the subjectivism of utility theory (di Patti, 2001). Others stress the static analysis of efficient allocation as the distinguishing feature of neoclassical economics.
>
> (Hennings, 1980)

In contrast to Colander, E. Roy Weintraub, for example, argues there are three fundamental assumptions underlying neoclassical economics: (1) People have rational preferences among outcomes. (2) Individuals maximize utility and firms maximize profits. (3) People act independently on the basis of full and relevant information (Weintraub 2007). Endres (1997: 2–8) argues for there being three branches of neoclassical economics: a Jevonian/Marshallian branch, a Walrasian/Paretian branch and an Austrian branch, each of which can be characterised differently.

4 While not writing down or drawing a demand curve, Lardner utilised the idea of a negative relationship between price and quantity. With regard to the railway that Lardner is concerned with, he writes, for example,

> [i]t is evident that, by lowering the tariff [price], the quantity of traffic, as well as the average distances, will be augmented, and this increase will go on even if we were to carry the diminution of the tariff to the extreme length of extinguishing it altogether, and transporting the traffic gratuitously. But at this imaginary limit the receipts would be nothing.
>
> On the contrary, if the tariff be augmented continually, the quantity of traffic, as well as the average distance it is to be carried, will be continually diminished; the

magnitude of the charge being such as a less and less quantity of traffic is capable of bearing. A limit will at length be attained, at which the traffic will altogether vanish, the tariff becoming so great, that no objects can bear it. Here, again, the receipts become nothing.

(Lardner 1850: 286–7)

and

[e]very increase of traffic produced by a diminishing tariff

(Lardner 1850: 290)

and

[a]ny diminution of r (the tariff) [price] must produce an increase either of D (the distance to which the traffic is carried), or of N (the quantity of traffic), or of both of these [an increase in these factors amounts to an increase in quantity demanded of railway services].

(Lardner 1850: 294)

5 While Lardner did not argue explicitly in terms of decreasing elasticity, he did come close:

[n]ow, if a less value still be assigned to the tariff, such as Om″, the receipts will be augmented, because the influence of the increased number of objects booked, and the increased distances to which they are carried, owing to the diminution of the tariff, will have a greater effect in increasing the gross receipts than the reduction of the tariff has in diminishing them. By thus gradually diminishing the tariff, the traffic will increase both in quantity and distance, and the gross receipts will be placed under the operation of two contrary causes, one tending to increase, and the other to diminish them. So long as the influence of the former predominates, the gross receipts will increase; but when the effect of the reduction of the tariff counterpoises exactly the effect of the increase of traffic in quantity and distance, then the increase of the gross receipts will cease. After that, the influence of the reduction of the tariff in diminishing the receipts will predominate over the influence of the increased traffic in augmenting them, and the consequence will be their diminution.

(Lardner 1850: 287–8)

Lardner was aware that there were two opposing forces acting on revenue and that it was the relative strength of these forces that determined the change in revenue. In modern terms, when demand is inelastic, the quantity effect dominates, and when demand is elastic, the price effect prevails.

6 The idea of a production function is even older than von Thünen:

the idea, if not the actuality, of such functions dates back at least to 1767 when the French physiocrat A. R. J. Turgot implicitly described total product schedules possessing positive first partial derivatives, positive and then negative second partial derivatives, and positive cross-partial derivatives. Thirty years later, Parson Thomas Malthus presented his famous arithmetic and geometric ratios (1798), which imply a logarithmic production function. Likewise, a quadratic production function underlies the numerical examples that David Ricardo (1817) used to explain the trend of the relative shares as the economy approaches the classical stationary state.

(Humphrey 1997: 53)

Schumpeter (2006: 249, footnote 5) summarised Turgot's contribution by noting that

> [t]he same thing may be expressed, by means of a different concept, in a somewhat different way. This concept, which emerged toward the end of the nineteenth century (see below, Part IV, ch. 7, sec. 8), is now being called the production function. This function expresses the technological relation that exists between the quantity of product and the quantities of the "factors" that co-operate in varying proportions to produce it. Reducing, for the sake of simplicity, the number of these factors to two, we may mark off the quantities of the product and of the two factors on the axes of a system of rectangular space co-ordinates. Every point in space that corresponds to any positive and finite values of those three quantities will then represent that quantity of product that can (at best) be produced by the corresponding quantities of factors, and the set of all these points will identify a surface in three-dimensional space, the production surface. Now let one of the factor quantities be held constant, and cut this surface by a plane at right angles to this factor's axis and go through the point on this axis that corresponds to the constant. The curve of intersection between the surface and the plane will represent Turgot's law of first increasing and then decreasing returns. Though Turgot did not discover either the production function or its geometric picture, the production surface as such, we may say that he discovered a property of it, viz., the form of one of its contours, and hence that he got hold of something, possession of which (with ordinary care and competence prevailing in our science) should have brought out the production function of today before the eighteenth century was out. The reason why this argument is being inflicted upon the reader at this stage is that the case is so revelatory of the "ways of the human mind," which rarely discovers the obvious and fundamental first. More often it gets hold of some particular aspect of an idea and then works back to the conceptions that hold priority in logic.

7 You do have to ask, does a theory of the entrepreneur need a theory of the firm? On the relationship between entrepreneurship and the theory of the firm, see Klein (2016) and Foss, Klein and McCaffrey (2019: chapter 6). Some see the two fields as quite separate, "[a]lso, while entrepreneurial behaviour is typically manifested in firms and firms are, as it were, tools of entrepreneurs, entrepreneurship theory and the theory of the firm are rarely integrated (Foss and Klein, 2005, 2012)" (Foss, Klein and Bjørnskov 2019).

8 $$\begin{aligned} r &= \frac{(\pi - hC)}{\beta}c \\ &= \frac{(\pi - h(\delta + c))}{\beta}c \quad (C = \delta + c) \\ &= \frac{(\pi - h\delta - hc)}{\beta}c \\ &= \frac{\pi c - h\delta c - hc^2}{\beta} \end{aligned}$$

9 $$\begin{aligned} &\frac{\partial r}{\partial c} = \frac{\pi - h\delta - 2hc}{\beta} = 0 \\ &\Rightarrow \pi - h\delta - 2hc = 0 \\ &\Rightarrow c = \frac{\pi - h\delta}{2h} \end{aligned}$$

10 Net revenue $= (T - \zeta ht)ch$
$= (T - (\delta + c)ht)ch$
$= (T - \delta ht - cht)ch$
$= Tch - \delta h^2tc - c^2h^2t$

11 $Th - h^2\delta t - 2ch^2t = 0$

$$\Rightarrow 2ch^2t = Th - h^2\delta t$$
$$\Rightarrow 2cht = T - h\delta t$$
$$\Rightarrow 2ch = \frac{T}{t} - h\delta$$
$$\Rightarrow ch = \frac{1}{2}\left(\frac{T}{t} - h\delta\right)$$

12 $\delta h + ch = \delta h + \frac{1}{2}\left(\frac{T}{t} - h\delta\right)$

$$\Rightarrow \quad \zeta h = \delta h + \frac{1}{2}\frac{T}{t} + \frac{1}{2}h\delta \;\; (\zeta = \delta + c)$$
$$= \frac{1}{2}\left(\frac{T}{t} + \delta h\right)$$
$$= \frac{1}{2}\left(\frac{T}{t} + \delta h\right)$$

13 $h\zeta + x\beta - M = h'\zeta' + (X - x)\beta$

$$\Rightarrow h\zeta + x\beta = h'\zeta' + (X - x)\beta + M$$
$$\Rightarrow 2x\beta = h'\zeta' - h\zeta + X\beta + M$$
$$\Rightarrow x = \frac{h'\zeta' - h\zeta + X\beta + M}{2\beta}$$
$$\Rightarrow x = \frac{h'\zeta' - h(\delta + c) + X\beta + M}{2\beta} \;\; (\zeta = \delta + c)$$
$$\Rightarrow x = \frac{h'\zeta' - h\delta - hc + X\beta + M}{2\beta}$$

14 $\dfrac{\partial xc}{\partial c} = \dfrac{X\beta + h'\zeta' - h\delta - 2hc + M}{2\beta} = 0$

$$\Rightarrow X\beta + h'\zeta' - h\delta - 2hc + M = 0$$
$$\Rightarrow 2hc = X\beta + h'\zeta' - h\delta + M$$
$$\Rightarrow c = \frac{X\beta + h'\zeta' - h\delta + M}{2h}$$

15 $c + \delta + \zeta = \dfrac{X\beta + h'\zeta' - h\delta + M}{2h} + \delta$

$$= \frac{X\beta + h'\zeta' - h\delta + M + 2h\delta}{2h}$$
$$= \frac{X\beta + h'\zeta' + h\delta + M}{2h}$$

16 $$0=\frac{h'\zeta'-h\zeta+X\beta+M}{2\beta}$$
$$=h'\zeta'-h\zeta+X\beta+M$$
$$\Rightarrow h\zeta=h'\zeta'+X\beta+M$$
$$\Rightarrow \zeta=\frac{h'\zeta'+X\beta+M}{h}$$

17 $$\delta+c=\frac{h'\zeta'+X\beta+M}{h}$$
$$\Rightarrow c=\frac{h'\zeta'+X\beta+M}{h}-\delta$$
$$=\frac{h'\zeta'-h\delta+X\beta+M}{h}$$

18 $$hc=\frac{P-h'c'}{2}$$
$$=\frac{P-\frac{P-hc}{2}}{1}$$
$$=\frac{P-\frac{1}{2}P+\frac{1}{2}hc}{2}$$
$$\Rightarrow 2hc=\frac{1}{2}P+\frac{1}{2}hc$$
$$\Rightarrow 2hc-\frac{1}{2}hc=\frac{1}{2}P$$
$$\Rightarrow \frac{3}{2}hc=\frac{1}{2}P$$
$$\Rightarrow hc=\frac{1}{3}P$$

19 $$h'c'=\frac{P-\frac{1}{3}P}{2}$$
$$=\frac{\frac{2}{3}P}{2}$$
$$=\frac{1}{3}P$$

20 See Spengler (1950) for the modern introduction of double marginalisation.
21 Marian Bowley makes the point that Cournot

> stated the solution [to the max profit problem] to be the equality of marginal revenue with marginal costs, for he showed that the monopolist would maximise his net returns when the increment to total receipts from an additional sale equalled the increment to total costs incurred thereby. Cournot did not give either increment a

name [. . .] nor did he point out that the increment to total revenue (marginal revenue) was a concept hitherto unlabelled in economic analysis.

(Bowley 1973: 171)

It took till around 1930 for marginal revenue to be rediscovered. Robbins (1970: 30) writes

> [m]uch has been made of the alleged discovery about the end of the twenties of the general formula for profit maximisation – marginal revenue equal to marginal cost. But this is historically untrue. The formula is implicit in Cournot's treatment of monopoly. A solution in terms of parallel tangents to the aggregate curves, which of course is exactly the same thing, is given in Auspitz and Lieden's famous *Untersuchungen über die Theorie des Preises*. Alfred Marshall states it quite explicitly in the Appendix to the *Principles*. . . . And it is not as though this has escaped notice – thought obviously the more recent "discoveries" had not heard of it: it is reproduced in one of the most widely used pre-1914 textbooks, Chapman's *Outlines of Political Economy*.

He also notes that a similar solution is algebra and geometry is given in Flux (1904: 293) (Robbins 1970: 30, footnote 4). In addition he explains that the parallel tangents solution was presented by Lardner (1850: 287–92) (Robbins 1970: 30, footnote 2).

22 $f(D_1 + D_2) + D_1 f'(D_1 + D_2) = f(D_1 + D_2) + D_2 f'(D_1 + D_2)$

$\Rightarrow D_1 f'(D_1 + D_2) = D_2 f'(D_1 + D_2)$

$\Rightarrow D_1 = D_2$

23 $2f(D) + Df'(D) = 0$

$$\Rightarrow 2p + D\frac{dp}{dD} = 0 \left(\text{since } p = f(D) \text{ and } \frac{df}{dD} = \frac{dp}{dD}\right)$$

$$\Rightarrow 2p\frac{dD}{dp} + D = 0 \left(\text{dividing by } \frac{dp}{dD}\right)$$

24 $f(D) + Df'(D) = 0$

$$\Rightarrow p + D\frac{dp}{dD} = 0$$

$$\Rightarrow p\frac{dD}{dp} + D = 0$$

25 But note that, as Gary-Bobo (1998: 519) reminds us, "[u]ndoubtedly, Cournot was considering perfect competition as a limiting case of oligopolistic competition, even if he did not state a convergence result explicitly".

26 The Bertrand 1883 review was the second review of Cournot's work. A Canadian mathematician, J.B. Cherriman, reviewed the book in 1857. See Dimand (1988) for details.

27 In the original French version of Cournot's book I consulted, the quote appears on page 89.

28 In the English translation, this reads, "[i]nstead of adopting $D = F(p)$ as before, in this case it will be convenient to adopt the inverse notion $p = f(D)$". This text appears on page 80.

29 See Chapter 5 for a discussion.

References

Backhouse, Roger E. (2002). *The Ordinary Business of Life: A History of Economics From the Ancient World to the Twenty-First Century*, Princeton, NJ: Princeton University Press.

Bertrand, Joseph (1883). 'Review of Cournot (1838) and Leon Walras, Théorie mathématique de la richesse sociale', *Journal des Savants*, September: 499–508.

Blaug, Mark (1972). 'Was There a Marginal Revolution?', *History of Political Economy*, 4(2) Fall: 269–80.

Blaug, Mark (1985). 'The Economics of Johann Von Thünen', *Research in the History of Economic Thought and Methodology*, 3: 1–25.

Blaug, Mark (1997). *Economic Theory in Retrospect*, 5th edn., Cambridge: Cambridge University Press.

Blaug, Mark (2001). 'No History of Ideas, Please, We're Economists', *Journal of Economic Perspectives*, 15(1) Winter: 145–64.

Boulding, Kenneth E. (1960). 'The Present Position of the Theory of the Firm'. In Kenneth E. Boulding and W. Allen Spivey (eds.), *Linear Programming and the Theory of the Firm* (1–17), New York: The Macmillan Company.

Bowley, Marian (1973). *Studies in the History of Economic Theory before 1870*, London: The Macmillan Press.

Calsoyas, C. D. (1950). 'The Mathematical Theory of Monopoly in 1839: Charles Ellet, Jr.', *Journal of Political Economy*, 58(2) April: 162–70.

Chamberlin, Edward H. (1933). *The Theory of Monopolistic Competition*, Cambridge, MA: Harvard University Press.

Cherriman, J. B. (1857). 'Review of Cournot (1838)', *Canadian Journal of Industry, Science and Art*, 9 new series: 185–94.

Coase, Ronald Harry (1937). 'The Nature of the Firm', *Economica*, n.s. 4(16) November: 386–405.

Colander, David (2000). 'The Death of Neoclassical Economics', *Journal of the History of Economic Thought*, 22(2) June: 127–43 .

Cournot, A. A. (1838). *Researches into the Mathematical Principles of the Theory of Wealth*, New York: Augustus M. Kelley Publishers, 1971.

Debreu, Gerard (1959). *Theory of Value*, New York: Wiley.

Dempsey, Bernard W. (1960). *The Frontier Wage: The Economic Organization of Free Agents*, Chicago: Loyola University Press.

Dimand, Robert W. (1988). 'An Early Canadian Contribution to Mathematical Economics: J.B. Cherriman's 1857 Review of Cournot', *Canadian Journal of Economics*, 21(3) August: 610–16.

Edgeworth, F. (1925). 'The Pure Theory of Monopoly'. In F. Y. Edgeworth (ed.), *Papers Relating to Political Economy* (vol. 1, pp. 111–42), Bristol: Thoemmes Press, 1993.

Ekelund, Robert B. Jr. and Robert F. Hébert (1999). *Secret Origins of Modern Microeconomics: Dupuit and the Engineers*, Chicago: University of Chicago Press.

Ekelund, Robert B. Jr. and Robert F. Hébert (2002). 'Retrospectives: The Origins of Neoclassical Microeconomics', *Journal of Economic Perspectives*, 16(3) Summer: 197–215.

Ekelund, Robert B. Jr. and Donald L. Hooks (1973). 'Ellet, Dupuit, and Lardner: On Nineteenth Century Engineers and Economic Analysis', *Nebraska Journal of Economics and Business*, 12(3) Summer: 43–52.

Ellet, Charles, Jr. (1839). *An Essay on the Laws of Trade, in Reference to the Works of Internal Improvement in the United States*, Richmond: P. D. Bernard.

Ellet, Charles, Jr. (1840). *The Laws of Trade Applied to the Determination of the Most Advantageous Fare for the Passengers in Rail Roads*, Philadelphia.

Endres, A. M. (1997). *Neoclassical Microeconomic Theory: The Founding Austrian Version*, London: Routledge.

Foss, Nicolai (1994). 'The Theory of the Firm: The Austrians as Precursors and Critics of Contemporary Theory', *The Review of Austrian Economics*, 7(1): 31–65.

Foss, Nicolai, P. G. Klein and Christian Bjørnskov (2019). 'The Context of Entrepreneurial Judgment: Organizations, Markets, and Institutions', *Journal of Management Studies*, 56(6) September: 1197–1213.

Foss, Nicolai J., Peter G. Klein and Stefan Linder (2015). 'Organizations and Markets'. In Peter Boettke and Christopher Coyne (eds.), *The Oxford Handbook of Austrian Economics* (272–95), Oxford: Oxford University Press.

Foss, Nicolai J., Peter G. Klein, and Matthew McCaffrey (2019). *Austrian Perspectives on Entrepreneurship, Strategy, and Organization*, Cambridge: Cambridge University Press.

Friedman, James W. (2000). 'The legacy of Augustin Cournot', *Cahiers d'Économie Politique*, 37(1): 31–46.

Gary-Bobo, Robert (1989). 'Cournot, A Great Forerunner of Mathematical Economics', *European Economic Review*, 33(2–3): 515–22.

Hennings, Klaus H. (1980). 'The Transition from Classical to Neoclassical Economic Theory: Hans von Mangoldt', *Kyklos*, 33(4) November: 658–81.

Humphrey, Thomas M. (1997). 'Algebraic Production Functions and Their Uses Before Cobb-Douglas', *Federal Reserve Bank of Richmond Economic Quarterly*, 83(1) Winter: 51–83.

Hutchison, T. W. (1953). *A Review of Economic Doctrines 1870–1929*, Oxford: Oxford University Press.

Jevons, W. Stanley (1871). *The Theory of Political Economy*, London: Macmillan and Co.

Klein, Peter G. (2016). 'Why Entrepreneurs Need Firms, and the Theory of the Firm Needs Entrepreneurship Theory', *Revista de Administração*, 51(3) July–September: 323–26.

Lardner, Dionysius (1850). *Railway Economy; A Treatise on the New Art of Transport, its Management, Prospects, and Relations, Commercial, Financial, and Social, with an Exposition of the Practical Results of the Railways in Operation in the United Kingdom, on the Continent, and in America*, London: Taylor, Walton, and Maberly.

Lloyd, Peter J. (1969). 'Elementary Geometric/Arithmetic Series and Early Production Theory', *Journal of Political Economy*, 77(1) January–February: 21–34.

Longfield, Mountifort (1834). *Lectures on Political Economy: Delivered in Trinity and Michaelmas Terms, 1833*, Dublin: William Curry, Jun. and Company.

Marshall, Alfred (1890). *Principles of Economics*, London: Macmillan and Co.

Maxwell, James A. (1958). 'Some Marshallian Concepts, Especially the Representative Firm', *Economic Journal*, 68(272) December: 691–8.

McNulty, Paul J. (1984). 'On the Nature and Theory of Economic Organization: The Role of the Firm Reconsidered', *History of Political Economy*, 16(2) Summer: 233–53.

Menger, Carl (1871). *Principles of Economics*, New York: New York University Press, 1976.

Mill, J. S. (1848). *Principles of Political Economy with Some of Their Applications to Social Philosophy*, 7th edn. 1873, re-edited by William J. Ashley 1909, New York: A. Kelley reprint, 1973.

Moss, Laurences M. (2010). 'Isaac Butt and the Early Development of the Marginal Utility Theory of Imputation', *American Journal of Economics and Sociology*, 69(1) January: 210–31. First published in *History of Political Economy*, 5(2) Fall 1973: 317–38.

Moss, Scott (1984). 'The History of the Theory of the Firm from Marshall to Robinson and Chamberlin: the Source of Positivism in Economics', *Economica*, n.s. 51(203) August: 307–18.

O'Brien, Denis P. (2003). 'Classical Economics'. In Warren J. Samuels, Jeff E. Biddle and John B. Davis (eds.), *A Companion to the History of Economic Thought* (112–29), Oxford: Blackwell Publishing Ltd.

O'Brien, Denis P. (2004). *The Classical Economists Revisited*, Princeton, NJ: Princeton University Press.

Pullen, John (2009). *The Marginal Productivity Theory of Distribution: A Critical History*, London: Routledge.

Puu, T. (1970). 'Ferguson, C. E.: "The Neoclassical Theory of Production and Distribution." Some Comments on Part I', *The Swedish Journal of Economics*, 72(3) September: 230–40.

Robbins, Lionel (1935). *An Essay on the Nature & Significance of Economic Science*, 2nd edn., Revised and Extended, London: Macmillan and Co. Limited.

Robbins, Lionel (1970). *The Evolution of Modern Economic Theory and Other Papers on the History of Economic Thought*, London: Macmillian.

Robinson, Joan (1933). *The Economics of Imperfect Competition*, London: Macmillan and Co., Ltd.

Schumpeter, J. A. (2006). *History of Economic Analysis*, London: Taylor & Francis e-Library. First published 1954.

Shackle, G. L. S. (1967). *The Years of High Theory: Invention and Tradition in Economic Thought 1926–1939*, Cambridge: Cambridge University Press.

Simpson, David (2013). *The Rediscovery of Classical Economics: Adaptation, Complexity and Growth*, Cheltenham, UK: Edward Elgar.

Spengler, Joseph J. (1950). 'Vertical Integration and Antitrust Policy', *Journal of Political Economy*, 58(4) August: 347–52.

Stigler, George J. (1955). 'The Nature and Role of Originality in Scientific Progress', *Economica*, n.s. 22(88) November: 293–302.

Walker, Paul (2018). *A Brief Prehistory of the Theory of the Firm*, London: Routledge.

Walras, Léon (1874). *Elements of Pure Economics: Or the Theory of Social Wealth.* Translated by William Jaffé, Homewood: Irwin, 1954.

Weintraub, Roy E. (2007). 'Neoclassical Economics', *The Concise Encyclopedia of Economics.* Available at: www.econlib.org/library/Enc1/NeoclassicalEcon omics.html

Wolfe, J. N. (1954). 'The Representative Firm', *Economic Journal*, 64(254) June: 337–49.

Zouboulakis, Michel S. (2015). 'Elements of a Theory of the Firm in Adam Smith and John Stuart Mill'. In George C. Bitros and Nicholas C. Kyriazis (eds.), *Essays in Contemporary Economics: A Festschrift in Memory of A. D. Karayiannis* (45–52), Cham: Springer.

Appendix

A very brief history of perfect competition

It was noted in the text (see page 92) that Cournot began the process that culminated in what we now know as the theory of perfect competition.[1] In this appendix we give a very brief outline of this process from Cournot to Knight.[2]

As noted in Chapter 4, in chapter 8 of Cournot (1838) Cournot considers the case of what he refers to as 'unlimited competition'. It is in this chapter that we see the argument that perfect competition is the limiting case of the entire spectrum of market structures defined in terms of the number of sellers. As the number of sellers increases, the output of the industry converges in the limit to the output of what we now refer to as a perfectly competitive industry. Cournot shows that in equilibrium the price will equal marginal cost.

Take, as an illustration, Cournot's special case of zero productions costs. From page 91 we know that when the number of firms is n, the first order condition is

$$D(p)+np\frac{dD(p)}{dp}=0,$$

which implies

$$np=\frac{-D(p)}{\frac{dD(p)}{dp}}.$$

This equation is represented in the diagram[3] labeled as Figure 4.5.[4] Note that $n = 1$ is the monopoly case, $n = 2$ the duopoly case and $n > 2$ is oligopoly.[5]

From this diagram we can see that as n increases, the price (p) tends towards zero, which is marginal cost (mc), and the perfectly competitive equilibrium price (p_{pc}) for this case. Market output (y) increases as n increases.

Theocharis (1983: 148–9) offers an interpretation of $\frac{-D(p)}{dD(p)/dp}$, for the monopoly case, in terms of demand elasticity:

> Cournot's $\frac{-F(p)}{F'(p)}\left[\frac{-D(p)}{dD(p)/dp}\right]$, in terms of which the analysis is carried out, can be shown to be related to the modern concept of demand elasticity. For if (i) $A=\frac{-F'(p)}{F(p)}$ is the 'relative rate of change of the quantity demanded in

response to the change in price', $\frac{-F(p)}{F'(p)}$ is the inverse of this, $\frac{1}{A}$. Under the usual definition of demand elasticity (ii) $\eta = -\frac{p}{F(p)} \cdot \frac{dF(p)}{dp} = -\frac{p \cdot F'(p)}{F'(p)} = pA$ From (i) we get (iii) $\frac{\eta}{A} = p$, from which it follows that where $p = \frac{-F(p)}{F(p)} = \frac{1}{A}$, $\eta = 1$. At this point, therefore, where according to Cournot, revenue is a maximum demand elasticity is equal to unity.

Therefore the $\frac{-D(p)}{dD(p)/dp}$ curve is the locus of points which correspond to the reciprocal of the semi-elasticity of *D*(*p*). The semi-elasticity of a function *D*(*p*) at *p* is $\frac{dD(p)/dp}{D(p)}$ which gives the percentage change in *D*(*p*) for a one *unit* change[6] in *p*.[7] Thus the reciprocal is the change in *p* required to get a 1% increase in *D*(*p*). For the monopoly case, the equilibrium price *p* has to be such that demand at that price will increase by 1% and the monopolist will supply that amount of extra output. For the duopoly case, the supply is greater for all $p > 0$ – see Figure 4.5 – than in the monopoly case, and thus the equilibrium price must be lower to ensure that the supply is demanded, or the lower the price, the greater the change in price has to be to achieve the 1% increase in *D*(*p*), that is, the lower the price the more inelastic is demand compared to higher prices. Again, in equilibrium, the price is such that demand will increase by 1%, and the two identical firms will be induced to supply the extra output. For three firms, output is greater still for all $p > 0$, and thus the equilibrium price is lower still. As in the previous cases, the increase in supply has to equal the 1% increase in demand. This pattern continues as *n* increases.

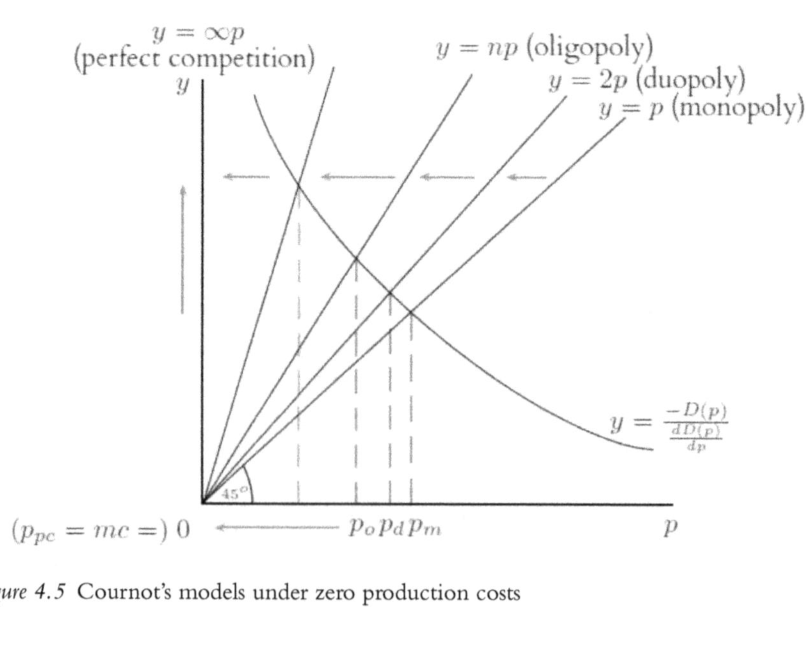

Figure 4.5 Cournot's models under zero production costs

For the case where there are n firms, the first order condition can be interpreted in terms of the standard demand elasticity,

$$np = \frac{-D(p)}{\frac{dD(p)}{dp}}$$

$$\Rightarrow p = \frac{1}{n}\frac{-D(p)}{\frac{dD(p)}{dp}}$$

which means we have, using (iii), that,

$$\frac{\eta}{A} = p = \frac{1}{n}\frac{-D(p)}{\frac{dD(p)}{dp}}$$

$$\Rightarrow \eta\frac{1}{A} = \frac{1}{n}\frac{1}{A}$$

$$\Rightarrow \eta = \frac{1}{n}.$$

Thus, for n firms, revenue is maximised where the demand elasticity is equal to $\frac{1}{n}$. Note that as $n \rightarrow \infty$ the demand elasticity goes towards zero, so the demand curve facing each firm becomes perfectly elastic.

In his essay on "Perfect Competition, Historically Contemplated" George Stigler noted what he saw as a shortcoming with Cournot's approach, namely that Cournot ignored the conditions of entry. This meant that Cournot's definition applied to industries with multiple firms but for which entry was not possible.

For William Stanley Jevons, the idea of competition was part of the notion of a market. Jevons's concept of a perfect market involves two conditions:

1 "there must be perfectly free competition, so that anyone will exchange with anyone else for the slightest apparent advantage" (Jevons 1965: 86).
2 "A market, then, is theoretically perfect only when all traders have perfect knowledge of the conditions of supply and demand, and the consequent ratio of exchange" (Jevons 1965: 87).

The importance of point 2 is the role that (perfect) knowledge plays in a perfect market.

Stigler (1957: 6) argues that Jevons made an unfortunate error by merging the concepts of the market and competition. He goes on to argue that both concepts are deserving of exhaustive, but separate, treatments.

The mixing of the market and competition is a pattern that has been followed by Jevons's successors, with regrettable consequences. By combining the two concepts economists began to see competition as an 'end-state'[8] replacing the 'competition as a process'[9] view of earlier writers. The view that competition is a process involving ongoing rivalry is inconsistent with an end-state view of competitive markets. Competition must have ended for the market to be in equilibrium.

Edgeworth (1881) offered a more rigorous definition of perfect competition.

> The *field of competition* with reference to a contract, or contracts, under consideration consists of all the individuals who are willing and able to recontract about the articles under consideration. . . .
>
> There is free communication throughout a *normal* competitive field. You might suppose the constituent individuals collected at a point, or connected by telephones – an ideal supposition, but sufficiently approximate to existence or tendency for the purposes of abstract science.
>
> A *perfect* field of competition professes in addition certain properties peculiarly favourable to mathematical calculation; namely, a certain indefinite *multiplicity* and *dividedness*, analogous to that *infinity* and *infinitesimally* which facilitate so large a portion of Mathematical Physics (consider the theory of Atoms, and all applications of the Differential Calculus). The conditions of a *perfect* field are four; the first pair referrable to the heading *multiplicity* or continuity, the second to *dividedness* or fluidity.
>
> I Any individual is free to *recontract* with any out of an indefinite number, *e.g.*, in the last example there are an indefinite number of Xs and similarly of Ys.
>
> II Any individual is free to *contract* (at the same time) with an indefinite number; e.g., any X (and similarly Y) may deal with any number of Ys. This condition combined with the first appears to involve the indefinite divisibility of each *article* of contract (if any X deal with an indefinite number of Ys he must give each an indefinitely small portion of *x*); which might be erected into a separate condition.
>
> III Any individual is free to *recontract* with another independently of, *without the consent* being required of, any third party, *e.g.*, there is among the Ys (and similarly among the Xs) no *combination* or precontract between two or more contractors that none of them will recontract without the consent of all. Any Y then may accept the offer of any X irrespectively of other Ys.
>
> IV Any individual is free to *contract* with another independently of a third party; . . .
>
> The failure of the first [condition] involves the failure of the second, but not *vice versa*; and the third and fourth are similarly related.
>
> (Edgeworth 1881: 17–19, emphasis in the original)

Stigler responds to this set of conditions by commenting,

> [t]he natural question to put to such a list of conditions of competition is: Are the conditions necessary and sufficient to achieve what intuitively

> or pragmatically seems to be a useful concept of competition? Edgeworth replies, in effect, that the conditions are both necessary and sufficient. More specifically, competition requires (1) indefinitely large numbers of participants on both sides of the market; (2) complete absence of limitations upon individual self-seeking behavior; and (3) complete divisibility of the commodities traded.
>
> (Stigler 1957: 7)

Edgeworth's list seems to be the origin of many of the modern briefs about the nature of perfect competition (Stigler 1957: 7).

When discussing the notions of competition utilised by some of the classical and early neoclassical writers, including Léon Walras, Peter Groenewegen argues that there was little support for the idea of perfect competition among these authors.

> First, and somewhat negative, support for the notion of what became known in the 1920s and 1930s as perfect competition (Knight 1921; Robinson, 1934, 1960) was pretty well non-existent for these economic writers, despite attempts to put words into the mouths of some of them (For Walras, this included Jaffé's attempt when translating the Eléments to smuggle in usage of the phrase "*perfect competition*" on Walras' part, unwarranted in terms of the French text. For Marshall, it included Stigler's remarks trying to impose a horizontal demand curve for the individual firm on him in a "*perfectly competitive*" industry as the general competitive case).
>
> (Groenewegen 2004: 11)

Groenewegen also notes

> that some of Walras' implied qualities making for a high degree of free competition in the market, resemble the attributes much later assigned as necessary and sufficient conditions for the theoretical construct of perfect competition. Following Knight (1921, pp. 76–86), as summarised by Joan Robinson (1934, 1960), these can be specified as "rational *conduct on the part of buyers and sellers, full knowledge, absence of frictions, perfect mobility and perfect divisibility of factors of production, and completely static conditions*" (Joan Robinson, 1934, 1960, p. 20). Knight (1921, p. 82) also stressed that if "*intercommunication is actually perfect, exchange can only take place at one price*". Buyers in the perfectly competitive market were therefore implicitly price-takers. It is interesting that "absence of [market] frictions" included with Knight's conditions for perfect competition, matches Walras' analogy of the frictionless world of mechanics with a freely competitive world in economic theory.
>
> (Groenewegen 2004: 4, emphasis in the original)

But is should also be noted that

> such parallels cannot be driven too far. For example, the horizontal demand curve for the individual firm as a characteristic of perfect competition is not to be found in Walras. Nor did Walras explicitly accept the notion of buyers as price takers as an essential characteristic of a freely competitive market, or view the competitive economic system in his Eléments as essentially static.
>
> (Groenewegen 2004: 4)

In an examination of perfect competition as it appeared in the work of the Italian economist Enrico Barone, Manuela Mosca and Michael E. Bradley (Mosca and Bradley 2013) consider Barone's analysis of the components necessary for perfect competition. Product homogeneity is seen as an implicit assumption in Barone's approach to perfect competition. It is unclear what role Barone assigned to a multiplicity of firms for competition. Barone does, at times, mention a multiplicity of firms as having a role in competition. But at other times he condemns the excessive number of firms in a market. Barone also sees in some cases the optimal number of firms as being determined endogenously. In fact, the "limit state of competition" can be such that the number of firms is reduced to just a few, all of the same size and type. Barone also seemed to believe that even when firms are few, they can continue to compete, but competition can also lead to a natural monopoly. But even when this occurs, the monopolist faces potential competitors.[10] Price taking behaviour is derived from having many firms in a market in some cases, while in other cases this behaviour does not depend on the number of firms. Thus, for Barone the relationship between the number of firms in the market and competition is not unequivocal. For Barone the most important condition for competition is free entry and exit. Barone places the most emphasis on free exit; he sees low-cost firms driving out higher costs ones. Mosca and Bradley (2013: 16) state that they found no mention of perfect information having a role in determining competition in Barone's works.

In a discussion of another Italian economist (and sociologist) Vilfredo Pareto, Dennis (1975: 264) points out that

> [t]he work of Vilfredo Pareto illustrated another trend in mature neoclassical thought, one which made skillful use of mathematical logic to the understanding of rational economic calculation, while, at the same time, reducing the word competition to a technically obscure component of the economists vocabulary.

Dennis goes on to say that Pareto confines himself to static partial equilibrium analysis and that he was only interested in the properties of equilibrium and not in how it arises.[11] Equilibrium served to define certain ideal results (Dennis 1975: 265).

Pareto examines two types of phenomena to do with market activity. He defines Type I situations as those where an individual "may be seeking only the satisfaction of his tastes, *given a certain state or condition of the market*" (Pareto 1972: 115, emphasis added), while Type II situations are those where "the individual is considered may seek to modify the conditions of the market in order to gain an advantage therefrom or any other purpose whatever" (Pareto 1972: 115). Dennis contends that " Pareto seizes upon this distinction to portray competition as an equilibrating tendency arising from passive response to external forces and nothing else" (Dennis 1975: 265–6). Importantly for our purposes, "Type I is found where there is competition among those who act according to it. . . . Moreover, Type I is more pure as competition is the more widespread and the more perfect" (Pareto 1972: 116). Type II phenomena are found "where competition does not exist and where there is engrossment, monopoly, etc." (Pareto 1972: 116).

Dennis (1975: 266) concludes that

> Pareto illustrated those two parallel trends which were to become so much more pronounced during the latter half of the 20th century:- the transformation of economic theory into a mathematical calculus of rational choice, devoid of behavioural explanation; and the metamorphosis of the word competition, away from being a term to describe market behaviour, into a technical term indicating the mathematically convenient condition that the set of equilibrium prices of an economy could be treated as "given".

American economist Henry Moore was among the earliest authors to write on the formal definition of competition. Moore (1906: 213) argues that

> competition is a blanket-term covering more or less completely at least the following [five] implicit hypotheses.

The five hypotheses can be summarised as (Moore 1906: 213–4),

1 Every economic factor seeks a maximum net income
2 There is but one price for commodities of the same quality in the same market
3 The influence of the product of anyone producer upon the price per unit of the total product is negligible
4 The output of anyone producer is negligible as compared with the total output
5 Each producer orders the amount of his output without regard to the effect of his act upon the conduct of his competitors

Turning to the works of Alfred Marshall, we find that Marshall utilises the notion of 'free competition' rather than that of perfect competition. Many authors have interpreted Marshall in terms of perfect competition, but as

Hart (2012: 82) points out, "[s]ubsequent reconstructions of Marshall's economics based on notions of 'perfect competition' are a fabrication, lacking any justification in terms of Marshall's own writings".

The market structure envisioned under free competition differs from that of the large numbers-homogeneous product-perfect knowledge characterisation of perfect competition:

> The assumption of perfect knowledge, which Marshall associates with "perfect" competition, is explicitly excluded from Marshall's definition of free competition (see Principles: 540). Instead, free competition was associated with freedom of entry and availability of information. While likely to be characterised by a large number of competitors, these encompass competitors with businesses of all sizes (Principles: 397).
>
> (Hart 2012: 82)

For Marshall,

> competition was correlated most directly with the ideal of economic freedom that was to enable individuals to develop and realise their capabilities and pursue a course of action selected to be of most benefit to themselves and to others with whom they interacted most closely. For the business enterprise, competition both allowed and inspired adaptation to the ever changing economic environment.
>
> (Hart 2012: 84)

Stigler (1957: 10) writes that

> [o]nly two new elements needed to be added to the Edgeworth conditions for competition in order to reach the modern concept of perfect competition. They pertained to the mobility of resources and the model of the stationary economy, and both were presented, not first, but most influentially, by John Bates Clark.

In his book 'The Distribution of Wealth', Clark sets out to analyse a stationary economy in which all dynamic forces are suppressed. "We must, in imagination, sweep remorselessly from the field the whole set of influences that we have called dynamic" (Clark 1899: 71). To achieve this aim the concept of competition is fundamental.

> there is an ideal arrangement of the elements of society, to which the force of competition, acting on individual men, would make the society conform. The producing organism actually shapes itself about this model, and at no time does it vary greatly from it.
>
> (Clark 1899: 68)

The mobility of resources is also basic.

> We must use assumptions boldly and advisedly, make labor and capital absolutely mobile, and let competition work in ideal perfection.
>
> (Clark 1899: 71)

One thing that was new in Clark's approach was the introduction of factor mobility as an assumption of competition, but Stigler (1957: 11) argues that Clark offers no explanation for the assumption.

Stigler continues by saying that

> [m]obility of resources had always been an implicit assumption of competition, and in fact the conditions of adequate knowledge of earning opportunities and absence of contrived barriers to movement were believed to be adequate to insure mobility. But there exist also technological limitations to the rate at which resources can move from one place or industry to another, and these limitations were in fact the basis of Marshall's concept of the short-run normal period. Once this fact was generally recognized, it became inevitable that mobility of resources be given an explicit time dimension, although of course it was highly accidental that instantaneous mobility was postulated.
>
> (Stigler 1957: 11)

The process started by Cournot ended with the work of Frank H. Knight. Knight's ending point was:

> [p]erfect competition is conditioned by the existence of a set of assumptions, the most important of which are the following: (1) "a perfect market for productive services . . ., that is, uniform prices over the whole field" (1921, 316); (2) complete rationality and perfect knowledge by free and independent individuals; (3) "perfect mobility in all economic adjustments, no cost involved in movements or changes" (1921, 77); (4) "virtually instantaneous and costless" exchange of commodities (1921, 78); (5) "perfect, continuous, costless intercommunication between all individual members of the society" (1921, 78); (6) perfect divisibility of commodities; and (7) "an indefinitely large number of competing organizations, each of the most efficient size" (1921, 316).
>
> (Marchionatti 2003: 58)

Since Knight established the basic definition of perfect competition the idea has been expressed in a number of different ways. The role of the large numbers assumption (point 7 in the Marchionatti quote) in the changing expression of perfect competition is highlighted by Dennis (1975: 278) when he writes,

> [f]rom the very beginning of economic theory, the phrase "more competition" was often meant to imply "more competitors," and the condition of

> large numbers was taken to measure the degree or intensity of competition. From this large-numbers condition arose the idea that no individual trader could significantly influence the general pattern of trading in any market, whence came the invalid inference that each trader by himself would feel "powerless" to influence events and therefore would passively accept the ruling price of the market as given. Eventually, such reasoning led to the more elaborate concept of the infinitely elastic demand constraint facing individual sellers. And, as the requirements of the mathematical method grew more rigorous, the phrase "perfect competition" began to connote this demand constraint alone, more than any specified pattern of market behaviour.

This point is perhaps best exemplified by Joan Robinson's 1934 definition of perfect competition,

> [w]hat do we mean by "perfect competition?" The phrase is made to cover so many separable ideas, and is used in so many distinct senses, that it has become almost valueless as a means of communication. It seems best therefore to begin with a definition. By perfect competition, I propose to mean a state of affairs in which the demand for the output of an individual seller is perfectly elastic.
>
> (Robinson 1934: 104)

But Dennis also notes that by this time there was nothing particularly radical in what Robinson was saying:

> [i]n 1934 this was not a startlingly new suggestion: it only made very explicit what had been more or less implied in much of the literature of the previous few years. Accordingly, the condition of infinite elasticity was not considered to be an inference drawn from the hypothesis of perfect competition. It had become part – a crucial part – of the very meaning of the phrase itself.
>
> (Dennis 1975: 279)

Since the introduction of the concept of transaction costs into economics by Ronald Coase in 1937, it has become common to say that the world of perfect competition is a world of zero transaction costs. Implicitly, George Stigler took advantage of this fact when he formulated the now famous Coase theorem: "[t]he Coase Theorem thus asserts that under perfect competition private and social costs would be equal" (Stigler 1966: 113). A more modern way of stating the theorem is "[i]n the absence of transaction costs, the allocation of resources is independent of the distribution of property rights" (Allen 2000: 12). But as Coase has noted, the perfect competition and the zero transaction cost statements are equivalent,

> Stigler states the Coase Theorem in the following words: ". . . under perfect competition private and social costs will be equal." Since, with zero

> transaction costs, as Stigler also points out, monopolies would be induced to "act like competitors," it is perhaps enough to say that, with zero transaction costs, private and social costs will be equal.
>
> (Coase 1988: 158)

The zero transaction cost nature of perfect competition has an important implication for the history of the theory of the firm, since it means there are no firms in the model. There is no need for firms, since without transaction costs consumers can organise production themselves.

> With perfect and costless contracting, it is hard to see room for anything resembling firms (even one-person firms), since consumers could contract directly with owners of factor services and wouldn't need the services of the intermediaries known as firms.
>
> (Foss 2000: xxiv)

If you look at points (3), (4) and (5) in the Marchionatti quote, you can see the importance of zero transaction costs.

For good or for ill, Cournot started a process that fundamentally changed the way mainstream economists think about the concept of competition.[12] Gone is the idea of competition as rivalry, as a process of discovery involving constant change, to be replaced by the idea of an end-state and equilibrium.

Notes

1 A second, related, question which is not discussed here has to do with what propositions can be derived from within the Perfect Competition Paradigm (PCP). Dardi (2012: 220) writes,

> [t]o begin with, I try to summarize what the PCP has yielded in terms of propositions concerning competitive economies. It is generally agreed that the PCP does not tell us much about how perfect competition works, but only (1) what its final consequences are supposed to be, and how they may vary as a function of structural (preferences and technology) and non-structural (initial endowments) characteristics of the economy; (2) that such consequences are logically viable in the sense that perfect competition does not clash with any inevitable in-built contradiction; and (3) that such consequences cannot be improved without conflict, in the sense that modifications that all traders would perceive as being improvements, or at least neutral, are not available.

2 One man not covered here, which may surprise some readers, is Arthur Cecil Pigou. But while Pigou helped popularise the idea, he did not play a role in its development. As George Stigler has put it, "[a]lthough Pigou was not concerned with the formal definition of competition, he must also be accounted an influential figure in the popularization of the concept of perfect competition" (Stigler 1957: 11, footnote 50).

3 This diagram is an adaptation of Figure 9.7 from Theocharis (193: 164), which is in turn an adaptation of Cournot's Figure 4.

4 $\left(\frac{-D}{D'}\right)' = \frac{-D'D' + DD''}{(D')^2}$ which is negative as long as $-D'D' + DD'' < 0$. This differentiation utilises the Quotient Rule: $\frac{d}{dx}\frac{f(x)}{g(x)} = \frac{f'(x)g(x) - f(x)g'(x)}{g^2(x)}$, see Chiang and Wainwright (2005: 158–9) for details.

5 As each 'firm' here is identical, they all have the same costs – zero; duopoly consists of two 'monopolists', oligopoly of *n* 'monopolists' etc.

6 Compare this with the standard elasticity which gives the percentage change in $D(p)$ for a 1% change in p.

7 Empirically, if we consider the log-linear regression, $\log(y) = \beta x$, the interpretation of β is as the percentage change in y that occurs when there is a one unit change in x – the semi-elasticity. To see this, note that the regression equation is the same as $y = \exp(\beta x)$, in which case $dy/dx = \beta \exp(\beta x)$ (remember if $y = \exp(ax)$ then $dy/dx = a \exp(ax)$, see Chiang and Wainwright (2005: 278–82) for details). Thus, the percentage change in y when x changes is $(dy/dx)/y = (\beta \exp(\beta x))/\exp(\beta x) = \beta$.

8 First, an end-state social theory attempts an understanding of social phenomena through a description of the features of a society at a specified point in time. It is a kind of photograph which reveals such elements as a society's distribution of income, wealth, power, prestige, status, the structures of the economic and political systems, and so forth. It is as if a society were like a video film which we 'freeze frame' at certain points to discover its structural features. Both analogies illustrate the static character of end-state analyses. They do not show how a particular end-state or 'outcome' (I use the two terms interchangeably) comes about; nor do they describe the mechanisms that are to determine future changes. Nevertheless, in economic theory at least there is an attempt to show how the actions of decentralised agents, buyers and sellers or savers and investors, motivated by self-interest, are co-ordinated. An economic end-state does have an explanation or rationale.

(Barry 1988: 25)

9 Considering competition as a process implies at first that competition is intrinsically a dynamic and complex phenomenon. In the real world, competition is taken to mean that range of actions aimed at ensuring the realization of the choices of a given firm while restraining at the same time the sphere of actions of its rivals. In the current sense of the word, competition is associated with the verb 'to compete' which involves a process of rivalry between firms for a market or for a productive resource (human, material or financial). This includes rivalry in prices, in improved techniques of production or products, in R&D or in advertising expenses, in the engagement of new productive or distributive activities or in the imitation of existing activities, in the implementation of new forms of organization in which customers, suppliers, partners or even competitors may be involved.

(Krafft 2000: 1)

10 Mosca and Bradley write "[w]e therefore deduce that Barone believed that there were potential competitors also in the case of scale economies and sunk costs, so that his theory cannot be thought of as analogous to that of contestable markets" (Mosca and Bradley 2013: 14, footnote 18).

11 Manuela Mosca takes a contrary position. In Mosca (2005) it is argued that Pareto had a process view of competition.

12 The Austrian School are one group of economists who reject the idea of perfect competition. See, for example, Hayek (1948).

References

Allen, D. W. (2000). 'Transaction Costs'. In Boudewijn Bouckaert and Gerrit De Geest (eds.), *Encyclopedia of Law and Economics* (Volume One: The History and Methodology of Law and Economics, pp. 893–926), Chelthenham: Edward Elgar Press.

Barry, Norman P. (1988). *The Invisible Hand in Economics and Politics: A Study in the Two Conflicting Explanations of Society: End-States and Processes*, London: The Institute of Economic Affairs.

Chiang, Alpha C. and Kevin Wainwright (2005). *Fundamental Methods of Mathematical Economics*, 4th edn., New York: McGraw-Hill/Irwin.

Clark, John Bates (1899). *The Distribution of Wealth: A Theory of Wages, Interest and Profits*, London: Macmillan & Co., Ltd.

Coase, R. H. (1988). *The Firm, the Market, and the Law*, Chicago: The University of Chicago Press.

Cournot, A. A. (1838). *Researches into the Mathematical Principles of the Theory of Wealth*, New York: Augustus M. Kelley Publishers, 1971.

Dardi, Marco (2012). 'The Perfect Competition Paradigm: Evolving from Its Ambiguities', *Cahiers d'économie Politique/Papers in Political Economy*, 2012/2(63): 219–31.

Dennis, K. G. (1975). 'Competition in the History of Economic Thought'. Doctoral dissertation, University of Oxford, Oxford, England.

Edgewoth, F. Y. (1881). *Mathematical Psychics: An Essay on the Application of Mathematics to the Moral Sciences*, London: C. Kegan Paul & Co.

Foss, Nicolai J. (2000). 'The Theory of the Firm: An Introduction to Themes and Contributions'. In Nicolai Foss (ed.), *The Theory of the Firm: Critical Perspectives on Business and Management* (xv–lxi), London: Routledge.

Groenewegen, Peter (2004). 'Notions of Competition and Organised Markets in Walras, Marshall and Some of the Classical Economists', paper presented at the 4th conference of the International Walras Association, Nice, France, September 23–24.

Hart, Neil (2012). *Equilibrium and Evolution: Alfred Marshall and the Marshallians*, Houndmills, Basingstoke, Hampshire: Palgrave Macmillan.

Hayek F. A. (1948). 'The Meaning of Competition'. In F. A. Hayek, *Individualism and Economic Order* (92–106), Chicago: University of Chicago Press.

Jevons, W. Stanley (1965). *The Theory of Political Economy*, 5th edn., New York: Augustus M. Kelley. First published 1871.

Krafft, Jackie (2000). 'Introduction'. In Jackie Krafft (ed.), *The Process of Competition* (1–9), Cheltenham: Edward Elgar.

Marchionatti, Roberto (2003). 'On the Methodological Foundations of Modern Microeconomics: Frank Knight and the "Cost Controversy" in the 1920s', *History of Political Economy*, 35(1): 49–75.

Moore, Henry L. (1906). 'Paradoxes of Competition', *The Quarterly Journal of Economics*, 20(2) February: 211–30.

Mosca, Manuela (2005). 'Competition and Monopoly Power in Vilfredo Pareto and Enrico Barone', paper presented at the 32nd Annual Meeting of the History of Economics Society, University of Puget Sound, Tacoma, WA, USA, June 24–27.

Mosca, Manuela and Michael E. Bradley (2013). 'Perfect Competition According to Enrico Barone', *Cahiers d'économie Politique/Papers in Political Economy*, 2013/1(64): 9–44.

Pareto, Vilfredo (1972). *Manual of Political Economy*. Translated by Ann S. Schwier, edited by Ann S. Schwier and Alfred N. Page, London: Macmillan. Translation based on the 1927 French edition. First published, in Italian, in 1906.

Robinson, Joan (1934)[1960]. 'What is Perfect Competition?', *Quarterly Journal of Economics*, 49(1) November: 104–20.

Stigler, George J. (1957). 'Perfect Competition, Historically Contemplated', *The Journal of Political Economy*, 65(1) February: 1–17.

Stigler, George J. (1966). *The Theory of Price*, 3rd edn., New York: The Macmillian Company.

Theocharis, Reghinos D. (1983). *Early Developments in Mathematical Economics*, 2nd edn., Philadelphia: Porcupine Press.

5 The representative firm

Introduction

Genuine attempts at developing a theory of the firm only started in the 1970s. Before then there were theories of production but little in the way of actual theories of the firm (Walker 2020a). The classical economists had a theory of production, but it was largely a theory of aggregate production. The early neoclassicals wrote little of substance on the firm. As was noted on page 22, Kenneth Boulding maintained that, "[i]t is well to remember that for all practical purposes there was no theory of the firm in economics before Marshall" Boulding (1952: 42). Terence Hutchison summarised the early neoclassical contributions to the theory of the firm and markets as

> Jevons has little on the firm. . . . Walras's assumptions of perfect competition (maintained virtually throughout) and of fixed technical "coefficients", limited his contribution to the analysis of firms and markets . . . . Pareto's contribution to the theory of firms and markets were not rounded off, and of very varying value.
>
> (Hutchison 1993: 307)

As noted by Boulding, perhaps the only exception to this dearth of work on the firm/micro-level production was Alfred Marshall. Marshall created the notion of a 'representative firm'. His aim was to construct an industry supply curve without having to having to assume that all firms are identical. But the idea was somewhat nebulous and came under frequent attack, as Lionel Robbins's famous comment exemplifies,

> [t]he Marshallian conception of a Representative Firm has always been a somewhat unsubstantial notion. Conceived as an afterthought – so far as I am able to discover it does not figure at all in the first edition of the Principles – it lurks in the obscurer corners of Book V like some pale visitant from the world of the unborn waiting in vain for the comforts of complete tangibility. Mr. Keynes has remarked that, "this is the quarter in

> which in my opinion the Marshall analysis is least complete and satisfactory and where there remains most to do," and others have not been lacking to express similar opinions.
>
> (Robbins 1928: 387)

Because of the ongoing criticism, the notion did not last very long in the economics literature. Marshall first used the expression 'representative firm' in the second edition of his *Principles of Economics* published in 1891, and the idea was driven out of the literature around 1928, when it was replaced by Pigou's 'equilibrium firm'.

Marshall's idea

The representative firm was part of Alfred Marshall's answer to the problem of constructing an industry supply curve which shows in a two-dimensional own-price/output space an inclusive relationship involving other prices and other quantities. In such an environment, a movement along the supply curve involves a change in many economic variables, such as input prices and other product prices.[1] This stands in sharp contrast to the now standard microeconomic textbook approach to industry supply in which all prices are assumed to be constant apart from the price of a particular commodity, and then output – of both the individual price-taking firm and of the industry – is taken to be a function of only that price (Opocher and Steedman 2008: 247).

Each firm's cost structure will depend, in part, on the size of the firm. Marshall knew that, even for a given industry, there were firms of many different sizes who would be able to access different levels of internal economies and thus be able to produce at different levels of costs. The problem this gives rise to is which of these firms, and thus cost levels, determines the market price of the good? Today, if we look at microeconomic textbooks, we find that the supply price is that of the marginal firm; firms who cannot produce at or below the cost level of the marginal firm will have to move to a lower cost production technique or leave, or not enter, the industry. But Marshall's investigations of industries told him that in any given industry there would be firms who had just entered the market and would be willing, in the short-term at least, to make a loss in the hope of gaining a foothold in the market and making profits later on. On the other hand, there would also be firms who are well established and would be making profits now. The industry supply price would be higher than the established firm's costs but lower than the new firm's costs. For Marshall, the representative firm is a firm whose costs of production are equal to the industry supply price.

To begin to make sense of the somewhat opaque idea of the representative firm, it is worth noting what it isn't:

> It is not some statistical construct; it is not, for example, created by dividing total supply by the number of firms in the industry. It is not a giant

> super-firm that is assumed to produce all of the aggregate output. It is not a particular real firm; Marshall writes (1920 [1961], p. 805), "We have to consider the conditions of the representative firm rather than a given individual firm".
>
> (Hartley 1996: 170)

Marshall made it clear that the representative firm was not an average firm, or at least, it was not a normal average[2] but a 'particular sort of average firm'.[3]

> Thus a representative firm is in a sense an average firm. But there are many ways in which the term "average" might be interpreted in connection with a business. And a representative firm is that particular sort of average firm, at which we need to look in order to see how far the economies, *internal and external*, of production on a large scale have extended generally in the industry and country in question. We cannot see this by looking at one or two firms taken at random: but we can see it fairly well by selecting, after a broad survey, a firm, whether in private or joint-stock management (or better still, more than one), that represents, to the best of our judgment, this particular average.
>
> (Marshall 2009: 265)

Hartley (1996) goes on to make the important point that Marshall created the representative firm to avoid having to assume that all firms were the same.[4]

> Marshall created the representative firm to abstract from the idiosyncrasies of individual firms and the vagaries of industry supply. His fundamental purpose was to avoid needing to assume all firms were alike. He wanted to be able to describe a single industry equilibrium with a single market price without having to assume that all firms were producing in exactly the same manner.
>
> (Hartley 1996: 171)

'Firms'[5] in the modern textbook theory are identical.

For Marshall, firms were dynamic, heterogeneous, in disequilibrium; they progressed through a life cycle in much the same way as people.

> They began young and vigorous, but after a period of maturity they became old and were displaced by newer more efficient firms.
>
> (Backhouse 2002: 179)

Marshall gave us the famous metaphor of an industry being like a forest – while it might appear unchanged if considered as a whole, the individual trees that make it up are constantly changing.[6] It was to reconcile his dynamic view of individual firms with the static view of industries that Marshall introduced the idea of the 'representative firm'.

> The representative firm is composed of the salient characteristics of all firms in the industry.
>
> (Moss 1984: 308)

and

> It would need to be in some sense "representative" both of the cost and of the sales position of other firms within the industry. For this to be true it would need to be "representative" with respect to its business ability, age, luck, size and its access to net external economies.
>
> (Williams 1978: 102)

As noted on pages 48–9, Marshall wrote about the representative firm in the following terms:

> [o]n the one hand we shall not want to select some new producer just struggling into business, who works under many disadvantages, and has to be content for a time with little or no profits, but who is satisfied with the fact that he establishing a connection and taking the first steps towards building up a successful business; nor on the other hand shall we want to take a firm which by exceptionally long-sustained ability and good fortune has got together a vast business, and huge well-ordered workshops that give it a superiority over almost all its rivals. But our representative firm must be one which has had a fairly long life, and fair success, which is managed with normal ability, and which has normal access to the economies, external and internal, which belong to that aggregate volume of production; account being taken of the class of goods produced, the conditions of marketing them and the economic environment generally.
>
> (Marshall 2009: 264–5)

Williams (1978: 101) argues that the output of the representative firm will change if and only if the output of the industry changes, and any alteration in output will be in the same direction for the representative firms as it is for the industry. Thus, if the output of the industry increases, this has to mean that the price exceeds the representative firm's unit normal expenses of production.[7]

D. H. Macgregor's interpretation of the representative firm is explained in the following paragraph:

> [t]he firm which is to be regarded as our unit is the "representative" firm, the structure which is typical of a period of economic development, which has access to all the normal economies of that period, and is of the size which is suited to their most efficient use. It has had a "fairly long life, and fair success," is "managed with normal ability," while its size takes account

of "the class of goods produced, the conditions of marketing them, and the economic environment generally".

(Macgregor 1906: 9)

Macgregor (1949) uses a version of Figure 5.1 to illustrate the properties of the 'representative firm'.

In the diagram the supply is denoted by 0*M* and the price by *MP*. The line *QR* (called the particular expenses curve)[8] shows the average costs at which different firms, placed from left to right in the order of their efficiencies, are able to produce. Those firms in the interval between *S* and *R* are high-cost suppliers who, given their current production methods, cannot cover their full costs of manufacture at the price *MP*. Such firms will have to either alter their methods of production to lower their costs and thus move to the *QR* portion of the curve, or they will be driven from the market. Other firms, some of the lower cost producers, that is, some of those firms between *Q* and *S*, will, for different reasons, suffer from lower efficiency and thus find themselves between *S* and *R*. In Figure 5.1, the price-determining cost[9] will be *MP* and the representative conditions are those around *S*, or in other words the representative firm is, roughly, the firm which has average total costs equal to the market price.

In Frisch (1950) we find two definitions of the representative firm. Frisch sees the representative firm as a way of reasoning about the adjustment of supply necessitated by the process of adaptation that occurs along the path leading to a long-run equilibrium. Frisch's 'general definition' of the representative firm is

> [t]he representative firm is to give a miniature illustration of the supply side, in the sense that if we want to know how total supply will react, *we may simply study how the representative firm will react.* The characteristics of the representative firm must be defined in accord with this aim. In general

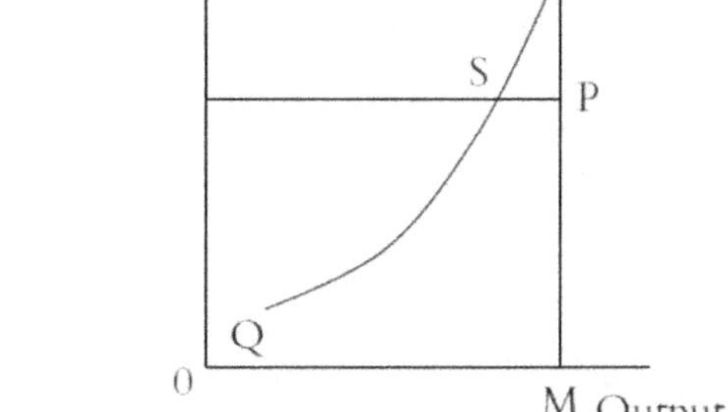

Figure 5.1 The representative firm

Source: A modified version of the diagram from D. H. Macgregor, *Economic Thought and Policy*, 1949, p. 44. By permission of Oxford University Press

> terms we can say that it must not be "some new producer just struggling into business," nor "a firm with . . . a vast business and huge well-ordered work-shops . . .," but "one . . . with a fairly long life and fair success, which is managed with normal ability and which has normal access to the economies external and internal which belong to that aggregate volume of production" (IV. XIII. 2. p. 317).
>
> (Frisch 1950: 512, emphasis in the original)

His 'more quantitative definition' is,

> [i]f we should try to formulate the definition in a more quantitative manner, we might say that the volume of production of the representative firm must vary *parallel* to the aggregate volume of production in the market, its unit cost must represent the average unit cost in the market, etc. The representative firm is in other words a *construction of the mind*, a device by which to reason quickly and conveniently on the evolution of the market as a whole. It is not certain that there will always be an actual firm in the market which may be picked out as representative. But if there are many firms in the market and each of them develops through a typical life-cycle, several of them will at some time or other in their development pass through a stage in which for a while they are similar to the representative firm. The size of the representative firm depends upon the size of the long-period aggregate production which we consider.
>
> (Frisch 1950: 512–13, emphasis in the original)

For Marshall, the analysis of the firm he undertook was driven by – and sought to rationalise – the studies of real firms he had undertaken. His view of industry, on the other hand, was as an abstract concept under the umbrella of which the many producers of a good or service could be organised to facilitate the analysis of the issue under investigation. The role of the representative firm was to link the dynamic view of the firm with the abstract view of the industry.

Hart (2003: 1140) argues that the representative firm allowed Marshall to have, simultaneously, the market in equilibrium and the firm in disequilibrium,

> [i]t [the representative firm] was an avenue through which Marshall conjectured a notion of equilibrium at a point in time for the industry as a whole, while at the same time individual firms were in disequilibrium, being subject to an "organic" process of change. The representative firm therefore meets at the junction of Marshall's biological and mechanical notions of opposed forces described in the introductory comments in book 4 of Principles.

T. W. Hutchison argued that the representative firm has no 'significant role in any purely abstract and precise model of the competitive industry'. He saw its usefulness in reducing the multiformity of the real world into a manageable range of representable forms (Hutchison 1993: 78).

From this perspective, the representative firm can be seen as a forerunner of the representative agent, the role of which is to stand in for the behaviour of the 'group', meaning the industry for Marshall and the economy for those utilising the representative agent (Blankenburg and Harcourt 2007: 46; Hartley 1996).

The cost controversy

What we now refer to as the 'cost controversy' was initiated in 1922 by the economic historian Sir John Harold Clapham when he attacked the use A. C. Pigou made of Marshall's distinction between constant, increasing and decreasing returns to scale industries. In his book *Wealth and Welfare*, published in 1912, Pigou made use of these distinctions when studying the effect of industries on the 'national dividend' (or GDP in today's terms). Pigou continued this usage in the 1920 edition of *The Economics of Welfare*. But his discussion was wholly abstract, and this abstract analysis became the target of Clapham's attack on Pigou, and thus Marshall, in his famous 1922 essay "On Empty Economic Boxes". Clapham argued that it was not in general possible to assign actual industries to any one of the three categories. If we were to open these conceptual 'boxes', Clapham asked, would we find anything 'real' inside? Clapham's aim was to show that these three categories could not be usefully used by an applied researcher.[10]

The cost controversy consisted of a series of papers – predominately published in the *Economic Journal* in the 1920s and early 1930s – debating aspects of Marshallian economics.

> The debate involved such Cambridge outsiders as Knight, Robbins, Young and Schumpeter; the insiders consisted of Clapham, Sraffa, Robertson and Shove. Critics harped on different aspects but agreed that this was the "least complete and satisfactory" area of Marshallian economics (Keynes 1951: 185; Schumpeter 1928: 369, fn.) and that the "doctrine of internal and external economies . . . seem[ed], indeed, radically in need of revision" (Robbins 1928: 398, n. 2).
>
> (Aslanbeigui 1996: 277)

The representative firm was a casualty of this controversy. Wolfe (1954) places responsibility for the expunging of the representative firm from the economics literature firmly at the feet of two papers, Sraffa (1926) and Robbins (1928). Wolfe summarised the situation thus:

> Marshall's whole account of supply price centred around the theory of the representative firm. This firm possessed both external and unexhausted internal economies. Its size and access to these economies depended on the output of the industry. And its cost of production governed the supply price of the industry. . . . It was generally agreed that the theory of the representative firm applied to conditions of what Marshall called "free

competition" and "long-run equilibrium." The meaning of these terms was the pivot upon which, it can now be seen, criticism has turned. Those who attacked Marshall assumed that he had in mind what we would now call perfect competition and static equilibrium. Using this interpretation, Mr. Sraffa showed that Marshall had apparently involved himself in a logical inconsistency. Unexhausted internal economies are not compatible with static equilibrium under perfect competition; the representative firm was not useful for determination of price under competitive conditions. But it was still used as a tool of the theory of distribution. It was here that Professor Robbins's intervention was decisive. He showed that with free mobility of resources and static equilibrium the representative firm was unnecessary for the theory of distribution, and might even prove misleading. Thus was the last important refuge of the theory of the representative firm denied it.

(Wolfe 1954: 337–8)

In his 1926 paper Sraffa raised two major objections to Marshall's theory.[11] Robinson (1971: 19) explains,

> [w]e have already seen that supply-and-demand analysis, despite its status as the textbook introduction to *all* price situations, if taken literally, really applies only to the special case of pure competition (that being the only case in which the back-ground of the supply curve can be explained). In brief, Sraffa's argument was this: 1) this supply-and demand, pure-competition package relies excessively on the law of diminishing returns, while at the same time it is blind to the observed fact of *increasing* returns; 2) the resulting analysis is based on such restrictive assumptions as to have little application to real-life situations.

To start with the first part of (1), we see that Sraffa asserted that there are incompatibilities between pure-competition and diminishing returns. He first noted that the law of diminishing returns developed in a context where more of a variable factor of production, for example, labour, was added to a fixed factor, for example, land, and at some point lower incremental per-unit returns, and thus increasing per-unit costs, would result. For example, Ricardo utilised such an argument to show how the distribution of income between workers and landowners would be affected by additional labour being applied to a fixed area of land. Sraffa (1926: 538–9) then argued that rising marginal cost and thus positively sloped supply curves resulting from diminishing returns are incompatible with partial equilibrium analysis.[12] First, he noted that for perfect competition we require that it must be possible to draw each of the demand and supply curves in such a manner that both the shape and position of the curves are unaffected by movements along the other curve. But this mutual independence of curves cannot be assumed if the production of a given commodity employs a considerable part of an input that is fixed in quantity. For any increase in the production of the commodity, there will be a corresponding increase in the unit price of the fixed factor due to competition for that input from other goods that utilise it. Thus, the prices of these other goods, be they substitutes or complements, will increase, and this will alter the conditions of demand for the original good.

But if, on the other hand, the first commodity employs just a small fraction of the available amount of the fixed factor, any increase in its use will have little effect on the factor's price or the average cost of production. This means that under perfect competition it is difficult to account for either an increasing average cost curve or an increasing marginal cost curve. This in turn implies that upward sloping supply curves are difficult to rationalise under perfect competition. A more modern way of saying this is to note that perfect competition applies to the input markets as well as the output markets, and thus an industry is able to purchase its inputs at the market price, which is independent of that industry's output. If all industries expand output, then we get decreasing returns, but this assumption violates the *ceteris paribus* assumption, because one thing being kept constant is the output of other industries.

Shackle (1967: 19) captures this point by saying,

> [i]f we allow ourselves to speak in modern terms of perfect competition, and mean by this that prices of both product and factors to the individual firm are independent of its output, then the conclusion of Mr Sraffa's argument at this stage is the failure of perfectly competitive assumptions to show any equilibrium of the individual firm. For both the demand curve for its product and the curve relating unit cost to output would be horizontal straight lines. This indictment of the perfectly competitive assumptions is Mr Sraffa's first objective.

When we turn to the second part of point (1), we see that Sraffa argued that there is an incompatibility between increasing returns to scale and perfect competition. The problem for the static theory of the industry is that a firm that faces a given price and produces under (internal) increasing returns to scale will increase its output without limit. If one firm expands to the point that it captures the whole market, what are we to make of perfect competition?[13] Assuming external increasing returns to scale meant reliance on a class of returns that were "seldom to be met with" (Sraffa 1926: 540).

Romney Robinson counters Sraffa's argument by noting two points. First he explains that in the short-run, at least, a firm's stock of plant and equipment is fixed, and this fact is enough to ensure, assuming a sufficient increase in the firm's level of output, higher per-unit costs, that is, diminishing returns. Second, Robinson explains that Sraffa's argument to do with the long-run amounts to little more than the claim that the long-run pure-competition supply curve is (approximately) flat (Robinson 1971: 20). Also, external increasing returns to scale may be "met with" more often than Sraffa assumed. As Carlo Cristiano has noted,

> [c]onsidered in retrospect, Chapman provided a clear example of an industry in which there are significant economies that are external to the firm but internal to the industry, precisely the case that Sraffa (1926) would later label as irrelevant because unrealistic.
>
> (Cristiano 2010: 18)

As part of a response to Clapham's claim of empirical irrelevance and Sraffa's claim of logical incoherence, Pigou argued that for carrying out comparative static analysis,

> Marshall's highly complex analytical starting point in a population of heterogenous disequilibrium firms was, strictly speaking, unnecessary. Pigou insisted on the possibility – and, indeed, desirability – of eliminating this complexity.
>
> (Foss 1994: 1121)

Pigou's response involved the introduction of the 'equilibrium firm', ostensibly as a way of eliminating this unnecessary complexity. Pigou described the equilibrium firm, at some length, as

> [m]ost industries are made up of a number of firms, of which at any moment some are expanding, while others are declining. Marshall, it will be remembered, likens them to trees in a forest. Thus, even when the conditions of demand are constant and the output of an industry as a whole is correspondingly constant, the output of many individual firms will not be constant. The industry as a whole will be in a state of equilibrium; the tendencies to expand and contract on the part of the individual firms will cancel out; but it is certain that many individual firms will not themselves be in equilibrium and possible that none will be. When conditions of demand have changed and the necessary adjustments have been made, the industry as a whole will, we may suppose, once more be in equilibrium, with a different output and, perhaps, a different normal supply price; but, again, many, perhaps all, the firms contained in it, though their tendencies to expand and contract must cancel one another, will, as individuals, be out of equilibrium. This is evidently a state of things the direct study of which would be highly complicated. Fortunately, however, there is a way round. Since, when the output of the industry as a whole is adjusted to any given state of demand, the tendencies to expansion and contraction on the part of individual firms cancel out, they may properly be regarded as irrelevant so far as the supply schedule of the industry as a whole is concerned. When the conditions of demand change, the output and the supply price of the industry as a whole must change in exactly the same way as they would do if, both in the original and in the new state of demand, all the firms contained in it were individually in equilibrium. This fact gives warrant for the conception of what I shall call the *equilibrium firm*. It implies that there *can* exist some one

> firm, which, whenever the industry as a whole is in equilibrium, in the sense that it is producing a regular output y in response to a normal supply price p, will itself also individually be in equilibrium with a regular output x_r. The conditions of the industry are compatible with the existence of such a firm; and the implications about these conditions, which, whether it in fact exists or not, would hold good if it did exist, must be valid. For the purpose of studying these conditions, therefore, it is legitimate to speak of it as actually existing. For any given output, then, of the industry as a whole, the supply price of the industry as a whole must be equal to the price, which, with the then output of the industry as a whole, leaves the equilibrium firm in equilibrium. The industry, therefore, conforms to the law of increasing, constant or decreasing supply prices according as the price which leaves the equilibrium firm in equilibrium increases, remains constant, or decreases with increases in the output of the industry as a whole.
>
> (Pigou 1928: 239–40)

Importantly, when considering industry equilibrium, Marshall had no need for an equilibrium firm. Long run equilibrium was achieved when market demand equalled market supply; there was no pretence that individual firms were in equilibrium. This point is one way in which Marshall differed from other approaches to the theory of the firm.

> One major departure by Marshall from many of the other leading theories of the period was over the relationship between the equilibrium of the industry and the equilibrium of the firms within the industry. The models of Cournot, Walras, and Edgeworth held, as a condition for equilibrium of the large group, that all the firms within the group should be in equilibrium.
>
> (Williams 1978: 74)

Another point worth emphasising is that the representative firm and the equilibrium firm are different concepts.

> It is essential to counter the claim, first stated directly by Robbins (1928, p. 387) that Marshall's *representative firm* and Pigou's (1928) *equilibrium firm* are essentially identical concepts. This rather unfortunate misconception has as its origin Pigou's (1927, p. 195) argument that "the representative firm must be conceived as one for which, under competitive conditions, there is, at each scale of aggregate output, a certain optimum size, trespass beyond which yields no further internal economies." Clearly, the equilibrium firm emerging from Pigou's analysis, which was assumed to be in equilibrium whenever the industry as a whole was in equilibrium, together with the associated "U" shaped long-run average cost curves, represent a significant point of departure from Marshall's thinking.
>
> (Hart 1996: 362, emphasis in the original)

Moss (1984: 313) notes the importance to Marshall of firms being different and that some of these differences are related to dynamics and time, all of which is missing from Pigou's concept.

> Pigou wrote . . . that Marshall conceived of his representative firm as an equilibrium firm. Unfortunately, Pigou gives no citation of Marshall's statement to this effect. And it is hard to see how the representative firm could stand in any logical relationship to the equilibrium firm. Whatever other properties it may have had, the representative firm was intended to entail characteristics of firms in different circumstances within a single industry and some of these characteristics were dynamic in the sense that they could not be discussed without considering the effects of the passage of time. Time clearly has no role in the Pigovian construction of the equilibrium firm. While Marshall's representative firm might reasonably have suggested to Pigou his conception of the equilibrium firm, the two concepts are hardly the same.

As noted previously, it was not Sraffa alone who expunged Marshall's representative firm from the economic record; Robbins (1928) was his willing accomplice.

In Marshall's approach to the firm, there is variety among firms in terms of their products, age, internal organization, innovation capabilities, etc. This variety causes problems. Foss (1994) writes

> [i]t is this element of variety among firms that explains the introduction of the representative firm – that firm that has cost of production equal to the industry average in long run equilibrium, is of average size, and earns "normal" profit. The representative firm is a heuristic fiction, not to be found in any given industry; however, what exactly is its analytical significance? Is it merely a statistical summary measure? Or, does it have analytical significance, as for example a device for comparative static analysis, knowledge of the cost structure of the representative firm allowing qualitative predictions about the average industry response if, for example, demand changes? All this is, as Lionel Robbins [1928] pointed out, unclear.
>
> (Foss 1994: 1120)

and then adds,

> Robbins pointed out the unclear analytical status of the representative firm. But more fundamentally, he made clear that (general) equilibrium was not inconsistent with variety among firms.
>
> (Foss 1994: 1120–1)

Schohl (1999: 71) sees Robbins as arguing that the use of the representative firms suppresses innovation just when it is most important,

> Lionel Robbins explained that the representative firm is not a necessary tool for equilibrium analysis and that it is even superfluous in Marshall's own analysis. Firstly, this conclusion is based on the observation that Marshall made no intensive use of his own conception. This is, secondly, consistent with equilibrium thinking because all that is required for equilibrium in the presence of heterogeneous factors is that differential rewards correspond to differential efficiencies. It is therefore simply not necessary to shift to an imaginary average consideration about firms, as it is unnecessary to introduce representative pieces of land, machines or workers (Robbins 1928, pp. 392–3). In addition . . . Robbins finds the representative firm even to be misleading because it "cloaks the essential heterogeneity of productive factors – in particular the heterogeneity of managerial ability – just at that point at which it is most desirable to exhibit it most vividly" (ibid., pp. 399–402). Again, the innovation issue provides a powerful argument against the applicability of the representative firm. This time it occurs in the shape of the innovative capabilities of corporate leaders to compete on modern industrial markets.

In giving a concise summary of Robbins's argument Marchionatti (2001: 62–3) writes,

> [i]n his article Robbins examined the places in which Marshall used the concept, from which his most relevant results were:
>
> - The representative firm is essentially a long-period conception with neither statistical significance nor practical usefulness.
> - The representative firm is not a necessary tool: "There is no more need for us to assume a representative firm or representative producer, than there is for us to assume a representative piece of land, a representative machine, or a representative worker. All that is necessary for equilibrium to prevail is that each factor shall get at least as much in one line of production as it could get in any other" (Robbins 1928: 393).
> - The representative firm is inessential to the hypothesis of stationariness as well as to the hypothesis of static equilibrium (which Marshall rejected because of "his curious predilection for biological analogies" or "for fear of becoming unintelligible to business men and economic historians" (ibid.: 395)). This is true both in the case of general equilibrium and of partial equilibrium.
> - The representative firm is not necessary also in the case of diminishing costs under competitive conditions. He questioned the existence of external economies' referring to the criticisms of Young and Knight (ibid.: 398–9).
> - Finally, the representative firm is a very poor tool for examining the problems of change and development. In a note, referring to the contemporary research programme of Allyn Young, at that time at the London School of Economics, he said that:

> In a world in which growth in the economic system proceeds just as much by way of differentiation and subdivision as by the expansion and development of particular economic units, the idea of a representative unit which preserves its essential identity while undergoing progressive expansion is apt to be very misleading. . . . In such a case to continue to speak of *the* representative firm of the industry . . . is to suggest a state of affairs having no counterpart in reality. . . . It is no accident, I suggest, that in *Industry and Trade* where problems of this sort are dealt with, the use of the representative firm is even more nebulous and half-hearted than in the *Principles*.
>
> (Robbins 1928: 402–3 note)

Robbins's rejection of the representative firm can also be seen as just one example of his more general dissatisfaction with partial equilibrium models and thus with much of Marshallian analysis. Robbins's biographer D. P. O'Brien writes, "[t]he representative firm was essentially a partial equilibrium concept; and Robbins was critical of partial equilibrium analysis as a whole" (O'Brien 1988: 89).

On his view of partial equilibrium, Robbins wrote,

> [i]t is, perhaps, worth stressing the point that the objection here implied is not to partial equilibrium analysis as such, but to partial equilibrium analysis unrelated to the general theory of equilibrium. It may be quite true that the general theory of equilibrium by itself is often too abstract and general for useful application. But it is equally true – and it is a thing which has often been forgotten in recent discussions – that partial equilibrium analysis unaccompanied by a continual awareness of the propositions of general equilibrium theory is almost certain to be misleading.
>
> (Robbins 1933: xv, footnote 3)

And, importantly for our discussion, Robbins went on to say, "[i]t may be asserted without fear of serious contradiction that most of the confusion in the recent cost controversy[14] has sprung from the attempt to make the constructions of partial equilibrium carry more than they can legitimately bear" (Robbins 1933: xv, footnote 3). Robbins favoured what has been referred to as 'Austrian general equilibrium'.[15] O'Brien (1988: 87) notes "[a] key role in Robbin's approach to microeconomics was . . . an emphasis upon general equilibrium – usually general equilibrium analysed in terms similar to those used by the Austrians and Wicksteed".

Hartley (1996: 172–4) summarises the British literature attacking the representative firm by arguing that it made four major claims. (1) Robbins claimed the representative firm was ephemeral. (2) He also argued that its use gained nothing.

> *There is no more need for us to assume a representative firm or representative producer, than there is for us to assume a representative piece of land, a representative machine, or a representative worker.*
>
> (Robbins 1928: 393, emphases in original, footnote deleted)

Marshall used the representative firm to show how heterogeneous firms could generate a single market price, but Sraffa (1926) argued that in equilibrium different producers could charge different prices for similar commodities. In modern terms, think, for example, of monopolistic competition. Thus there is no need for the representative firm. (3) Young (1928) showed that the representative firm cannot account for economic expansion other than that generated by the expansion of current manufacturing processes. Marshall's view was that as an industry grew, the representative firm grew proportionally. This is what is meant by the supply curve remaining relevant. Young (1928) pointed out that as the economy grew the division of labour expanded, so that commodities once produced by one firm could now be made by multiple firms, each single firm specialising in producing just one part of the good. Young (1928: 538) writes

> [w]ith the extension of the division of labour among industries the representative firm, like the industry of which it is a part, loses its identity. Its internal economies dissolve into the internal and external economies of the more highly specialized undertakings which are its successors, and are supplemented by new economies.

Thus, if we have growth, we must ask what happens to the representative firm? During a period of growth, the representative firm may cease to be representative. Even if all firms are the same and growth occurs due to an increase in the number of firms, then the representative firm does not grow with the industry. (4) Robbins (1928: 399) writes

> [b]ut it is possible, I think, to condemn it [the representative firm] on grounds more general than this. The whole conception, it may be suggested, is open to the general criticism that it cloaks the essential heterogeneity of productive factors – in particular the heterogeneity of managerial ability – just at that point at which it is most desirable to exhibit it most vividly.

The reason Marshall created the representative firm in the first place was to create a single supply curve with heterogeneous firms. Implicit in this formulation is the idea that the supply curve will be the supply curve of the representative firm. But why? Why not some other firm – the marginal firm, for example? Marshall argues that if a manager sees the representative firm making profits, he will enter the market. This increases supply and forces down the market price.

This process will end when the price equals the costs of the representative firm, and hence this firm's profits will be zero. But for price to equal the costs of the representative firm, all mangers would have to be of average ability. If there were managers of superior or inferior ability, the supply price could be forced away from the representative firm's cost to some other firm's costs, for example, the marginal firm's costs. But by assuming that managers are all average, Marshall is forgetting the heterogeneities he began with.

Attacks on the representative firm came from America as well as the United Kingdom. Davenport (1908: 378) makes clear that he thinks the concept is obscure and lacking in tangibility.

> In substance this is evidently an opportunity-cost analysis of the reasons for the movement of entrepreneur ability and entrepreneur capital from one industry to another; it has no necessary relevancy to the representative or to the average firm, and depends for its correctness upon no assumption of this sort. Accurately, however, it does imply a firm or a situation where the wages of superintendence are only just large enough, etc., – "the price the expectation of which will just suffice to maintain the existing aggregate of production," a marginal-cost price, as it would seem. But this appears not to be Marshall's idea, nor is it possible – to this writer at least – to make out quite precisely what the idea is; the notion of the representative firm appears to lack something in point of theoretical tangibility.

Silberling (1924: 438) wrote,

> [t]he attempt, however, to account for a theoretical equilibrium price under such conditions [decreasing costs] on the basis of the costs of some "representative" firm (which for Marshall is after all nothing but an average firm) is as misleading as it is superfluous.

Conclusion

The criticisms of Sraffa and Robbins received support from many quarters. John Maynard Keynes, for example, then editor of the *Economic Journal*, was in sympathy with Robbins's paper. In a letter to Robbins, dated 14 March 1928, Keynes wrote

> [i]t is a very interesting piece of work, which much wanted doing, and for my part I am in sympathy with it. I should like to do away with the representative firm altogether, and I believe you are right in arguing that it really serves no useful purpose.
>
> (Keynes Papers, EJ/1/3, quoted in Marchionatti 2001: 62)

The criticisms were also remarkably effective, Maxwell (1958: 691) comments that

> [i]n a recent article in the ECONOMIC JOURNAL (June 1954) on "The representative firm," Mr. J. N. Wolfe alleged that Mr. Sraffa and Professor Robbins had, in articles written more than twenty-five years age,' driven this Marshallian concept from the pages of the text-books.

Blaug (1985: 422) explains

> L. Robbins' critique of "The representative firm", *EJ*, 1928, . . . succeeded in virtually eliminating the concept from the literature".

Williams (1978: 100) writes

> [a]ssessed as an expositional tool, the representative firm must be regarded as a failure. Against the onslaught by Robbins, the concept crumbled remarkably quickly.

O'Brien (1984: 32) argues

> [t]he "representative firm" was virtually eliminated from the literature by Lionel (now Lord) Robbins in an article published in the Economic Journal of 1928.

Looking back at the publication of Robbin's paper, J. N. Wolfe commented that

> [i]t is now more than twenty-five years since Professor Robbins's famous article on the representative firm finally drove that concept from the pages of economic text-books.
>
> (Wolfe 1954: 337)

So the representative firm was driven out of the economics literature with little difficulty. Today, the textbook model of the 'firm' is based not on Marshall but rather on Pigou. The equilibrium firm has become the standard.

While studies of real world industries influenced Marshall's approach to the theory of the firm, there is a tension between his desire to base his representative firm on real firms and the use of an implicitly zero transaction cost framework for his theoretical modelling of the firm. If we accept that Marshall worked within a zero transaction cost framework,[16] then there is no role for firms to play.[17] That zero transaction costs result in firms having no role in production is most clearly seen in the (neoclassical) textbook perfect competition model. With regard to the partial equilibrium approach to the firm, G. L. S. Shackle notes,

> [t]he firm's essential function is to take decisions. It must decide what commodity to produce; what quantities of factors to use, according to what

> technique, in making this commodity; and how much of this commodity to put on the market on each unit of time.
>
> (Shackle 1968: 35)

But to carry out this function, all that is needed in a single decision maker, a single person; no real firm is needed. Decisions are made, but no real problems are solved. Klein (1996: 5) summarises the situation as,

> [i]n neoclassical economic theory, the firm as such does not exist at all. The "firm" is a production function or production possibilities set, a means of transforming inputs into outputs. Given the available technology, a vector of input prices, and a demand schedule, the firm maximizes money profits subject to the constraint that its production plans must be technologically feasible. That is all there is to it. The firm is modeled as a single actor, facing a series of relatively uncomplicated decisions: what level of output to produce, how much of each factor to hire, and so on. These "decisions," of course, are not really decisions at all; they are trivial mathematical calculations, implicit in the underlying data. In the long run, the firm may also choose an optimal size and output mix, but even these are determined by the characteristics of the production function (economies of scale, scope, and sequence). In short: the firm is a set of cost curves, and the "theory of the firm" is a calculus problem.

This result – that zero transaction costs implies we have production without firms – means that Marshall's representative firm is a theory of production rather than being a firm in any real sense or in the modern theoretical sense. While what Marshall offers can be seen as a theory of production, it is a theory that has no need for firms. The 'firms' that lie along the particular expenses curve are just collections of the factors of production bought together and controlled by market contracts organised to produce the goods desired by consumers. As was explained in the Appendix to Chapter 4, with zero transaction costs comes perfect contracting, and we know that,

> [w]ith perfect and costless contracting, it is hard to see room for anything resembling firms (even one-person firms), since consumers could contract directly with owners of factor services and wouldn't need the services of the intermediaries known as firms.
>
> (Foss 2000: xxiv)

Also, Marshall's theory cannot answer the three basic question that underlie the post-1970 theory of the firm: (1) why do firms exist? (2) what determines the boundaries of the firm? and (3) what determines the internal structure of the firm?

Marshall's 'firms' are just collections of cost curves; they have no real existence, no boundaries and no internal organisation. Such 'firms' are consistent with production taking place via a series of sophisticated market contracts. Thus, the Marshallian modelling process can be interpreted as one which begins with production involving real firms but ends with a model of production involving no firms at all.

While no model of the firm, including the representative firm, makes much sense in a world of zero transaction costs, Ravix (2012) argues that the representative firm does make sense when Marshall's work on the firm and industrial organisation is placed in an evolutionary context. As Metcalfe (2007: S3) has written about the representative firm,

> [i]t [the representative firm] is the most immediate expression of Marshall's evolutionary turn of mind but it would never make sense in the context of a non-evolutionary account of order and transformation.

To understand the firm we must understand the production process and institutional forms. Central to this is the concept of dynamic economics centred on the relationship between organisation and knowledge. As Marshall himself has written,

> [c]apital consists in a great part of knowledge and organization: and of this some part is private property and other part is not. Knowledge is our most powerful engine of production; it enables us to subdue Nature and force her to satisfy our wants. Organization aids knowledge; it has many forms, e.g. that of a single business, that of various businesses in the same trade, that of various trades relatively to one another, and that of the State providing security for all and help for many. The distinction between public and private property in knowledge and organization is of great and growing importance: in some respects of more importance than that between public and private property in material things; and partly for that reason it seems best sometimes to reckon Organization apart as a distinct agent of production.
>
> (Marshall 2009: Book IV, Chapter 1, p. 115)

One important point for our understanding of Marshall's analysis is the often-overlooked relationship between internal business organisation and external trade connections and internal and external economies. Marshall sees an increase in labour and capital giving rise to improved organisation, which in turn increases the efficiency of the work of capital and labour. This results in increasing returns. Marshall argues that a firm will set out to extend both its internal and external organisation. External organisation meaning the firm's network of social, technical and commercial arrangements that provide the connections between a firm and its customers, suppliers and rivals. The representative firm can be utilised to bridge the gap between Marshall's dynamic analysis of the industry and his static analysis of equilibrium.

Metcalfe (2007: S3) argues that both the static marginal firm and the dynamic representative firm are needed for Marshall's value theory,

> [w]e need the marginal firm to distinguish different instantiations of long period order, and we need the representative firm not simply to deal with the messy facts of heterogeneous firms but rather to understand the dynamic consequences of their variation for the transformation of the prevailing order.

The entry/exit decision of firms is based on the expected profit to be earned in a particular industry. This expected profit is calculated by comparing the firm's revenues with the costs of creating and maintaining a representative firm.

Ravix (2012: 53) goes on to point out that the evolutionary aspects of Marshall's work explains why modern theories of the firm based on Marshall's analysis can go beyond the standard transaction cost approach to the firm. Transaction costs can explain vertical integration (the 'make-or-buy' decision) but little more. To explain how the structure of the industry is determined by the decisions made by firms, it is necessary to place the organisation of the industry in its dynamic context. In this situation there are problems pertaining not just to issues to do with costs but also to questions with regard to a firm's activities and capabilities. To be able to expand industrial organisation to take into account firms' strategies and firms' interactions, we need to consider how firms choose their activities and the manner in which they develop their competencies. Ravix (2012: 53–4) writes that,

> [t]he main result of the neo-Marshallian theory of the firm is that the simple firm–market dichotomy is only a subcase of the division of labour among different business institutions that involves firm, market and cooperation as alternative and complementary modes of organizing industrial activities. As Richardson writes, "(t)he dichotomy between firm and market, between directed and spontaneous co-ordination, is misleading; it ignores the institutional fact of inter-firm co-operation and assumes away the distinct method of co-ordination that this can provide" (Richardson, 1972, p. 895).

The evolutionary framework inherited from Marshall allows the modern theory of the firm to develop by integrating into industrial organisation the division of labour, substitutions and re-combinations of firms and business institutions and to see how these concepts simultaneously determine the boundaries of firms and the entry and exit of firms into and from the market.

Notes

1 For more on Marshall's industry supply curve, see Opocher and Steedman (2008) and Williams (1978: 87–102). For Marshall, a supply schedule does not show how much an industry will supply at any given price but rather what is the minimum price at which

producers are willing to produce a particular quantity. This minimum price must cover the average costs of the highest cost producer and the supply curve shows how these costs change as the industry output increases.

2 Another point to consider is that Marshall was trained as a mathematician, having achieved the rank of Second Wrangler in the 1865 Cambridge Mathematical Tripos, and so it seem reasonable to assume that if he had meant the "average" firm he would have used the term.

3 Marshall's view of what constitutes the representative firm changed over time. In this respect, the controversial notion of the 'representative firm' is central. His taste for economic facts compelled Marshall to consider industries that comprise different firms: hence the necessity of some average, abstract representation (incidentally, in the PTDV ['The Pure Theory of Domestic Values'] and in the MSS ['manuscripts on value', see Opocher and Steedman (2008: 248, footnote 2)], Marshall argued precisely in terms of an average of actual firms) (Opocher and Steedman 2008: 250, footnote 7). By the time of his in the 1890s, Marshall's view had changed, now the representative firm is, as noted on pages 126–7, '. . . not some statistical construct; it is not, for example, created by dividing total supply by the number of firms in the industry' (Hartley 1996: 170). The representative firm has become a 'particular sort of average firm', see page 127.

4 It is normally assumed that all firms are identical since having firms that are different can lead to a discontinuous industry supply curve.

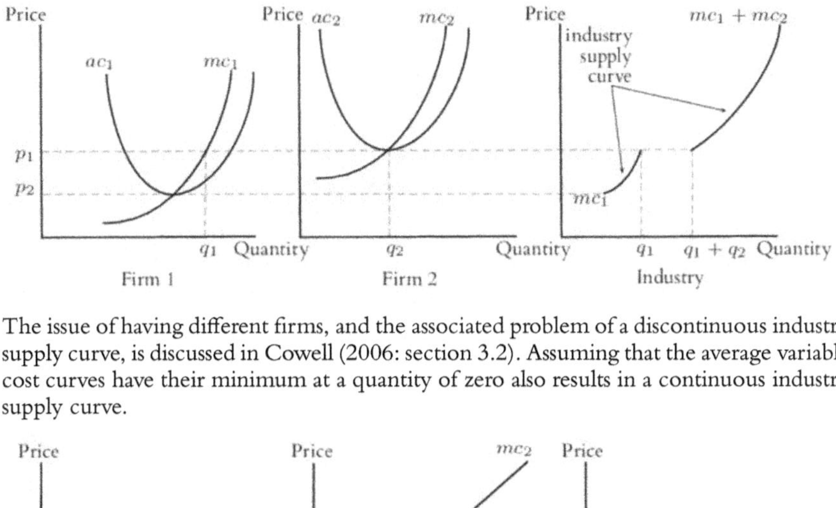

The issue of having different firms, and the associated problem of a discontinuous industry supply curve, is discussed in Cowell (2006: section 3.2). Assuming that the average variable cost curves have their minimum at a quantity of zero also results in a continuous industry supply curve.

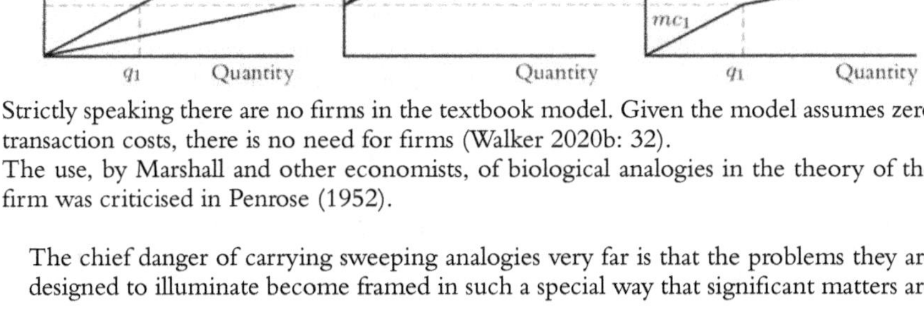

5 Strictly speaking there are no firms in the textbook model. Given the model assumes zero transaction costs, there is no need for firms (Walker 2020b: 32).

6 The use, by Marshall and other economists, of biological analogies in the theory of the firm was criticised in Penrose (1952).

> The chief danger of carrying sweeping analogies very far is that the problems they are designed to illuminate become framed in such a special way that significant matters are

> frequently inadvertently obscured. Biological analogies contribute little either to the theory of price or to the theory of growth and development of firms and in general tend to confuse the nature of the important issues.
>
> (Penrose 1952: 804)

7 Williams (1978: 101) also notes that

> a firm's long-period supply price (average of normal expenses) includes income forgone by investing capital in this particular enterprise. So when industry output is stable, the representative firm must be earning its opportunity income on capital. This opportunity income is the definition of the normal rate of interest or, if earnings of management are counted in, of profit.

and

> the representative firm will have a supply curve found by the vertical summation of the supply schedules of the factors it uses, when the factor supply schedules plot the amount of the factor needed to produce a unit of a given quantity of output against the supply price of that quantity of the factor. This exercise does not give any indication of the supply schedules of firms within the industry in question, but it possibly helps to illustrate the meaning of the costs of particular factors per unit of output.

8 Marshall called *QR* the 'particular expenses curve' (Marshall 2009: 668). Jacob Viner defines the curve as

> [t]o a curve representing the array of actual average costs of the different producers in an industry when the total output of the industry was a given amount, these individual costs being arranged in increasing order of size from left to right, Marshall gave the name of "particular expenses curve".
>
> (Viner 1932: 44; footnotes removed)

For greater detail, see Appendix 1, Walker (2020b).

9

> Recent economists, while adhering to the doctrine of marginal cost as a price-determinant in the case of commodities subject to the law of diminishing returns, have been disposed to accept Marshall's theory of the representative firm in the case of commodities subject to the law of constant or decreasing cost. It is not towards the cost of production to the least efficient producer that price gravitates, they say, but to that of the well-established, solid business man – the man doing a conservative, prosperous, but not phenomenally brilliant business.
>
> (Wright 1919: 560)

10 Knight (2016: 51) notes that Clapham "was an early critic of Pigou's increasing reliance on abstract theoretical analytics without reference to historical data, although, of course, Clapham was similarly critical of Marshall".

11 Sraffa began this assault on Marshall's theory with a paper in Italian, Sraffa (1925). The first few pages of Sraffa's 1926 paper are a summary of the arguments made in the 1925 paper. An English translation of Sraffa (1925) appeared as Sraffa (1998). For a comparison of Sraffa (1926) with Sraffa (1925), see Maneschi (1986).

12 See Robinson (1969: 116–9) and Shackle (1967: 13–21) for more detailed discussion.

13 In today's terminology, this is the problem of natural monopoly. For an introduction to the theory of natural monopoly, see Sharkey (1982).

14 Given that the introduction is dated October 1932, the 'recent cost controversy' is most likely the papers from the *Economic Journal*, starting with Clapham (1922), and including Robbins (1928), some of which were discussed earlier.

15 Mark Blaug explains that 'Austrian general equilibrium' isn't general equilibrium in the sense of Walras; rather, it is what he calls 'total equilibrium' analysis. By this term he means "any kind of economics that stresses the interdependencies between different markets and particularly factor markets and product markets" (Blaug 1990: 185).

16 It does not matter whether we think of Marshall's framework is one of perfect competition, as many of those who attacked the representative firm thought, or as one of imperfect competition, as some thought – see, for example, Hollander (1961) – both frameworks are implicitly zero transaction cost frameworks.

17 The main point of Coase (1937) was that firms make no sense in a world of zero transaction costs.

References

Aslanbeigui, Nahid (1996). 'The Cost Controversy: Pigouvian Economics in Disequilibrium', *The European Journal of the History of Economic Thought*, 3(2) Summer: 275–95.

Backhouse, Roger E. (2002). *The Ordinary Business of Life: A History of Economics from the Ancient World to the Twenty-First Century*, Princeton, NJ: Princeton University Press.

Blankenburg, Stephanie and Geoffrey Harcourt (2007). 'The Debates on the Representative Firm and Increasing Returns: Then and Now'. In Philip Arestis, Michelle Baddelely and John S. L. McCombie (eds.), *Economic Growth, New Directions in Theory and Policy* (44–64), Cheltenham, UK: Edward Elgar Publishing Ltd.

Blaug, Mark (1985). *Economic Theory in Retrospect*, 4th edn., Cambridge: Cambridge University Press.

Blaug, Mark (1990). 'Comment on O'Brien's "Lionel Robbins and the Austrian Connection"'. In Bruce J. Caldwell (ed.), *Carl Menger and His Legacy in Economics: Annual Supplement to Volume 22, History of Political Economy* (185–8), Durham: Duke University Press.

Boulding, Kenneth E. (1952). 'Implications for General Economics of More Realistic Theories of the Firm', *American Economic Review*, 42(2) Papers and Proceedings of the Sixty-fourth Annual Meeting of the American Economic Association May: 35–44.

Clapham, J. H. (1922). 'Of Empty Economic Boxes', *Economic Journal*, 32(127) September: 305–14.

Coase, Ronald Harry (1937). 'The Nature of the Firm', *Economica*, n.s. 4(16) November: 386–405.

Cowell, Frank (2006). *Microeconomics: Principles and Analysis*. Oxford: Oxford University Press.

Cristiano, Carlo (2010). 'Marshall at Cambridge'. In Tiziano Raffaelli, Giacomo Becattini, Katia Caldari and Marco Dardi (eds.), *The Impact of Alfred Marshall's Ideas The Global Diffusion of his Work* (17–39), Cheltenham, UK: Edward Elgar Publishing Ltd.

Davenport, H. J. (1908). *Value and Distribution: A Critical and Constructive Study*, Chicago: University of Chicago Press.

Foss, Nicolai J. (1994). 'The Biological Analogy and the Theory of the Firm: Marshall and Monopolistic Competition', *Journal of Economic Issues*, 28(4) December: 1115–36.

Foss, Nicolai J. (2000). 'The Theory of the Firm: An Introduction to Themes and Contributions'. In Nicolai Foss (ed.), *The Theory of the Firm: Critical Perspectives on Business and Management* (xv–lxi), London: Routledge.

Frisch, Ragnar (1950). 'Alfred Marshall's Theory of Value', *Quarterly Journal of Economics*, 64(4) November: 495–524.

Hart, Neil (1996). 'Marshall's Theory of Value: The Role of External Economies', *Cambridge Journal of Economics*, 20(3) May: 353–69.

Hart, Neil (2003). 'Marshall's Dilemma: Equilibrium versus Evolution', *Journal of Economic Issues*, 37(4) December: 1139–60.

Hartley, James E. (1996). 'The Origins of the Representative Agent', *Journal of Economic Perspectives*, 10(2) Spring: 169–77.

Hollander, Samuel (1961). 'The Representative Firm and Imperfect Competition', *Canadian Journal of Economics and Political Science*, 27(2) May: 236–41.

Hutchison, T. W. (1993). *A Review of Economic Doctrines 1870–1929*, Bristol: Thoemmes Press. First published 1953.

Klein, Peter G. (1996). 'Economic Calculation and the Limits of Organization', *The Review of Austrian Economics*, 9(2): 3–28.

Knight, Karen (2016). 'A.C. Pigou, a Loyal Marshallian?', *History of Economics Review*, 64(1) August, 42–63.

Macgregor, D. H. (1906). *Industrial Combination*, Kitchener, Ontario: Baroche Books, 2001.

Macgregor, D. H. (1949). *Economic Thought and Policy*, Oxford: Oxford University Press.

Maneschi, Andrea (1986). 'A Comparative Evaluation of Sraffa's "The Laws of Returns under Competitive Conditions" and Its Italian Precursor', *The Cambridge Journal of Economics*, 10(1) March: 1–12.

Marchionatti, Roberto (2001). 'Sraffa and the Criticism of Marshall in the 1920s'. In Terenzio Cozzi and Roberto Machionatti (eds.), *Piero Sraffa's Political Economy: A Centenary Estimate* (43–80), London: Routledge.

Marshall, Alfred (2009). *Principles of Economics*, Unabridged 8th edn., New York: Cosimo, Inc. Eighth edition first published 1920. First edition 1890.

Maxwell, James A. (1958). 'Some Marshallian Concepts, Especially the Representative Firm', *The Economic Journal*, 68(272) December: 691–98.

Metcalfe, J. S. (2007). 'Alfred Marshall's Mecca: Reconciling the Theories of Value and Development', *Economic Record*, 83(Supp.): 1–22.

Moss, Scott (1984). 'The History of the Theory of the Firm from Marshall to Robinson and Chamberlin: the Source of Positivism in Economics', *Economica*, n.s. 51(203) August: 307–18.

O'Brien, Denis P. (1984). 'The Evolution of the Theory of the Firm'. In Frank H. Stephen (ed.), *Firms, Organization and Labour: Approaches to the Economics of Work Organization* (25–62), London: Macmillan Press.

O'Brien, Denis P. (1988). *Lionel Robbins*, London: The Macmillian Press.

Opocher, Arrigo and Ian Steedman (2008). 'The Industry Supply Curve: Two Different Traditions', *The European Journal of the History of Economic Thought*, 15(2) June: 247–74.

Penrose, E. T. (1952). 'Biological Analogies in the Theory of the Firm', *American Economic Review*, 42(5) December: 804–19.

Pigou, A. C. (1928). 'An Analysis of Supply', *Economic Journal*, 38(150) June: 238–57.

Ravix, Jacques-Laurent (2012). 'Alfred Marshall and the Marshallian Theory of the Firm'. In Michael Dietrich and Jackie Kraff (eds.), *Handbook on the Economics and Theory of the Firm* (49–54), Cheltenham, UK: Edward Elgar.

Robbins, Lionel (1928). 'The Representative Firm', *Economic Journal*, 38(151) September: 387–404.

Robbins, Lionel (1933). 'Introduction'. In Phillip H. Wicksteed, *The Common Sense of Political Economy and Selected Papers and Reviews on Economic Theory* (vol. I, pp. v–xxiii), edited with an introduction by Lionel Robbins, London: George Routledge & Sons, Ltd.

Robinson, Joan (1969). *The Economics of Imperfect Competition*, 2nd edn., London: The Macmillan Press Ltd.

Robinson, Romney (1971). *Edward H. Chamberlin*, New York: Columbia University Press.

Schohl, Frank (1999). 'The Paradoxical Fate of the Representative Firm', *Journal of the History of Economic Thought*, 21(1) March: 65–80.

Shackle, G. L. S. (1967). *The Years of High Theory: Invention and Tradition in Economic Thought 1926–1939*, Cambridge: Cambridge University Press.

Shackle, G. L. S. (1968). *Economic for Pleasure*, 2nd edn., Cambridge: Cambridge University Press.

Sharkey, William W. (1982). *The Theory of Natural Monopoly*, Cambridge: Cambridge University Press.

Silberling, Norman J. (1924). 'Graphic Illustration of the Laws of Price', *American Economic Review*, 14(3) September: 417–42.

Sraffa, Piero (1925). 'Sulle relazioni fra costo e quantità prodotta', *Annali di Economia*, 2: 277–328.

Sraffa, Piero (1926). 'The Laws of Returns under Competitive Conditions', *Economic Journal*, 36(144) December: 535–50.

Sraffa, Piero (1998). '"On the Relations Between Cost and Quantity Produced", English translation by John Eatwell and Alessandro Roncaglia'. In L. L. Pasinetti (ed.), *Italian Economic Papers* (vol. 3, pp. 323–63), Bologna: Il Mulino and Oxford: Oxford University Press.

Viner, Jacob (1932). 'Cost Curves and Supply Curves', *Zeitschrift für Nationalökonomie*, 3 September: 23–46.

Walker, Paul (2020a). 'A Brief Prehistory of the Theory of the Firm: Revised Edition', Working Paper. Available at: http://ssrn.com/abstract=2911699

Walker, Paul (2020b). 'The Theory of the Firm: An Overview of the Economic Mainstream: Revised Edition', Working Paper. Available at: http://ssrn.com/abstract=2000431

Williams, Philip L. (1978). *The Emergence of the Theory of the Firm: From Adam Smith to Alfred Marshall*, London: The Macmillan Press.

Wolfe, J. N. (1954). 'The Representative Firm', *Economic Journal*, 64(254) June: 337–49.

Wright, Philip G. (1919). 'Cost of Production and Price', *Quarterly Journal of Economics*, 33(3) May: 560–67.

Young, Allyn A. (1928). 'Increasing Returns and Economic Progress', *Economic Journal*, 38(152) December: 527–42.

6 The neoclassical model under fire 1940–1970

Introduction

The neoclassical model of production, often mischaracterised as a theory of the firm,[1] that appears in most undergraduate microeconomic textbooks had largely developed by the 1940s. It grew out of Pigou's notion of the equilibrium firm which he introduced in Pigou (1928).[2] Importantly, the construct of the equilibrium firm allowed Pigou to utilise marginal and average cost curve diagrams to develop the idea of industries producing under increasing returns but where any economies of scale are external to the firm but internal to the industry. When outlining the conditions for a firm being in equilibrium Pigou notes that these requirements involve the significant condition that all the internal economies of scale are exhausted so that all economies have to be external. Pigou maintained that the equilibrium firm produced at its minimum efficient scale so that the output level of the equilibrium firm, for a many-firm industry, would occur where the marginal cost curve cuts the average cost curve (i.e. $p = \frac{F(y)}{y} = F'(y)$) (Pigou 1928: 254). See Figure 6.1.

To get from the equilibrium firm to the textbook firm, the important innovation came when it was assumed that industries were comprised entirely of equilibrium firms. In their development of imperfect competition and monopolistic competition, respectively, Robinson (1933) and Chamberlin (1933) made this move. For them, industries are composed entirely of equilibrium firms which have identical cost curves, and firms, as production functions, faced household preference (demand) functions. But as Moss (1984: 314) points out,

> [b]y assuming that every firm in the industry has an identical cost curve, Robinson and Chamberlin stood Pigou's construction of the equilibrium firm on its head. Where Pigou argued that an equilibrium firm could be derived from the laws of returns obeyed by any particular industry, Robinson and Chamberlin defined the industry on the basis of a population of equilibrium firms.

With this change, which took place in the 1930s, in the interpretation of the relationship between the equilibrium firm and the industry, the neoclassical approach to the firm had developed. Puu (1970: 230) highlights this point,

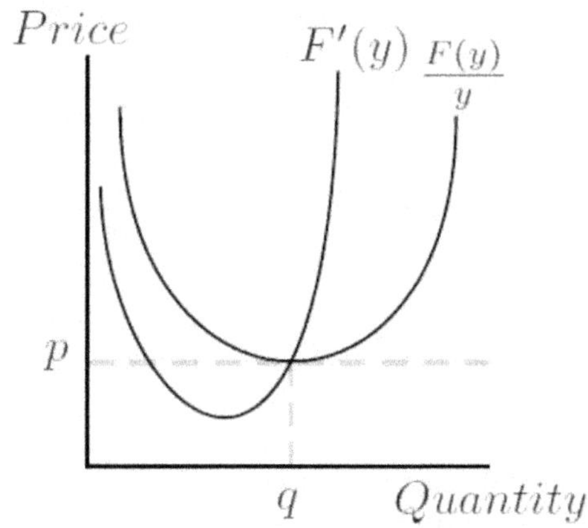

Figure 6.1 The equilibrium firm

the theory of the firm had, in substance, been developed to its present state by 1940.

While the marginalist model became the dominant model of the firm during the 1930s, the basic tenants of this new orthodoxy were the subject of a number of controversies from the beginning. As Anna Koutsoyiannis has noted,

> [i]n 1939 there started a gradually mounting dissatisfaction with the traditional neoclassical theory of the firm, its assumptions and its marginalistic behavioural rules.
>
> (Koutsoyiannis 1979: 256)

During the period 1940–1970, controversies occurred in both the United Kingdom and the United States.

The full cost and marginalist controversies

Of the early attacks on the neoclassical model the most famous were the 'full cost controversy'[3] in the United Kingdom and, in the United States, the related 'marginalist controversy' (Mongin 1992, 1998).

The full cost controversy was begun by the publication of R. L. Hall and C. J. Hitch's 1939 paper, 'Price Theory and Business Behaviour'. This paper surveyed businessmen with regard to their firm's pricing policies and found that firms set prices in a 'full cost' way by estimating an average-cost amount at a reference level of output and adding to it a fixed percentage – referred to as the mark-up. The controversy arose because this full cost approach to pricing was seen as a challenge to the usual marginalist (neoclassical) profit-maximising view of the firm. In particular, full cost pricing challenges two basic tenets of standard economic theory:

1 that both demand and supply conditions, or costs, affect the pricing decision – remember Marshall's famous "two blades of the scissors" analogy, and
2 that the solution of all price problems occurs when marginal revenue equals marginal cost

An implication of this is that long-run profit maximisation would only be achieved in the lucky case where the mark-up bears the 'correct' relationship to the firm's perceived elasticities of demand.

As an illustration of this point consider this example from Koutsoyiannis (1979: 278–80). Koutsoyiannis assumes that the firm uses the mark-up rule $P = AVC + GPM$, where AVC is average variable costs and GRM is the gross profit margin. It is assumed that the firm's aim is to maximise long-run profits. What Koutsoyiannis shows is that this pricing rule means the firm implicitly 'guesses' at the demand elasticity, provided that the AVC is constant over the relevant values of output.

To show this note that the neoclassical profit maximising condition is

$$MC = MR. \tag{6.1}$$

Note also that marginal revenue can be written as[4]

$$MR = P\left(1 - \frac{1}{e}\right) \tag{6.2}$$

where e is the demand elasticity, that is, $e = -\frac{dQ}{dP}\frac{P}{Q}$.

If $MC > 0$ then $MR > 0$ for profit maximisation. This implies that profits are maximised with $|e| > 1$, since if (1) $e = 1$ then $MR = 0$ or (2) if $e < 1$ then $MR < 0$, and in either case $MC \neq MR$.

Also, a number of empirical studies have suggested that the AVC curve has a range of quantities over which the minimum of AVC occurs,[5] see Figure 6.2.

Figure 6.2 Empirical AVC and MC curves

So it is not too extreme to assume that the minimum of AVC is flat. An implication of this is that over the flat region of AVC we have[6]

$$AVC = MC \tag{6.3}$$

Substituting 6.3 and then 6.2 into 6.1 gives $AVC = MR$ and $AVC = P\left(1-\frac{1}{e}\right) = P\left(\frac{e-1}{e}\right)$.

Solving this for P gives $P = AVC\left(\frac{e}{e-1}\right)$. Given that we have $|e| > 1$, the term in the parentheses is always greater than 1. This means we can write $\left(\frac{e}{e-1}\right) = (1+k)$ where $k > 0$. This, in turn, gives $P = AVC(1 + k)$, where k is the gross profit margin.

A simple example of this is, if the firm sets 20% of its AVC as the gross profit margin, then $(1+k) = 1+0.20 = \left(\frac{e}{e-1}\right)$. Solving this for e gives an elasticity of demand of 6.

Thus, Koutsoyiannis has shown that setting the gross profit margin amounts to estimating the price elasticity of demand correctly and applying the standard neoclassical analysis. Therefore, the full cost pricing approach and the neoclassical approach are equivalent. But it can be argued that this is a special case; it highlights just how stringent the informational requirements are for full cost and marginal cost pricing to be equivalent. Such conditions are unlikely to be met in any real-world situations. Thus, in general, full cost pricing does challenge the neoclassical analysis.

Interestingly, in a much more recent paper, Gramlich and Ray (2016), it is argued that full cost pricing may simply be a practical way to implement the neoclassical optimal pricing. It is noted that firms are unlikely to have the information about their demand curves that is required for optimal economic pricing, but they may well have information regarding their equilibrium income. This information can be used, along with full cost pricing techniques, to find their optimal price. A full cost pricing algorithm which converges to the optimal price is proposed. This helps resolve some of the apparent tensions between the two pricing methods.

But while some economists attacked the neoclassical theory, it was not without its defenders. The most famous of these was Machlup (1946). Machlup's rejoinder was not solely directed towards the full cost arguments; he also responded to a paper by labour economist R. A. Lester in which Lester argued that the marginalist theoretical predicts regarding the relationship between wages and employment could not be found in the data (Lester 1946). Lester's paper started the 'marginalist controversy'. Lester argued that

> his empirical research raised "grave doubts as to the validity of conventional marginal theory and the assumptions on which it rests" in the following ways: (1) market demand was more important in determining a firm's volume of employment than wage rates; (2) the firm's cost structure was not that suggested by "conventional marginalism" and its capital-labor ratio was not tied to its wage rate structure; and (3) "the practical problems involved

> in applying marginal analysis to the multi-process operations of a modern plant seem insuperable, and business executives rightly consider marginalism impractical as an operating principle in such manufacturing establishments" [Lester 1946, pp. 81–82].
>
> (Lee 1984: 1114)

Lester found that firm's most frequent reaction to an increase in relative costs were, in order, to,

> (1) increase production efficiency, (2) implement labour-saving devices, (3) make increased sale efforts, (4) change the price or quality of products, and finally (5) reduce output and employment. Lester was struck by the fact that adjustment (5), which is the competitive adjustment par excellence, came last in the list, and that adjustments (3) and (4), which are predicted by the imperfect or monopolistic competition models, fared just a little better. He interpreted (1), and ambiguously (2), as indicating unexploited profit possibilities before the relative cost change.
>
> (Mongin 1998: 278)

Lester's conclusion was, in line with Hall and Hitch, that businessman do not adjust their behaviour, in this case their employment levels in response to changes in wages and productivity, in a manner consistent with the neoclassical theory.

In his response to both Hall and Hitch and Lester, Machlup

> managed to dispute the quality and relevance of the evidence, and at the same time, to claim that data on price-setting were compatible with several of the available models of imperfect competition; he also sketched a general decision-theoretic argument to the effect that "rules of thumb" (the expression in Hall and Hitch) often reflect an underlying optimizing process. Most of the later neoclassical arguments are already in Machlup's proteistic plea. His general conclusion was that the current theory of the firm hardly needed revising even if the allegedly damaging findings were taken at face value.
>
> (Mongin 1992: 314–15)

These controversies were, for all intents and purposes, ended in June 1952 by a presentation made at the Conference on Business Concentration and Price Policy. Richard B. Heflebower presented a paper at the conference in which he argued that full cost pricing could be viewed in marginalist terms (Heflebower 1955). Heflebower maintained that profit maximisation was to be understood in a long-run sense and that oligopoly should became the main theoretical focus for economists. He wrote,

> The conclusion that emerges is that full cost as a determinant of the level of price is most significant where the market structure approximates a pure

> oligopoly. In such cases price decisions involve collusion in the sense of a high degree of "conjectural interdependence" typically aided, perhaps, by consultation.
>
> (Heflebower 1955: 378)

He added that the full cost doctrine did not constitute a well-developed body of price theory and that the empirical work on which it was based was "spotty in quality and in its representation of situations" (Heflebower 1955: 391). Heflebower's questioning of the data on which proponents of full cost pricing relied was not the first such attack; a few years earlier Bernard F. Haley had also questioned the quality of the survey data relied upon by these studies:

> [t]hose responsible for the studies have relied so heavily upon the answers of their respondents alone, however, that it probably would be unwise to give too much weight to their conclusions until these studies have been supplemented by further research in the behavior and motivation of entrepreneurs with respect to price policy.
>
> (Haley 1948: 13)

Importantly for the history of the development of the theory of the firm, the neoclassical theory survived these controversies relatively unscathed. As Mongin (1998: 280) has pointed out, for the majority of economists at the time,

> drastic adjustments in the theory of the firm were not needed to resolve the marginalist controversy.

Overall,

> [a]lthough no contribution to the AER controversy [the marginalist controversy] can be said to be decisive, it can be conjectured that it influenced American economists into thinking that Robinson's and Chamberlin's initial models had to be refined, but that the profit-maximizing framework was flexible enough to accommodate the available evidence.
>
> (Mongin 1998: 279)

and even Ronald Coase saw no reason for a change in thinking:

> [i]t is clear from Heflebower's masterly survey that many of the arguments used by supporters of the full cost principle are in no way inconsistent with orthodox economic theory.
>
> (Coase 1955: 393)

In other words, these controversies had little impact on neoclassical thinking about the theory of the firm.

While the papers discussed so far represent some of the major contributions to the full cost and marginalist controversies, they are not the only ones. Papers such as Drucker (1958), Margolis (1958) and Means (1958) all offer criticisms of the neoclassical theory of the firm and look for ways to improve that theory. The general approach of these papers is summarised by Bodenhorn (1959)[7] as

1 the standard theory makes incorrect assumptions,
2 the theory does not properly describe decision-making procedures within firms, and
3 because of (1) and (2) the theory does not make correct predictions of firm behaviour

But Bodenhorn argues, firstly, that these criticisms are not damaging to the standard theory and, secondly, that the counterproposals offered by the critics do not look like much of an improvement.

With regard to the idea that the traditional theory makes incorrect assumptions, Bodenhorn argues that all assumptions must be incorrect to some degree. Thus, the criticism that the assumptions of the standard theory are incorrect is trivial and, of course, the same criticism can be made of any theory, including those alternatives that the critics propose. This defence is in line with Milton Friedman's hugely influential 1953 essay 'The Methodology of Positive Economics' (Freidman 1953). The background to the essay was the attacks that had been launched against some of the key assumptions of marginalist theory, including the use of unrealistic assumptions. Part of Friedman's aim was to convince economists that such assumptions are not an issue.

As to the third point, that because of points (1) and (2) it follows that the predictions of the neoclassical theory must be wrong, Bodenhorn argues this conclusion is not justified. Empirical testing will determine the validity or falsehood of predictions. For example, Means (1958: 167) argues that the standard theory is wrong because "[t]here is nothing in the classical theory of the profit-maximization form which would lead one to expect prices and wages to behave as inflexibly as they really do", as shown by the empirical evidence.

As to the second claim, Bodenhorn argues that the critics miss the point of the traditional theory. The neoclassical model is not a model of intra-firm decision making but rather one of market behaviour, that is, it is a theory about prices and quantities. Thus, even if true, such a criticism is irrelevant. The idea that critics of the neoclassical model of the firm misunderstand the model is also used, some years later, in Fritz Machlup's 1967 Presidential Address to the American Economics Association, where he defends the standard theory against the behavioural and managerial theories that follow.

A number of suggestions were put forward by the various critics of the traditional theory to improve the analysis of the firm. One such suggestion concerned the use of more realistic assumptions concerning both the motivation of the firm's management and the decision-making methods within the firm. The main aim of the critics was to alter the profit maximisation assumption and to take into account decision-making under uncertainty. Drucker (1958), for example, suggested replacing the profit maximisation assumption with the idea that firms seek to achieve the smallest amount of profit consistent with the firm's continued existence. This level of profit is just one of five different areas where satisfactory performance is needed for survival. One problem with Drucker's approach is that it is not clear whether his objective is normative, to explain what the firm *ought to do*, or positive, to explain what firms *actually do*.

Means (1958) suggested improving the standard theory by incorporating the politics of the firms as well as the economics of the firm. He sees the firm as an organisation that must take into account the conflicting as well as the common interests of shareholders, workers, consumers and management.

While Margolis (1958) also challenges the profit maximisation assumption, he does not give a clear alternative. The best he does is to accept, undefined, 'satisfactory profits' as an objective. In Margolis's model, the amount and accuracy of information available to decision makers is limited. The best they can hope for is information on actual sales, prices, purchasers' characteristics, inventory movements and memory of the firm's past. In addition, as they operate under uncertainty, the rules and tools they use must be different from those of the traditional theory. Given that knowledge is imperfect, Margolis argues that profit maximisation must be abandoned. As the management of a firm does not have the information needed to consider all possible alternatives, the firm cannot, and does not even seek to, maximise profits.

R. A. Gordon joined the assault on the neoclassical model in 1948. A list of the criticisms[8] articulated in Gordon (1948) would begin with the argument that the economic environment in which a firm operates is so complex that making marginal adjustments – that is, equating the relevant marginal magnitudes – is simply beyond the capacity of the firm's management. The continuously changing nature of the economic environment means that long-run demand and costs cannot be estimated with enough accuracy to allow for marginalist principles to be applied; that is, firms do not have the information necessary to set $MR = MC$. Also, this complexity means that a firm's management cannot learn from the firm's past experience because the economic environment changes continuously, thereby invalidating any extrapolation of the past. Gordon goes on to claim that empirical studies show that average-cost pricing is often used by firms. He argues that such pricing is the best alternative to marginalism, in particular for multiproduct firms, where marginal costs cannot be estimated for all products. The average-cost rule utilising a standard normal level of output is considered more realistic in that it stresses the importance of maintaining production at a level that satisfies demand rather that at the profit maximising level. An average-cost rule makes sense here since it leads to prices that are similar for all firms, meaning that firms can concentrate on the level of sales at this given price. It is claimed that the elasticity of demand is of less importance to firms than shifts in demand.

Gordon also argues that empirical studies show that companies follow a multitude of goals, at least some of which are not compatible with or may be competing with profit maximisation. Further, he claims that 'local' problems that can arise in particular parts of a firm at any given time are dealt with in a manner not necessarily consistent with profit maximisation.

A more radical claim by Gordon is that marginalism can be, in certain circumstances, rendered tautological. For example, if we accept, as do some Austrian-influenced economists, that demand and cost functions are subjectively conceived by entrepreneurs, then any observed behaviour by a firm can be consistent with profit maximisation, since any action by the firm is compatible with the equality of some subjective marginal cost and revenue functions. In a similar vein, it can be argued that building additional objectives into a firm's cost and revenue functions can result in marginalism being reduced to a tautology. Any argument that states 'whatever the firm does is profit maximising since the firm is just taking subsidiary objectives into account' is tautological, since it implies that whatever the firm does is done to maximise profits. Lastly, the adjustment of demand and supply curves to take into account expectations about future changes in the business environment can also lead to tautological predictions. The equality of marginal costs and revenue arising from suitably expectation-augmented cost and revenue functions can always be explained in terms of profit maximisation.

Additional papers related to the neoclassical controversies include Oliver (1947), Cooper (1949a, 1949b, 1951) and Earley (1955, 1956). Oliver maintains that if marginalists wish to reject the results of papers like Hall and Hitch (1939) and Lester (1946), then the burden of proof is on them.

> [Oliver] argued that while it was acceptable to be skeptical of the results presented by Lester (1946) and Hall and Hitch (1939), the simple fact that present economic theory is built upon the marginalist framework is not enough to prove its validity. In his words "if business men *say* that they think in average-cost terms, then, if the burden of proof rests upon anyone at all (and it should not in economic discussion), it rest on the marginalists who do not believe the business man, rather than on the economic iconoclasts who . . . take him at his word".
>
> (Altomonte, Barattieri and Basu 2012: 5–6)

The Cooper papers look at the role of management in the firm. The management of a firm is seen as being divided into two parts: top- and lower-echelon management. Each echelon has its own, but related, functions, and each has its own, but related, channels and types of information. It is argued that the implications of this division of management for the behaviour of costs, production and prices is not considered in the neoclassical theory of the firm.

The Earley papers consider the implications of cost accounting for marginal analysis. On the basis of survey evidence, Earley reported that 'modern' [circa 1950s] accounting methods provide management with information on both marginal costs and revenues and that this information is utilised by the firm's managers in their decision making, cf. the Gordon arguments given earlier.

Enke (1951) argues that, given that firms face uncertainty about the future, profit maximisation does not give entrepreneurs a clear and unequivocal criterion for selecting a given course of action from all those available to them.

> the [profit-maximising] motive does not even provide an entrepreneur with a criterion for preferring certain policies to others, unless he is willing to ascribe a unique outcome to each policy; if he admits uncertainty, and even if he assumes overlapping frequency distributions for each outcome, there is no rational and unambiguous way to determine which is the "best" policy to adopt.
>
> (Enke 1951: 576)

Managerial, behavioural and X-inefficiency theories of the firm

Critiques of the neoclassical model of the firm did not stop after the full cost and marginalist controversies petered out. Further challenges to the orthodoxy arose in the 1950s and 1960s from economists who developed the managerial, behavioural and X-inefficiency theories of the firm. In terms of the history of the theory of the firm, these three sets of models are particularly significant, since they represent some of the first attempts to look inside the black box of the neoclassical 'firm', even if their ultimate impact on mainstream economics has also been limited. In the rest of this section, we will briefly review each of these three approaches to the firm in turn.[9]

The behavioural theories see the firm as a coalition of self-interested groups, the conflicting demands of which have to be harmonised via an ongoing bargaining process within the firm, while the managerial models, along with the behavioural models, see the firm as being manager controlled rather than owner controlled, meaning the managers have the ability to pursue their own agendas. In the X-inefficiency theory, the firm is seen as being technically inefficient and thus non-cost minimising and non-profit maximising.

Like the neoclassical model, the managerial models work within a maximising framework, the difference being that they maximise some form of management utility function rather than profit. The behavioural models, unlike both the neoclassical and managerial models, seek a 'satisfactory' level of their objective rather than a maximum. The X-inefficiency model also works from within a maximising framework but shows how profit maximisation can be consistent with technological inefficiency.

6.3.1 Behavioural models

The development of the behavioural theories of the firm can be traced back to the 1950s, with the seminal paper of Simon (1955) standing out. In this paper Simon elaborated one of the foundational models of bounded rationality. The model highlights the 'cognitive' limits to human cognition and that these cognitive limits result in limits to rationality. Importantly, 'bounded rationality' underlies 'satisficing' behaviour.[10] But the work which is most commonly associated with the behavioural approach to the firm is the 1963 book *A Behavioral Theory of the Firm* by R. M. Cyert and J. G. March.[11] The aim of the Cyert and March book, and much of the literature that followed from it, was to develop a theory of the firm which is based on decision making within the firm, and this is just one element that sets it apart from the neoclassical theory.

An important underlying assumption of behavioural models is that there is a separation between ownership and control, so that a firm's owners no longer exercise direct control over the firm's managers. Behavioural theorists perceive the firm as consisting of antagonistic self-interested groups who constantly attempt to influence the firm's decisions on variables such as price, output etc. The emphasis in behavioural models is on these internal relationships within the firm, with little being said about the external relationships that exist between firms. The firm is seen as having a multiplicity of different goals which are set and amended by the firm's top management via an incessant process of bargaining among the different factions that make up the firm.

An important point of difference between the behavioural theories and the neoclassical theories of the firm is that for behavioural theories, the goals of the firm are prescribed in 'aspirational' terms rather than in formal maximisation terms. The instruments of the behavioural theories are the same as those for the neoclassical theories insofar as they both consider output, price and sales strategy[12] as the major instruments.

The difference between the theories lies in the way it is assumed that a firm determines the values for these instruments. For the neoclassical model, values are selected to maximise long-run profits, while for the behavioural model, the values chosen are the satisficing levels. Here it is assumed that the firm seeks levels of the relevant variables, for example, profits, sales, rate of growth etc., which are 'satisfactory' rather than the maxima. Such satisficing behaviour is seen as 'boundedly rational', bounded since information is limited, time is limited and the computational abilities of the firm's management are limited.

For Cyert and March, there are two forms of uncertainty which can adversely affect the firm. Firstly, there is market uncertainty. This arises from changes in market conditions such as changes in tastes, products and methods of production. Insofar as such uncertainty can be dealt with, it is, within the behavioural approach, coped with by search activity, investment on R&D and by concentrating on short-term planning. This concentration on short-term planning is another point of demarcation between the behavioural approach and the neoclassical model. In the neoclassical world, the emphasises is on the long-term.

The second type of uncertainty is that which arises from the behaviour of a firm's competitors. This form of uncertainty is avoided, in the Cyert and March view, by firms operating within a 'negotiated environment', that is, firms act collusively.

Another distinctive feature of the behavioural theory is that it assumes that firms can learn from experience. When a firm starts out it is not a rational institution in the sense of neoclassical 'global rationality'. Over the long-run the firm may approach global rationality, but in the short-run there is a necessary process of learning to go through. A firm will make mistakes; there is a process of trial and error via which the firm learns and adapts to its business environment. The firm effectively has memory, and it can use past experiences to help it adapt to changing circumstances. Compare this with R. A. Gordon's argument, noted earlier, that the complexity of the economic environment is such that a firm's management cannot learn from the firm's past experience.

The neoclassical model of the firm pays no specific attention to the decision-making process that determines the allocation of resources within the firm. This process is, however, central to the behavioural model. The neoclassical firm reacts to its environment, that is, it reacts to market pressure. The neoclassical theory examines the price mechanism and its role in the allocation of resources for the economy. The behavioural theory, on the other hand, examines the allocation of resources within the firm, with less attention being paid to industry or economy-wide resource allocation.

When considering the intra-firm allocation of resources, Cyert and March refer to payments made to groups within the firm over and above those needed to keep the group as part of the organisation as 'slack'. This means that slack is the same as 'economic rent' which accrues to a factor of production in the standard theory of the firm.

The important point about the behavioural use of slack is its role in stabilising the activities of the firm. Changes in slack payments during strong and weak business periods allows the firm to maintain its aspiration levels despite changes to the general business environment.

6.3.2 Managerial models

Another set of models which were developed ostensibly in the 1960s to address some of the perceived shortcomings of the neoclassical approach are the managerial models of the firm.[13] Again, in this set of models it is assumed that there are moral hazard problems between the owners of the firm and the managers of the firm, that is, there is a separation between ownership and control. It is argued that the owners of firms have lost, at least to a significant degree, control of the firm's managers, resulting in the managers having de facto control of the firm. The unifying theme underling this literature is that the managers will exploit their effective control and pursue non-profit objectives, although the managers' behaviour is generally subject to some kind of performance constraint involving a profit related variable, that is, the owner's de jure control places some limits on the managers' freedom of action.

While the heyday of the managerial models was the 1960s, there were a few contributions to this literature before then. The most notable, and influential, of these works was Berle and Means (1932). Berle and Means open their book by contending that over the decades just prior to the 1930s, there had been an increasing concentration of capital in the United States which had led to a situation where a small number of firms had acquired a vast amount of power. Ongoing growth in the size of these firms meant that the ability of shareholders to effectively control them was being continuously eroded. Shareholdings were being dispersed among an increasing number of small shareholders who lacked both the incentives and ability to monitor the firm's management. This handed control of the firm to its managers, which in turn created a moral hazard problem between the owners and the managers, since the managers' interests were not fully aligned with those of the shareholders. The firm's owners prefer profits to be maximised and returned to them as dividends, while the managers were more likely to favour reinvesting them or using them to fund utility-enhancing privileges such as some form of 'perks' and/or higher salaries.

Another proto-managerial model of the firm was De Scitovszky (1943). In this model, there is an entrepreneur whose utility depends on both income and leisure, and thus they face an income/leisure trade-off defined by the profit function of the firm; the opportunity cost of leisure is profit. De Scitovsky shows that the entrepreneur will maximise utility at a point involving more leisure and less profit than would occur at the profit maximising point.

More recent work which has explicitly developed the managerial models of the firm are Baumol (1959, 1962), Marris (1964) and Williamson (1964, 1970).[14]

Within the neoclassical approach to production it is implicitly assumed that there are no moral hazard problems between the owners and managers, that is, the managers act purely in the interest of the firm's owners. Given that the owners can observe and control the managers' behaviour, they can induce the managers to maximise profit.[15] In contrast to this, the managerial approach to the firm assumes that ownership and control are separated and that managers just like all other economic agents act to further their self-interest. But in these models, unlike the behavioural approach, the maximising assumption is still used. The question this gives rise to is, what is maximised?

The answer given in Baumol (1959) is that managers will maximise the firm's sales subject to a profit constraint. In Baumol (1962), a dynamic model is developed in which the objective of the firm is to maximise the growth rate of sales. In Marris (1964), it is also assumed that managers maximise growth, but this time subject to a rate of return constraint. Marris shows that the manager has an incentive to grow the firm past its profit maximising size, since larger firms pay higher managerial salaries.

While intuition may suggest that having a growth maximisation aim would lead to different behaviour by a firm compared to that of a profit maximising one, work by Robert Solow (Solow 1971) shows that each type of firm would react in a qualitatively similar manner to changes in parameters such as changes in factor prices, exercise tax or a profit tax.

In Williamson (1964, 1970), a more general form of managerial utility function is assumed. In these models, the firm's managers make a trade-off between profits and 'slack'. For the static version of the model, slack can be taken either as excessive administrative staff or as managerial emoluments (corporate personal consumption). In the dynamic-stochastic version, slack comes in the form of internal inefficiency and so has much in common with Leibenstein's (1966) notion of X-inefficiency; see the next section. Williamson claims that behaviour in his discretionary models is qualitatively different from that of models, which assume profit maximisation, sales maximisation or growth maximisation, although aspects of this claim have been disputed; see, for example, Rees (1974).

The most famous rejoinder to the managerial and behavioural attacks on the neoclassical model came in Fritz Machlup's 1967 Presidential Address to the American Economics Association. Machlup opened his address by arguing that there was confusion as the role of the firm in neoclassical price theory.

> My charge that there is widespread confusion regarding the purposes of the "theory of the firm" as used in traditional price theory refers to this: The model of the firm in that theory is not, as so many writers believe, designed to serve to explain and predict the behavior of real firms; instead, it is designed to explain and predict changes in observed prices (quoted, paid, received) as effects of particular changes in conditions (wage rates, interest rates, import duties, excise taxes, technology, etc.). In this causal connection the firm is only a theoretical link, a mental construct helping to explain how one gets from the cause to the effect. This is altogether different from explaining the behavior of a firm. As the philosopher of science warns, we ought not to confuse the explanans with the explanandum.
>
> (Machlup 1967: 9)

Next, he argued that the behavioural and managerial attacks missed their target, since they were working at a different level of analysis relative to that of the neoclassical model. The neoclassical model is a model aimed at the level of the industry, while the behavioural and managerial models are models aimed at the level of the individual firm, and thus, Machlup contents, the latter cannot be a genuine theoretical rival to the former.[16]

Lee (1984: 1122) sees a connection between the 'marginalist controversy' of the 1940s and 1950s and the slightly later behavioural and managerial models of the firm. He contends that the marginalist controversy influenced works such as Baumol (1959), Cyert and March (1963) and Marris (1964). The authors of these works knew of the controversy, and their work showed, by introducing non-profit maximising objectives of different kinds, how an extended neoclassical model could be consistent with full cost pricing.

Thus, by generalising the neoclassical model, albeit in different ways, these authors managed both to reconcile the standard neoclassical model with full cost pricing and to make the model more realistic. But these results did not bring about any real change in the mainstream modelling of the firm since, as Mongin (1998: 280) notes,

> it would be a mistake to believe that these writers [the behaviourists/managerialists] were representative of the majority of the economics profession.

The majority view was that drastic change to the orthodox theory of the firm was unnecessary to counter the attacks on it, and so the managerial and behavioural theories were largely ignored.

6.3.3 X-inefficiency

A basic assumption of the neoclassical model of production is that production is carried out in a technically efficient manner.[17] Leibenstein (1966) challenges this assumption. First he argues that the empirical evidence suggests that producers typically do not achieve technical efficiency and he called this technical inefficiency, 'X-inefficiency'.[18] Secondly, he argues, in terms of a theoretical explanation for this inefficiency, that there are four major reasons for X-inefficiency:

1 Human beings are different from other factors of production in important ways:

> Machines have a potential output which can be achieved by pressing the right switches. Human beings by contrast can adjust the quality and pace of their work in line with their own preferences. By supervision, by punishments and incentives, human effort can be varied. There is no reason why a shop-floor worker, or manager, should have a utility function which coincides with that of the firm as a whole or of its shareholders. Employees may be compelled to produce a minimum output – or lose their job. There may also be a maximum output of which they are capable given all the right sticks and carrots. But between these levels they can choose to vary the amount of time they spend on various activities, the pace at which they work and the quality of the work they do. There is no single-valued relationship between the number of man-hours purchased and the quality or quantity of effort that is expended in production. As a result, it is unlikely that every employee's choices will be exercised in such a way as to give maximum output per unit of input. So X-inefficiency almost always exists.
>
> (Hawkins 1973: 50)

That is, labour contracts are (1) incomplete and (2) must deal with moral hazard issues. Labour contracts do not and cannot completely specify what is to be done by employees; only a limited number of actions can be contracted on. The contract may specify a minimum contractible performance level, but performance beyond that is voluntary. Employees will expend effort above the minimum level only if they want to, and they may not want to.[19] Also, the hiring of labour involves the hiring of time on the job, but the intensity of effort is endogenous, since effort is not fully observable, that is, there are, in addition to incompleteness issues, principal agent problems to contend with. Both these issues mean that employee effort will be at a level less than the efficient level

2 Not all of the factors of production needed to achieve technical efficiency are markable, and thus some of these factors may not be available to a producer. In particular, significant problems can arise when there are market imperfections in the market for management, meaning the quality of managers is hard to assess ex ante, that is, there are adverse selection problems in the market for managers
3 The production function is not completely specified nor completely known by the producer. Prior experience and ability to experiment are factors affecting the producer's knowledge of the production process. But if the producer does not fully understand the production function, it will struggle to achieve fully efficient production
4 If there are strategic interactions between producers and uncertainty about competitors' reaction to a move by any given producer, then tacit collusion and imitation between producers can result, and this could prevent producers from achieving fully efficient production. Put simply, competition matters for efficiency

In later work, Leibenstein (1975, 1976) expanded the theory of X-inefficiency. He noted that organisations are collections of individuals, each of whom has their own self-interest and whose efforts on behalf of the organisation are variable. Leibenstein emphasises the variability of effort by the individual rather than the mutuality of individuals' interests within the organisation. Individuals will pursue their own interests, which may (or may not) contribute to the interests of the organisation in its entirety. But there are constraints placed on the individual's actions by the organisation.

> The "tightness" of these constraints depends upon the nature of the job being done, the system of payments (e.g. payment by results, payment by time, etc.), and the type of organization. Two important factors in determining the tightness of the constraint are likely to be the strength of the competition in the markets where the firm operates, and its degree of success.
>
> (Sawyer 1979: 131)

It is worth noting that the degree of X-inefficiency is related to the concept of 'slack' employed in the previous sections. It arises in this context due to the pursuit of self-interest by individuals, variations in their effort and incomplete monitoring of individuals. In the behavioural theory, it arises because of the bargaining processes within the organisation, while in the managerial models it is due to pursuit of self-interest by managers. But the presence of slack, for whatever reason, suggests the non-minimisation of costs and thus the non-maximisation of profits.

Conclusion

One conclusion that follows from the inquiries reported on in this chapter is that although all the critics set out to challenge the neoclassical model of production, they often, albeit implicitly, also attacked each other. A number of the elements of the numerous alterative models put forward by the critics contradict each other. So while the critics all agreed that the neoclassical model needed to be reformed, they could not agree on what those reforms should entail.

Another, more obvious, conclusion is that whatever the nature of the challenges, they had little long-term affect. The behavioural, managerial and X-inefficiency theories can be seen as attempts to move away from the industry-level approach to the firm of the neoclassical model and to a theory of the firm at the level of the individual firm, a theory which, as Oliver Williamson has said of the Cyert and March (1963) book,[20] was an attempt to

> pry open what had been a black box, thereupon to examine the business firm in more operationally engaging ways.
>
> (Williamson 1996b: 150)

But these attempts met with scant success in the economics arena. Interaction with people such as Herbert Simon, Richard Cyert and James March while he was at Carnegie-Mellon University did play a role in Williamson's post-1970 development of the transaction cost approach to firm (Williamson 1996b), but apart from this, the impact of the behavioural, managerial and X-inefficiency theories on the mainstream economic theories of the firm has been, at best, limited.

The earlier full cost and marginalist controversies tried to highlight the empirical shortcomings of the neoclassical model, in particular the failure of empirical studies to support profit maximisation. A new, supposedly more empirically supported theory was put forward. But all this also met with scant success in actually changing the standard pre-1970 approach to the theory of the firm.

Thus, while under fire, the neoclassical theory took few casualties. As has already been remarked upon in this chapter, little changed in the mainstream approach to the modelling of the firm because of the many challenges to the theory. The orthodoxy survived all the attacks launched upon it mostly intact. It managed to absorb the critics' ideas, and these ideas supplemented, extended, developed and sometimes corrected the standard theory, but seldom did they subvert it. These controversies have now been largely forgotten.

In the late 1950s, G. W. Guillebaud and Milton Friedman made an interesting point about economics in general:

> [t]he new ideas and new criticisms, which then seemed to threaten to overturn the old orthodoxy, have, in the outcome, been absorbed within it and have served rather to strengthen and deepen it, by adding needed modifications and changing emphasis, and by introducing an altered and on the whole more precise terminology.
>
> (Guillebaud and Friedman 1958: vi)

While these observations where made about the development of economics as a whole midway through the twentieth century, it can be argued that such conclusions apply with full force to the specific case of the development of the theory of the firm before the 1970s.

Notes

1 The neoclassicals were not interested in the firm as such; they were, to abuse Marshall's famous analogy, more interested in the forest than in the trees. At a more technical level, as has been noted previously, Foss (2000) highlights the point that the neoclassical model is consistent with there being no firms at all, since in a world of zero transaction costs, and therefore complete contracts, consumers can produce for themselves.

> With perfect and costless contracting, it is hard to see room for anything resembling firms (even one-person firms), since consumers could contract directly with owners of factor services and wouldn't need the services of the intermediaries known as firms.
>
> (Foss 2000: xxiv)

2 See pages 134–5 for more detail on the equilibrium firm.

3 Notes on the full cost controversy by G. B. Richardson appear as Appendix 12 of Arena (2011).

4 Revenue is given by $R = P \cdot Q$, so marginal revenue is given by $\frac{dR}{dQ} = P + Q\frac{dP}{dQ} = P\left(1 + \frac{Q}{P}\frac{dP}{dQ}\right)$. As the own-price elasticity is given by $e = -\frac{P}{Q}\frac{dQ}{dP}$ then $\frac{Q}{P}\frac{dP}{dQ} = -\frac{1}{e}$ and thus $P\left(1 + \frac{Q}{P}\frac{dP}{dQ}\right) = P\left(1 - \frac{1}{e}\right)$.

5 When summarising the early statistical studies done on cost curves, Johnston (1960) writes

> [t]wo major impressions, however, stand out clearly. The first is that the various short-run studies more often than not indicate constant marginal cost and declining average cost as the pattern that best seems to describe the data that have been analyzed. The second is the preponderance of the L-shaped pattern of long-run average cost that emerges so frequently from the various long-run analyses.
>
> (Johnston 1960: 168)

More recently, Miller (2000) has noted

> [f]irst, as taught, increasing then diminishing returns for a firm produce the U-shaped average variable cost curve (AVC), with its associated, rising MC curve piercing the minimum. This prediction is not supported by over 60 years of empirical studies of short-run cost curves, studies which almost invariably show horizontal AVC = MC over a significant range of possible rates of output.
>
> (Miller 2000: 120)

6 If AVC = constant, then total variable cost (TVC) is constant × Q, and so marginal cost is $\frac{dTVC}{dQ}$ = constant, and thus $AVC = MC$.

7 Margolis (1959) is a response to Bodenhorn (1959).

8 See Koutsoyiannis (1979: 265–7) for more detail.

9 A good intermediate level discussion of these models is given in Sections E and F of Koutsoyiannis (1979).

10 Bounded rationality "refers to behavior that is intendedly rational but only limitedly so; it is a condition of limited cognitive competence to receive, store, retrieve, and process information. All complex contracts are unavoidably incomplete because of bounds on rationality" (Williamson 1996a: 377).
11 For a review of Cyert and March, after 50 years, from the perspective of organisational economics, see Gibbons (2013).
12 Sales strategy here includes all activities of non-price competition, such as advertising, salesmanship, service, quality etc.
13 For a full treatment of dynamic models of the managerial firm, see Ekman (1978).
14 Alchian (1965) gives a brief critique of the Marris (1964) and Williamson (1964) models.
15 Implicitly, the contract between the owners and the managers is complete.
16 A related 'level of analysis' attack has been made on the 'present' theories of the firm, as highlighted by Foss and Klein (2008: 429): "the critics are protesting the application of concepts designed for analysis of *markets exchange* to the study of firm organization". That is, concepts appropriate at the market level are not appropriate at the firm level.
17 This section is based on Sawyer (1979: section 8.4).
18 A more formal model of X-inefficiency is given in Crew (1975: 110–5).
19 For a formal modelling of such ideas, see Hart and Moore (2008) and the literature on the 'reference point' approach to contracting. For a brief introduction to the application of these ideas to the theory of the firm, see Walker (2020: section 4.1.2.1).
20 For retrospective look at *A Behavioral Theory of the Firm* after 45 years see Augier and March (2008).

References

Altomonte, Carlo, Alessandro Barattieri and Susanto Basu (2012). 'The Macroeconomic Effects of "Full Cost Pricing": A Case for Revisiting the Marginalist Controversy?', Working Paper, August 28.

Arena, Lise (2011). 'From Economics of the Firm to Business Studies at Oxford: An Intellectual History (1890s–1990s)'. Unpublished doctoral dissertation, University of Oxford, Oxford, England.

Augier, Mie and James G. March (2008). 'A Retrospective Look at *A Behavioral Theory of the Firm*', *Journal of Economic Behavior & Organization*, 66(1) April: 1–6.

Baumol, William J. (1959). *Business Behavior, Value and Growth*, New York: Macmillian. (Revised edition, 1967).

Baumol, William J. (1962). 'On the Theory of Expansion of the Firm', *American Economic Review*, 52(5) December: 1078–87.

Berle, Adolf Augustus Jr. and Gardiner C. Means (1932). *The Modern Corporation and Private Property*, New York: Macmillan.

Bodenhorn, Diran (1959). 'A Note on the Theory of the Firm', *Journal of Business*, 32(2) April: 164–74.

Chamberlin, Edward H. (1933). *The Theory of Monopolistic Competition*, Cambridge, MA: Harvard University Press.

Coase, Ronald Harry (1955). 'Comment' (on Heflebower (1955)). In *UniversitiesNational Bureau Committee for Economic Research, Business Concentration and Price Policy* (392–94), Princeton, NJ: Princeton University Press.

Cooper, W. W. (1949a). 'Theory of the Firm: Some Suggestions for Revision', *American Economic Review*, 39(6) December: 1202–22.

Cooper, W. W. (1949b). 'Theory of the Firm: Some Suggestions for Revision, II', Commission Discussion Papers: Economics: No. 255, March 29.

Cooper, W. W. (1951). 'A Proposal for Extending the Theory of the Firm', *Quarterly Journal of Economics*, 65(1) February: 87–109.

Crew, Michael A. (1975). *Theory of the Firm*, London: Longman.

Cyert, Richard M. and James G. March (1963). *A Behavioral Theory of the Firm*, Englewood Cliffs, NJ: Prentice-Hall, Inc.

De Scitovszky, T. (1943). 'A Note on Profit Maximisation and its Implications', *The Review of Economic Studies*, 11(1) Winter: 57–60.

Drucker, Peter (1958). 'Business Objectives and Survival Needs: Notes on a Discipline of Business Enterprise', *Journal of Business*, 31(2) April: 81–90.

Earley, James S. (1955). 'Recent Developments in Cost Accounting and the "Marginal Analysis"', *Journal of Political Economy*, 63(3) June: 227–42.

Earley, James S. (1956). 'Marginal Policies of "Excellently Managed" Companies', *American Economic Review*, 46(1) March: 44–70.

Ekman, Elan V. (1978). *Some Dynamic Economic Models of the Firm: A Microeconomic Analysis with Emphasis on Firms that Maximize Other Goals Than Profit Alone*, Stockholm: Economic Research Institute at the Stockholm School of Economics.

Enke, Stephen (1951). 'On Maximizing Profits: A Distinction Between Chamberlin and Robinson', *American Economic Review*, 41(4) September: 566–78.

Foss, Nicolai J. (2000). 'The Theory of the Firm: An Introduction to Themes and Contributions'. In Nicolai Foss (ed.), *The Theory of the Firm: Critical Perspectives on Business and Management* (xv–lxi), London: Routledge.

Foss, Nicolai J. and Peter G. Klein (2008). 'The Theory of the Firm and Its Critics: A Stocktaking and an Assessment'. In Eric Brousseau and Jean-Michel Glachant (eds.), *New Institutional Economics: A Guidebook* (425–42), Cambridge: Cambridge University Press.

Friedman, Milton (1953). 'The Methodology of Positive Economics'. In Milton Friedman, *Essays in Positive Economics* (1–43), Chicago: Chicago University Press.

Gibbons, Robert (2013). 'Cyert and March (1963) at Fifty: A Perspective from Organizational Economics', Working Paper, April 7. Available at: http://web.mit.edu/rgibbons/www/.

Gordon, R. A. (1948). 'Short-Period Price Determination in Theory and Practice', *American Economic Review*, 38(3) June: 265–88.

Gramlich, Jacob and Korok Ray (2016). 'Reconciling Full-Cost and Marginal Cost Pricing', *Journal of Management Accounting Research*, 28(1) Spring: 27–37.

Guillebaud, G. W. and Milton Friedman (1958). 'Introduction to the Cambridge Economic Handbooks by the General Editors'. In E. A. G. Robinson, *The Structure of Competitive Industry*, revised and reset edn. (v–vii), Welwyn, Herts, England: James Nesbet & Co. Ltd.; Cambridge: Cambridge University Press.

Haley, Bernard F. (1948). 'Value and Distribution'. In Howard S. Ellis (ed.), *A Survey of Contemporary Economics* (vol. I, pp. 1–48), Homewood, IL: Richard D. Irwin.

Hall, R. L. and C. J. Hitch (1939). 'Price Theory and Business Behaviour', *Oxford Economic Papers*, 1939(2) May: 12–45.

Hart, Oliver D. and John Moore (2008). 'Contracts as Reference Points', *Quarterly Journal of Economics*, 123(1) February: 1–48.

Hawkins, C. J. (1973). *Theory of the Firm*, London: The Macmillian Press.

Heflebower, Richard B. (1955). 'Full Costs, Cost Changes, and Prices'. In *Universities-National Bureau, Business Concentration and Price Policy* (359–92), Princeton, NJ: Princeton University Press.

Johnston, J. (1960). *Statistical Cost Analysis*, New Yok: McGraw-Hill Book Company, Inc.

Koutsoyiannis, A. (1979). *Modern Microeconomics*, 2nd edn., London: The Macmillan Press Ltd.

Lee, F. S. (1984). 'The Marginalist Controversy and the Demise of Full-Cost Pricing', *Journal of Economic Issues*, 18(4) December: 1107–32.

Leibenstein, Harvey (1966). 'Allocative Efficiency vs. X-Efficiency', *American Economic Review*, 56(3) June: 392–415.

Leibenstein, Harvey (1975). 'Aspects of the X-Efficiency Theory of the Firm', *Bell Journal of Economics*, 6(2) Autumn 1975: 580–606.

Leibenstein, Harvey (1976). *Beyond Economic Man*, Cambridge, MA: Harvard University Press.

Lester, Richard A. (1946). 'Shortcomings of Marginal Analysis for Wage-Employment Problems', *American Economic Review*, 36(1) March: 63–82.

Machlup, Fritz (1946). 'Marginal Analysis and Empirical Research', *American Economic Review*, 36(4) September: 519–54.

Machlup, Fritz (1967). 'Theories of the Firm: Marginalist, Behavioral, Managerial', *American Economic Review*, 57(1) March: 1–33.

Margolis, Julius (1958). 'The Analysis of the Firm: Rationalism, Conventionalism, and Behaviorism', *Journal of Business*, 31(3) July: 187–99.

Margolis, Julius (1959). 'Traditional and Revisionist Theories of the Firm: A Comment', *Journal of Business*, 32(2) April: 178–82.

Marris, Robin L. (1964). *The Economic Theory of Managerial Capitalism*, London: Macmillan.

Means, G. C. (1958). 'Looking Around', *Harvard Business Review*, 36(3) May–June: 27–180.

Miller, Richard A. (2000). 'Ten Cheaper Spades: Production Theory and Cost Curves in the Short Run', *The Journal of Economic Education*, 31(2) Spring: 119–30.

Mongin, Philippe (1992). 'The Full-Cost Controversy of the 1940s and 1950s: A Methodological Assessment', *History of Political Economy*, 24(2) Summer: 311–56.

Mongin, Philippe (1998). 'The Marginalist Controversy'. In John B. Davis, D. Wade Hands and Uskali Mäki (eds.), *Handbook of Economic Methodology* (277–81), Cheltenham, UK: Edward Elgar Publishing Ltd.

Moss, Scott (1984). 'The History of the Theory of the Firm from Marshall to Robinson and Chamberlin: The Source of Positivism in Economics', *Economica*, n.s. 51(203) August: 307–18.

Oliver, H. M. (1947). 'Marginal Theory and Business Behavior', *American Economic Review*, 37(3) June: 375–83.

Pigou, A. C. (1928). 'An Analysis of Supply', *Economic Journal*, 38(150) June: 238–57.

Puu, T. (1970). 'Ferguson, C. E.: "The Neoclassical Theory of Production and Distribution." Some Comments on Part I', *The Swedish Journal of Economics*, 72(3) September: 230–40.

Rees, Ray (1974). 'A Reconsideration of the Expense Preference Theory of the Firm', *Economica*, 41(163) August: 295–307.

Robinson, Joan (1933). *The Economics of Imperfect Competition*, London: Macmillan and Co., Ltd.

Sawyer, Malcom C. (1979). *Theories of the Firm*, London: Weidenfeld and Nicolson.

Simon, Herbert A. (1955). 'A Behavioral Model of Rational Choice', *Quarterly Journal of Economics*, 69(1) February: 99–118.

Solow, Robert (1971). 'Some Implications of Alternative Criteria for the Firm'. In R. Marris and A. Wood (eds.), *The Corporate Economy: Growth, Competition, and Innovative Potential* (318–42), London: Macmillan.

Walker, Paul (2020). 'The Theory of the Firm: An Overview of the Economic Mainstream: Revised Edition', Working Paper. Available at: http://ssrn. com/abstract=2000431

Williamson, Oliver E. (1964). *The Economics of Discretionary Behavior: Managerial Objectives in a Theory of the Firm*, Englewoods Cliffs, NJ: Prentice-Hall.
Williamson, Oliver E (1970). *Corporate Control and Business Behavior*, Englewoods Cliffs, NJ: Prentice-Hall.
Williamson, Oliver E. (1996a). *The Mechanisms of Governance*, Oxford: Oxford University Press.
Williamson, Oliver E. (1996b). 'Transaction Cost Economics and the Carnegie Connection', *Journal of Economic Behavior & Organization*, 31(2) November: 149–55.

7 Conclusion

When discussing the place of production (and the related area of entrepreneurship) within modern economic theory, Coase and Wang (2011: 1) write

> [b]ut the gain in rigor achieved in modern price theory comes with a heavy price tag. The most obvious and serious omission in price theory is that it sees no role for production, let alone entrepreneurship. How goods and services are actually produced, how new goods and services and new ways of production are constantly invented in the economy, how production and innovation are organized, and what forces are at work are rarely on the research agenda in economics. It is extraordinary that the process of production is virtually invisible in economic theory.

The invisibility of the production process within contemporary price theory is strange given the indisputable importance of production to the economy. An obvious question is, how did such a perplexing situation evolve? Clearly, in reality, production and entrepreneurship are important economic activities, but not, it seems, so important that economists cannot ignore them. Contemporary economics offers little in the way of a satisfactory explanation for this incongruous divergence between theory and practice. As noted in the Introduction, the history of economic thought in general and the history of thought to do with production and the firm in particular are marginalised areas in modern economics.[1] Modern economists show little interest in the evolution of economic thought and thus in providing an explanation for the progression of thought to do with production. The chapters offered here are an attempt to provide an introduction to some of the topics that make up the history of thought to do with the theory of production and the theory of the firm in the hope that this will convince readers that the field is one which should be given greater prominence in the research and teaching activities of contemporary economists.

The chapters contained in this book discussed some of the major steps along the path towards the creation of the standard neoclassical theory of production. They outline the process of moving from a normative to a positive method of analysis; the progress of the division of labour approach to the firm and the beginnings of the development of the neoclassical theory of market structure and production in the early to mid-1800s; the short-lived Marshallian approach to production involving the 'representative firm'; and some of the criticisms of the neoclassical approach to production that originated in the period 1940 to 1970.

One conclusion that can be drawn from the analysis presented in the preceding chapters is that the methods of inquiry employed in the examination of production have changed significantly, if slowly, over time. In the beginning, a normative approach predominated; questions had to do with what 'should' be produced, not with how commodities were actually being produced. What types of employment and goods fitted into the ethical or religious perspective of the time was the principal concern. But starting in the sixteenth century, a more positive view of production, albeit mainly aggregate production, began to emerge. The mercantilists and the physiocrats started the slow process of developing a positive approach to production.

We can also conclude that the normative view of production held sway for so long not because scholars did not have the tools to develop a more positive approach but rather because they did not use the tools they did have to analyse production. As has been shown by work starting in the twentieth century, the (manufacturing) division of labour can provide a basis for a theory of production. Ancient philosophers were aware of the concept of the division of labour and discussed the social version of it at some length. But this discussion did not evolve into a (positive) theory of either production or the firm.

The now standard textbook approach to the theory of production in different market structures and to input utilisation is that associated with the neoclassical economists, but this theory was largely developed before the 'neoclassical revolution' of the 1870s. Work starting in the late 1830s created the standard approach to firm behaviour in different market structures. The theory of monopoly, oligopoly and the beginnings of the theory of perfect competition along with the marginal productivity theory of distribution all came into existence before the 1870s. One may conclude, therefore, that the tools of neoclassical economics were available well before 1870, and thus the 'revolution' started earlier than is normally assumed.[2]

The major, and perhaps only, pre-twentieth century theory of firm-level production was that of the 'representative firm'. While the founders of the marginal revolution, and most of their followers, wrote little on production or the firm,[3] Alfred Marshall created the representative firm to enable him to be able to derive a market supply curve without having to assume that all firm were the same. For Marshall, firms were heterogeneous with a dynamic life cycle. The representative firm allowed Marshall to integrate his dynamic view of the firm with his static view of industry. But the representative firm did not last long in the economics literature being replace by the equilibrium firm in the late 1920s. It was this adoption of the equilibrium firm that led to the theory of production we see in all microeconomics textbooks today.

The now familiar textbook model of production had largely developed by the 1940s, but this new orthodoxy did not go unchallenged. There were several attacks on the neoclassical approach to production during the period

1940–1970. In the United Kingdom, there was the full cost controversy, while in the United States there was the related marginalist controversy. A few years after these controversies concluded, the mainstream model was again assailed, this time by the behavioural, managerial and X-inefficiency theories.

The important point about all these attacks, however, is just how ineffectual they were. The orthodoxy survived all the attacks launched upon it largely intact. It was not until the 1970s, when the transaction cost, principal-agent and incomplete contracts approaches to the theory of the firm started to be developed, that a genuine theory of the firm started to appear.[4] Post-1970, the emphasis shifted from questions about how producers acted in their factor and product markets to questions about the existence, boundaries and internal organisation of firms. There are now also attempts to integrate the theory of the entrepreneur with the theory of the firm. So the Coase and Wang concerns are starting to be addressed.

The relationships between the different sets of scholars whose work has been discussed in the previous chapters are highlighted by Figure 7.1. This figure shows the major lines of influence among the various schools of thought considered in the preceding chapters. Importantly, it shows that the ideas of the ancient Indians and Chinese had little direct influence on European economic thinking. It was ideas from the ancient Greeks, disseminated by Muslim scholars, that influenced the European writers the most. An obvious example from the preceding discussion is that it was the Greek and Muslim analysis of the division of labour that came down to the European scholars rather than that of the Chinese and Indian writers. The Greeks and the Muslims influenced the mercantilists, and the physiocrats and the mercantilists also influenced the physiocrats. One link between Chinese and European thought came via the influence of ancient Chinese thinking on the physiocrats.[5] The mercantilists and the physiocrats in turn influenced the ideas of the classical economists. The classical economists then influenced the neoclassical economists whose ideas feed into modern mainstream thought. And these contemporary ideas will develop into something new.

If we look at the contemporary economics literature, we see that the theory of the firm has largely developed within the orthodox structures. Foss and Klein (2006) have noted that there has been a close relationship between advances in the general economic mainstream and the development of the theory of the firm,

> the evolution of the theory of the firm has never taken place far away from the economic mainstream. On the contrary, it has in fact been much driven by advances in the mainstream, and the relatively limited borrowing from other disciplines that has taken place has usually been strongly adapted to conform to central mainstream tenets. To be sure, the theory of the firm may have been revolutionary in the (somewhat limited) sense of introducing new explananda to economics, but it is generally true to say that it has not been revolutionary in the sense of representing a radical break with any of the main tenets of mainstream economics.
>
> (Foss and Klein 2006: 3–4)

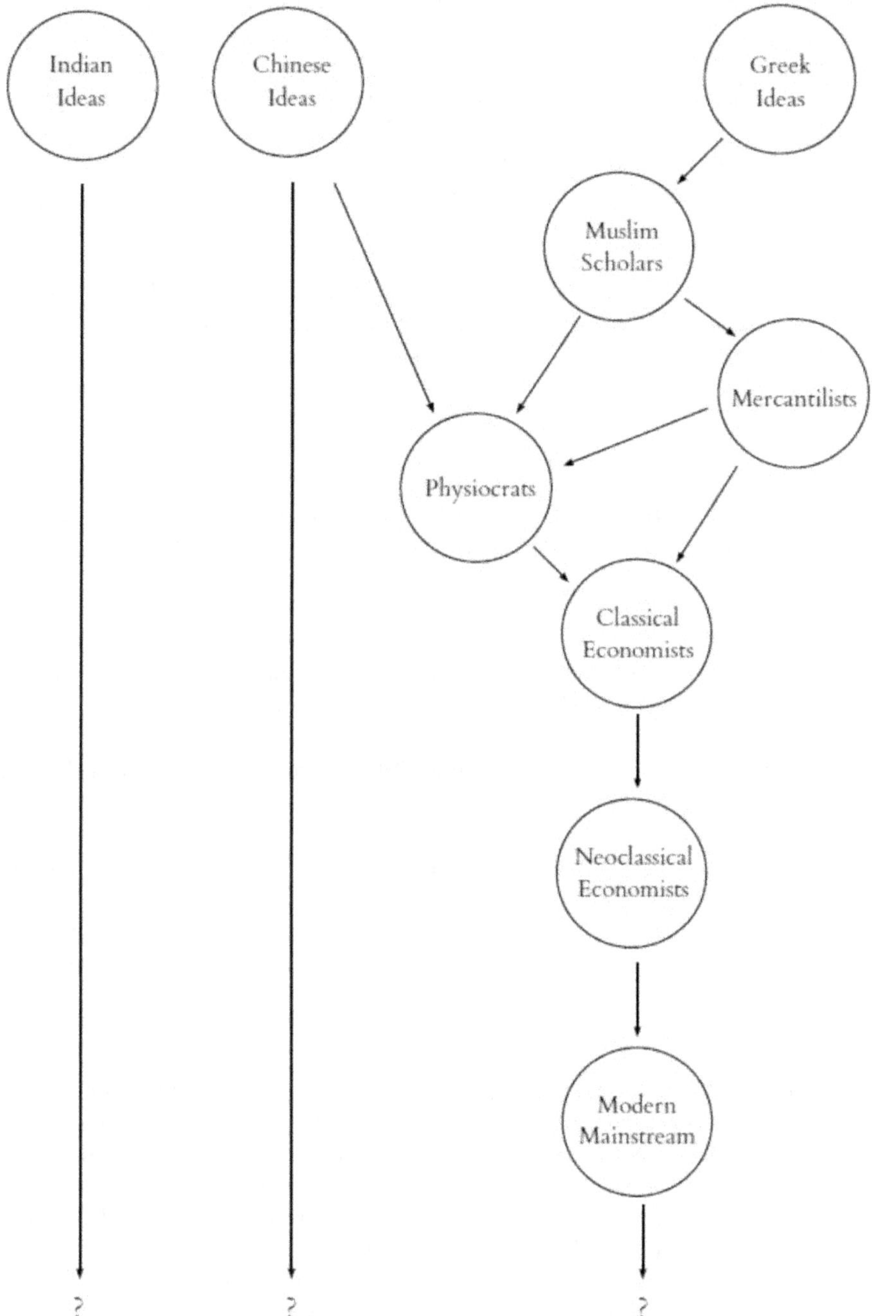

Figure 7.1 The influence of ideas

An implication of this is that the heterodox approaches to the firm have had little direct effect on the development of the economic theory of organisations. As has been noted in previous chapters, the heterodox approaches to the firm have made little progress in changing the mainstream. Thus, the concentration on the mainstream literature may do little damage to the story of the emergence of the theory of the firm. While the development of the theory of the firm has been limited in general, in relative terms, the mainstream literature is still ahead of that of the heterodox literature. When discussing Austrian economics, Per Bylund writes

> [b]ut despite the focus in Austrian economics on . . . "mundane economics," and the fact that "the Austrians [have] so many necessary ingredients for a theory of the firm" . . ., there is no Austrian theory of the firm.
>
> (Bylund 2011: 191)

and

> [w]hereas the theory of the firm has been a neglected area of study in mainstream economics, it has been missing from the Austrian economics literature.
>
> (Bylund 2011: 191)

Another example is the old institutionalists. When reviewing their contribution to the theory of the firm, Hodgson (2012: 55) writes

> we search in vain for a well-defined "theory of the firm" within the old institutional economics.

Carl M. Guelzo argues that one of the leading old institutionalists, John R. Commons,

> did not construct a rigorous theory of the firm since this was never his purpose.
>
> (Guelzo 1976: 45)

Interestingly management has proved a more receptive environment than economics for the development of many of the heterodox approaches to the firm, and thus the impact of these theories has been much greater in management than in economics. For example, Argote and Greve (2007: 337) go so far as to claim that *A Behavioral Theory of the Firm* (Cyert and March 1963) continues to be one of the most influential management books of all time.

A similar point has been made about the influence of the later resource-based view of the firm. Wernerfelt (2016: 3) argues that this approach to the firm has been very influential in management:

> "A Resource-Based View of the Firm" (RBV), a paper I wrote in 1984, has gone on to become very influential in the management literature. It introduced ideas that are taught in strategy, personnel, marketing, and often several other fields, in virtually every MBA program in the world.

The RBV approach has negligible impact on mainstream economics, however.

All this being said, there are a few areas where heterodox thinking is beginning to have an impact on mainstream thought. A prominent example of this is the integration of the theory of the entrepreneur with the theory of the firm, a point noted earlier. The introduction of the entrepreneur confronts the neoclassical model since in a zero transaction costs world there is no role for an entrepreneur. Under zero transaction costs, consumers can contract directly with the owners of the factors of production to bring about the creation of any commodities required, and thus there is no need for a middleman such as the entrepreneur. Three examples of the approaches that have been taken to the entrepreneur and the firm are Silver (1984), Spulber (2009) and Foss and Klein (2012).[6] Each can be seen as extending the mainstream approach to the firm by introducing the entrepreneur into the analysis, albeit in different ways. Silver (1984) offers a study of the entrepreneur and the boundaries of the firm, if not a full-blown theory of the firm and the entrepreneur, or more specifically, Silver offers a theory of the entrepreneur and vertical integration. Foss and Klein wish to explain the formation, determination of the boundaries and the internal organisation of the firm, all while emphasising the role of the entrepreneur. Spulber seeks to explain why firms exist, how firms are established, and what firms contribute to the economy. He sets out to create an approach to microeconomics in which entrepreneurs, firms, markets, and organisations are all endogenous. The Silver, Spulber and Foss and Klein contributions open important new lines of inquiry for the theory of the firm, since Hamlet really does need the Prince of Denmark.[7] It can be argued that the discussion of the entrepreneur, the formation of firms and, via them, the creation of markets, has now, finally, become a respectable mainstream activity. Such work will only grow in the future.

As to what this future, the question marks in Figure 7.1, will ultimately turn-out to be is inherently uncertain. Will the current mainstream be subverted by the introduction of new elements into the theory of production and the firm, or will these elements simply broaden the range of topics that the mainstream theory can handle? If we apply Alfred Marshall's reasoning to do with the development of economics at the end of the nineteenth century to the growth of the theory of production and the firm at the beginning of the twenty-first century, then the latter seems more likely than the former.

> Some of the best work of the present generation has indeed appeared at first sight to be antagonistic to that of earlier writers; but when it has had time to settle down into its proper place, and its rough edges have been worn away, it has been found to involve no real breach of continuity in

> the development of the science. The new doctrines have supplemented the older, have extended, developed, and sometimes corrected them, and often have given them a different tone by a new distribution of emphasis; but very seldom have subverted them.
>
> (Marshall 2009: v)

Notes

1 As was pointed out in the Introduction, there are just four books which deal with the history of the theory of production or the firm. The four are Cannan (1893), which covers the English literature from 1776 to 1848; Stigler (1941), which looks at the theory of production during the period 1879 to 1895; Williams (1978), which discusses the theory of the firm/firm level production from Smith to Marshall; and Walker (2018) which covers the theory of the firm/firm level production up until 1970.

2 Ekelund and Hébert (2002) is one example of this idea being argued.

3 T. W. Hutchison summarised the early neoclassical contributions to the theory of the firm and markets as

> Jevons has little on the firm. . . . Walras's assumptions of perfect competition (maintained virtually throughout) and of fixed technical 'coefficients', limited his contribution to the analysis of firms and markets . . . . Pareto's contribution to the theory of firms and markets were not rounded off, and of very varying value.
>
> (Hutchison 1953: 307)

When referring to Jevons, Blaug (1997: 293) writes, "he never developed a theory of the firm" and "[h]e showed no awareness of the need for a theory of the firm".
Hutchison (1953: 308) says about the Austrian School that

> [t]he Austrian School, with the exception of Auspitz and Lieben, did not concern themselves much with the analysis of markets and firms, except in respect to their general principle of imputation.

4 Ricketts (2019) and Walker (2020) discuss the contemporary theory of the firm.

5 See Maverick (1938) and Tan Min (2014) for discussions of this link.

6 For a more complete discussion of these works, see Walker (2020: section 4.1.2.2).

7 William Baumol noted more than 50 years ago, the entrepreneur has no place in formal neoclassical theory.

> Contrast all this with the entrepreneur's place in the formal theory. Look for him in the index of some of the most noted of recent writings on value theory, in neoclassical or activity analysis models of the firm. The references are scanty and more often they are totally absent. The theoretical firm is entrepreneurless – the Prince of Denmark has been expunged from the discussion of *Hamlet*.
>
> (Baumol 1968: 66)

References

Argote, Linda and Henrich R. Greve (2007). 'A Behavioral Theory of the Firm 40 Years and Counting: Introduction and Impact', *Organization Science*, 18(3) May-June: 337–49.

Baumol, William J. (1968). 'Entrepreneurship in Economic Theory', *The American Economic Review*, 58(2) Papers and Proceedings of the Eightieth Annual Meeting of the American Economic Association, May: 64–71.

Blaug, Mark (1997). *Economic Theory in Retrospect*, 5th edn., Cambridge: Cambridge University Press.

Bylund, Per L. (2011). 'Division of Labor and the Firm: An Austrian Attempt at Explaining the Firm in the Market', *Quarterly Journal of Austrian Economics*, 14(2): 188–215.

Cannan, Edwin (1893). *A History of the Theories of Production and Distribution in English Political Economy From 1776 to 1848*, London: Percival & Co. Second edition 1903, third edition 1917.

Coase, Ronald H. and Ning Wang (2011). 'The Industrial Structure of Production: A Research Agenda for Innovation in an Entrepreneurial Economy', *Entrepreneurship Research Journal*, 1(2): Article 1.

Cyert, Richard M. and James G. March (1963). *A Behavioral Theory of the Firm*, Englewood Cliffs, NJ: Prentice-Hall, Inc.

Ekelund, Robert B. Jr. and Robert F. Hébert (2002). 'Retrospectives: The Origins of Neoclassical Microeconomics', *Journal of Economic Perspectives*, 16(3) Summer: 197–215.

Foss, Nicolai J. and Peter G. Klein (2006). 'The Emergence of the Modern Theory of the Firm', Center for Strategic Management and Globalization, Copenhagen Business School, SMG Working Paper 1/2006, January.

Foss, Nicolai J. and Peter G. Klein (2012). *Organizing Entrepreneurial Judgment: A New Approach to the Firm*, Cambridge: Cambridge University Press.

Guelzo, Carl M. (1976). 'John R. Commons and the Theory of the Firm', *The American Economist*, 20(2) Fall: 40–6.

Hodgson, Geoffrey M. (2012). 'Veblen, Commons and the Theory of the Firm'. In Michael Dietrich and Jackie Kraff (eds.), *Handbook on the Economics and Theory of the Firm* (55–61), Cheltenham, UK: Edward Elgar Publishing Ltd.

Hutchison, T. W. (1953). *A Review of Economic Doctrines 1870–1929*, Oxford: Oxford University Press.

Marshall, Alfred (2009). *Principles of Economics*, Unabridged 8th edn., New York: Cosimo, Inc. Eighth edition first published 1920. First edition 1890.

Maverick, L. A. (1938). 'Chinese Influences Upon the Physiocrats', *The Economic Journal*, 48 (Supplement) February: 54–67.

Ricketts, Martin (2019). *The Economics of Business Enterprise: An Introduction to Economic Organisation and the Theory of the Firm*, 4th edn., Cheltenham, UK: Edward Elgar.

Silver, Morris (1984). *Enterprise and the Scope of the Firm: The Role of Vertical Integration*, Oxford: Martin Robertson.

Spulber, Daniel F. (2009). *The Theory of the Firm: Microeconomics with Endogenous Entrepreneurs, Firms, Markets, and Organizations*, Cambridge: Cambridge University Press.

Stigler, George J. (1941). *Production and Distribution Theories: The Formative Period*, New York: The Macmillan Company.

Tan, Min (2014). 'The Chinese Origin of Physiocratic Economics'. In Cheng Lin, Terry Peach and Wang Fang (eds.), *The History of Ancient Chinese Economic Thought* (82–97), London: Routledge. Originally published in 1990 as '重农学派经济学说的中国渊源', *Economic Research Journal* (经济研究), Issue 6: 66–76.

Walker, Paul (2018). *A Brief Prehistory of the Theory of the Firm*, London: Routledge.

Walker, Paul (2020). 'The Theory of the Firm: An Overview of the Economic Mainstream: Revised Edition', Working Paper. Available at: http://ssrn.com/abstract=2000431

Wernerfelt, Birger (2016). *Adaptation, Specialization, and the Theory of the Firm: Foundations of the Resource-Based View*, Cambridge: Cambridge University Press.

Williams, Philip L. (1978). *The Emergence of the Theory of the Firm: From Adam Smith to Alfred Marshall*, London: The Macmillan Press.

Index

www.ingramcontent.com/pod-product-compliance
Lightning Source LLC
LaVergne TN
LVHW021128300926
849160LV00010B/918
9780367722494